TERRORISM: THE CUBAN CONNECTION

TERR🌐RISM: THE CUBAN CONNECTION

Roger W. Fontaine

CRANE RUSSAK & COMPANY

NEW YORK · PHILADELPHIA · LONDON

USA	Publishing Office:	Crane, Russak & Company 3 East 44th St., New York, NY 10017
	Sales Office:	Taylor & Francis • Philadelphia 242 Cherry St., Philadelphia, PA 19106-1906
UK		Taylor & Francis Ltd. 4 John St., London WC1N 2ET

Terrorism: The Cuban Connection

Copyright © 1988 Crane, Russak & Company

First published 1988
Printed in the United States of America

Library of Congress Cataloging in Publication Data

Fontaine, Roger W.
  Terrorism : The Cuban connection.

  (The International book series on terrorism)
  Bibliography: p.
  Includes index.
  1. Terrorism. 2. Terrorists—Training of—Cuba.
3. Intelligence service—Cuba. 4. Cuba—Foreign
relations. I. Title. II. Series.
HV6431.F65 1988 303.6'25'097291 87-18088
ISBN 0-8448-1521-7
ISBN 0-8448-1522-5 (pbk.)

Contents

Contents

Introduction

Cuba's aiding and abetting terrorism is still poorly understood, and that is no accident. It is one mark of Fidel Castro's remarkable career that he has successfully cloaked his support of terrorists with the romantic garb of the heroic guerrilla.

Thus, in contrast to other states sponsoring terrorism—Iran, Libya, Syria, even the Soviet Union—Cuba's involvement in terrorism has never made headlines and more importantly has avoided nearly all serious inquiry.[1]

Indeed, even though the Castro regime has practiced terrorism in increasingly sophisticated ways for several decades, no single study has yet been devoted to the subject. Whole books have been written on the regime—even on its foreign policy—without the topic ever being raised, much less discussed at length. Moreover, that singular lack of curiosity continues to mark Cuban studies while the Castro regime has steadily expanded its scope for terrorism to a nearly world-wide basis. And it has done so in close cooperation with a number of governments and far more groups intent on seizing power through force.

The secrecy in which a Marxist police state shrouds its political games, both foreign and domestic, can explain this, but only in part. The Soviet Union, after all, is the premier regime of this sort, and *its* involvement in terrorism has been exposed in recent years, albeit gradually and only reluctantly by the Western media.

As a result, Fidel Castro is rarely, if ever, considered to be in the same league as Libya's Muammar Qaddafi or Syria's Hafez Assad. In fact, Castro has been involved in terrorism longer than either Arab leader has been in power.

Moreover, and in contrast, especially to the erratic Qaddafi, Castro employs terrorism with far greater skill, much less publicity, and considerably more success than the clown prince of the Mediterranean. And the Cuban Maximum Leader does so quite consciously and nearly always at the intended expense of his North American adversaries.

Cuban use of terrorism, however, is a complex story. It is not the only instrument of violence in Havana's armory. And Castro, even in his early days in power, did not rely simply on force to achieve his objectives. Nor did he do so while struggling against the hated usurper President Fulgencio Batista.

Nor has Castro's targets for subversion, including the use of terrorism, been confined to right-wing military dictatorships as had been popularly assumed. From the beginning, Havana has attempted to overthrow a variety of governments, both dictatorships and democracies, both struggling and well-established. Thus for every General Rafael Trujillo of the Dominican Republic, there has been a Romulo Betancourt of Venezuela or a Jose Napolean Duarte of El Salvador who has been in Castro's gunsights.

Moreover, Cuban-sponsored terrorism has rarely dislodged a military dictator (Somoza being the single and outstanding exception). The Argentine generals, for example, were driven from power because of their own folly in attempting to take the Falkland Islands by force, rather than by the Montoneros, among others. But terrorism did destroy the Uruguayan democracy for a decade and contributed greatly to the destruction of Chile's old political institutions, which culminated in the overthrow of Salvador Allende in 1973 by the armed forces.

But terrorism was not borrowed from abroad by the Cuban leadership. It is, for example, highly unlikely that Castro or any within his revolutionary entourage, including Ernesto "Che" Guevara, obtained their views on terrorism from V. I. Lenin or other classical revolutionaries.

For one thing, Cuban history is replete with examples most notably in the early 1930s, when groups of young Cubans struggled against another dictator, General Gerardo Machado. They invented many of the techniques of modern urban terrorism (co-ordinated bombing, for example) which Cuban advisers have since passed on in scores of training camps around the world to thousands of Argentines, Brazilians, Chileans, Colombians, Ecuadorans, Hondurans, Nicaraguans, Salvadorans, and Uruguayans, to name a few in Latin America, not to mention Basques, Namibians, Palestinians, West Germans, and Yemenis.

For another, Castro himself wrote and spoke publicly of terrorism even before he began his insurrection against Batista. Ironically, at the time, he opposed its use. He was not responding to some theoretical question, but to the revival of terrorist methods employed 20 years earlier—this time by another generation of student revolutionaries anxious to overthrow Batista who seized power in a March 1952 coup d'etat.

Moreover, the use of terrorism is not something the Cubans adopted immediately after 1959. In theory and often in practice, Castro and his closest followers were wedded to the *foco,* the belief that radical revolution could only occur when a group of rural guerrilla fighters took up arms against the government of the day. That belief was profoundly shaken by "Che" Guevara's pathetic stab at guerrilla warfare in Bolivia in 1967, even though the Castro camp had received earlier signals that such a simple-minded approach would not work.

Although the use of the rural guerrilla war strategy has never been entirely abandoned in either theory or practice, Cuba's sponsoring of urban-based terrorism became more and more a substitute although it has never been formally acknowledged by Havana. Nevertheless, terrorism— primarily urban-based terrorism—came to be, through earlier failure, the principal weapon in Cuba's arsenal as it continued to promote anti-American insurgencies around the world.

There is irony in this. The Castro–Guevara doctrine of guerrilla warfare was most crisply articulated by a young Frenchman Regis Debray in his small book *Revolution within a Revolution.* It asserted the necessity for creating the *foco* and sneered at the "revolutionary" efforts of more conventional Latin American communist parties. But Debray's thesis was not only simple-minded, it was profoundly wrong. That was so, in large part, because it became enmeshed in Castro's own web of deception over how Batista was really defeated.

Castro (and Guevara) insisted, of course, that their small, unconventional, and lightly armed Rebel Army was responsible for beating Batista's huge, heavily armed conventional armed forces. That central myth of the Cuban revolution entirely ignored the major contribution of the urban-based insurrectionary forces—many of them not under Castro's control—which operated most effectively in Havana and Santiago, the two principal cities on the island. The urban rebels, whose efforts are still not well known outside a handful of specialists, were, in fact, instrumental in Batista's defeat. Their often-times sophisticated and careful use of terrorism created the climate of counter-repression and demoralization on the part of the regime that allowed Castro's tiny forces to march into Havana unopposed in the first week of January 1959.[2]

In short, what other Latin American guerrillas were expected to do, that is, organize a largely unsupported rural *foco* and win power, had not happened before, even in Cuba, and many of these *guerrileros,* including

"Che" Guevara would pay—often with their lives—in a vain attempt to recreate a myth.[3]

Terrorism: A Definition

Scholars and analysts have struggled to define the term "terrorism" with indifferent success. Indeed, as Chalmers Johnson has pointed out, the 1972 United States Draft Convention on Terrorism failed to rally support in the United Nations because of difficulties in defining the terms.[4]

Therefore, at the risk of seeming "lame, even academic" (to quote Johnson, the mundane job of stating what terrorism is at the beginning is important. That is so particularly with the Cubans who have long employed a variety of instruments to achieve their objectives by force. A study of history and use of these instruments could fill several volumes. Terrorism is only one of them and, therefore, must be distinguished from the rest for the purpose of this study.

Although definitions abound, a useful one defines terrorism as political action employing extraordinarily violent means to achieve the largely psychological effect of intimidation and demoralization on the part of a nation's regime and its populace. Terrorism is also, as it has often been observed, the weapon of the weak—that is, it is used by groups and individuals who have little in the way of raw conventional military power.

Terrorism is also cheap. Training and supplying small groups of men and women with light arms and explosives are far easier to do than building a complex rural guerrilla army, hence, terrorism's popularity especially with states like Cuba who have aided and abetted terrorists over many years and in many countries.

Terrorism is almost always the monopoly of urban insurrectionists. Rural terrorism is a phenomenon nearly non-existent. That is so for several reasons. Guerrilla warfare belongs to the countryside where rebels seek out army and police patrols in a military effort to wear down the regime's security apparatus. A bomb set off in a cow pasture has little or no impact on anyone.

A bomb exploded in a crowded city, however, can have enormous impact on population and regime alike, and that is why the urban terrorist will invariably employ such methods to get attention, to demoralize, to provoke counter-terrorism on the part of the government which may, in turn, fatally undercut its own legitimacy—all at relatively low cost to Havana, Teheran, or Tripoli.

Cuba's Development of Terrorism

The Castro regime's use of terrorism has developed slowly over the years, and its present popularity with Havana rests on the relative success it has enjoyed and the failure of other Cuban instruments of force and coercion.

Although official historians of the Cuban revolution do not like to admit it, Castro's 26th of July organization committed acts of terrorism in the cities. Nor was the Rebel Army completely free of it either. Raul Castro, for example, kidnapped a group of Americans and Canadians in order to forstall the *batistiano* air forces' expected carpet bombing of suspected rebel positions. Castro's brother also organized one of the postwar era's earliest international plane hijackings, which resulted in the wreck of the aircraft and the deaths of 17 people in 1958.[5]

Thus, although acquainted with the basic techniques of terrorism through direct experience or by example, the Castro regime only gradually developed its preference for terrorism as a means to achieve its ends.

The very first attempts at promoting revolution in 1959 were simply to send expeditions of rebels—Cubans and locals—to countries like Panama and the Dominican Republic—although, in the case of the latter, the invaders were expected to touch off urban violence.

These primitive stabs at exporting revolution directly failed disastrously, and, accordingly, Havana reshaped its strategy along more subtle, if not more successful, lines. It did not, however, then or now, become "pragmatic," that is, abandon the larger ambitions of the *commandante-en-jefe,* as innumerable observers over the years have wanted to believe.

Instead, after 1960 and for nearly the next decade, Castro and his inner circle pursued revolution, largely but not exclusively in Latin America, through the support of rural guerrilla organizations. Resources were scarce, but the efforts were sincere. And in the end, they had one thing in common: they all failed.

Ernesto Guevara's half-baked attempt in Bolivia is, of course, notorious, but other examples of fomenting revolution before 1967 are numerous. Among the most serious were in Guatemala, Peru, and Venezuela.

The struggle in Venezuela between 1962 and 1967, however, was closest to Fidel Castro's heart and one he chose to hold up as the example *par excellence* for orthodox Latin American communist parties to follow.

Moscow's protégés refused, and Castro's quarrel with the Venezuelan Communist Party (the PCV) would become venomous, resulting in his open break with the PCV and, in turn, most of the region's communist parties.

That dispute is well-known to experts. What is less well-known is the Venezuelan insurgency was only in part a rural effort, unlike the rather feeble rural efforts of Hugo Blanco in Peru and "Che" Guevara in Bolivia.

Instead, in Venezuela much of the battle to overthrow two democratically elected governments was conducted in the capital Caracas and featured some of the most bloody urban terrorism experienced on the continent in the last quarter century. Moreover, it had the full support of Havana although Castro at the time, and since publicly, offered his approval of the *guerrillero* and passed over in near silence the atrocities of the urban terrorists. And as Castro no doubt noted at the time, while both city and countryside efforts failed, the urban terrorists proved far more dangerous to the government of Presidents Romulo Betancourt and Raul Leoni than the guerrillas operating in distant Falcon province ever were.

Nevertheless, in the 1960s, the bulk, perhaps 80 percent, of Cuban-supported insurgencies in Latin America was rural-based rather than urban in nature. In the next decade, the proportion would be reversed.

What accounts for the change? The failures of the 1960s, most prominently Guevara's, account for much of it. Fidel Castro does not enjoy losing, even if it means abandoning the strategy he proclaimed loudly, if mistakenly, to be his historic road to power.

Nowhere did he state that more vociferously than at the January 1966 Tricontinental Conference in Havana or the subsequent meeting of the Latin American Solidarity Organization (OLAS) held also in the Cuban capital 18 months later.

Still, it made no difference. Three months after Castro's sound and fury at OLAS—bombast that was amplified by his handpicked collection of international sycophants, "Che" Guevara was dead, leaving only three surviving Cubans of his little band desperately seeking safety in Chile.

Besides failure, there were the preferences of the local revolutionaries themselves to consider. Fighting, even living in the *campo,* is not pleasant. Conducting warfare in the cities of Latin America is far more agreeable especially to the upper middle-class youngsters who had always been drawn to the romance of revolution in the region.[6]

Moreover, in the very late 1960s and early 1970s when the next round of Cuban-sponsored insurrections was fought—Brazil, Uruguay, Argentina, and, to some extent, Chile—they occurred in countries that were already predominantly urban in nature. It manifestly made no sense to fight a war where no one lived, as the urban terrorist theorists who would replace Guevara and Debray would repeatedly point out.

This was enough to convince Havana, although Castro was careful never to endorse outright urban terrorism. He and his propaganda apparatus were vocal, however, in their support of Brazil's Carlos Marighella, the Uruguayan Tupamaros, and most clearly of all, the Chilean *Movimiento Izaquierdista Revolucionario* (MIR).

In the end, however, the urban terrorists of the Southern Cone in the 1970s enjoyed no more success than did their rural *companeros* further north in the 1960s, although they too had a gaggle of Western intellectuals insisting that urban warfare was the only way for the left to seize power, while they excused the terrorists' every act of murder and robbery.

For Castro, however, the experiment in outright terror was hardly a total loss. By degrees, no doubt, the Cuban leader learned that the Tupamaros and the Montoneros did not bomb and machinegun in vain. Although, the terrorists may not have seized power or even come close, they did undermine the governments they were attacking, thus preparing the way perhaps for future insurrectionists.

In the meantime, the self-styled "urban guerrillas" with no war to pursue at home could be usefully employed elsewhere. Not surprisingly then, South American terrorists were by the late 1970s to be found in Central America and even in the Middle East acting as "internationalists" while they remained under the firm control of Havana.

This long-term strategy formed out of necessity more than abstract strategizing can now be seen at work in Chile. That country and its military government has long been the *bete noire* of Fidel Castro. The Cuban leader has never made his loathing of the regime and desire for its destruction a state secret. Nor has he ever played down his support of armed rebels in that country.

Among those he had favored most is the MIR which has experienced more ups and downs than any of Latin America's numerous guerrilla/ terrorist groups.

The *miristas,* after their reversals of the mid-1970s, for example, were to be found in widely scattered areas of the world working with Havana. Two years ago, they and another Chilean rebel group sponsored by the newly militant Chilean Communist Party (PCCh) began to receive high priority Cuban support, including training and arms, for another stab at revolution in Chile.

It is clearly Castro's hope that the MIR and the PCCh's so-called Manuel Rodriguez Patriotic Front will revive the prospects of the extreme left in southern South America, while the fortunes of the Central American protégés appear to be at a low ebb.

Havana's calculation is simple: the Pinochet regime is vulnerable. Attacking it with armed force will further discredit it with more moderate Chileans and thus polarize further the Chilean political community. In time, Havana hopes the rebels will ride to power with the assistance of other anti-government elements much as the Sandinistas did in Nicaragua ten years ago.

But that is for the future. In any case, Havana after much trial and error continues to support armed revolutionaries, principally, but not exclusively, in Latin America. In practice, that has meant aiding urban terrorists as much or more than the theoretically favored rural guerrillas.

That is true for Central America today. The Nicaraguan Sandinistas seized power in an insurrection against an unpopular dictator which featured a good deal of urban warfare with its consequent high loss of life. In El Salvador, the Cuban-backed rebel coalition, the Farabundo Marti National Liberation Front (FMLN) began its revolt with acts of urban terrorism, and, while the effort in the countryside was important in the early 1980s, reversals in the *campo* had led the FMLN once more to emphasize urban operations with the apparent full blessing of Havana.

Other Cuban-sponsored revolutionaries in Costa Rica, Guatemala, and Honduras have also attempted to wage war in the form of urban terrorism as well. Only in Guatemala has any serious effort been made to supplement it with guerrilla action in the countryside.

Cuban Terrorism: The Network

Cuba does not work alone. In marked contrast to the 1960s, Fidel Castro has pragmatically shifted from being the Peck's bad boy of the communist world—he has not hurled an insult at a Latin American communist in years—to a valued and disciplined member of the anti-American team.

The turning point was 1968. Guevara was dead. The hot air, moist with revolutionary rhetoric of the Tricontinental Conference and the OLAS, had dissipated. More important, the Soviets were fed up with Castro's antics and were prepared to take action—specifically, slowing down shipments of petroleum to Havana.

It was the one import that the beleaguered Cuban economy was absolutely dependent on. There were no substitutes for energy-starved Cuba or other suppliers then willing to sell oil at below-market prices as the Soviets had done for years.

The Cuban leader got Moscow's message, and outsiders first realized the altered nature of the relationship when Castro, in effect, laboriously defended the Soviet invasion of Czechoslovakia in a speech in August 1968.

But the Cubans were not the only ones to change. The Soviets also learned that actively supporting revolutionary organizations, including terrorist groups, could be of strategic advantage to Moscow, providing it were done prudently. In the next ten years, the cooperation between Cuba and the Soviet Union became closer and more extensive. The high point of that cooperation in the use of armed force to attain their objectives came in the mid- and late 1970s as Cubans and Soviet forces acted to protect proto-Marxist regimes in Angola, Ethiopia, and Mozambique with conventional military forces.

With the victory of the Sandinistas in Nicaragua and further turmoil touched off in the rest of Central America, Moscow and Havana also worked and continue to work closely to promote revolution—this time through a combination of urban terrorism and rural guerrilla warfare.

But the network does not end with a single Moscow and Havana axis. Soviet and Cuban officers labor together in a score of far-flung training camps, cooperating with other certified communist states and non-communist but anti-American regimes like Libya and organizations like the Palestine Liberation Organization.

One small part of Cuba's new style of internationalism can be gathered from its efforts in remote South Yemen. According to Claire Sterling:

> Barely two months after [the Yom Kippur] war, in December 1973, forty Cuban experts in terrorist warfare arrived secretly in South Yemen. With

them was an East German specialist in the field named Hans Fiedler, who
had been in Cuba since 1971. Landing in Aden, they were at once whisked
upcountry to a Palestinian guerrilla camp run by Naif Hawatmeh. Second,
in importance only to Habash and Haddad in the Rejection Front, Hawatmeh had been an orthodox Communist all his political life.[7]

Twelve years after that trip to Aden, the network remains very much
in business, with the Cubans acting as one of its most valued members.
Thus, far from abandoning either his ambitions or penchant for making
trouble, Fidel Castro has become a disciplined sponsor of the selective
use of violence, including terrorism, to achieve his and the Soviet bloc's
goals—goals which are nearly always at the expense of the West.

The Instruments of Terrorism

Cuba, over the years, has developed a number of secret services that have
trained and supported guerrillas and terrorists in scores of countries since
1959.

Havana has also been successful in keeping its covert operations truly
secret, in glaring contrast to its principal adversary's penchant for making
the private, public.

Consequently, relatively little is known about who and what in the Cuban government support the terrorist apparatus. U.S. and other Western
intelligence agencies have gleaned some knowledge, largely from a handful of defectors, but much remains a mystery.

The two intelligence services involved in Cuban-sponsored terrorism,
the *Direccion General de Inteligencia* (DGI) and the *Departamento de
America* (AD), have received, by far, the most publicity recently, although they are not the only agencies within the regime that are in the
business.

The DGI, organized in 1961, is the oldest, largest, and best known of
Castro's intelligence services involved in aiding and abetting terrorist groups
that have found favor with the Cuban leader.

The DGI is also the service that corresponds most closely to an orthodox intelligence agency. It collects intelligence, conducts espionage, and
is involved in counter-intelligence activities throughout the world. Its agents
usually work under cover as Cuban diplomats and their *Centros* corre-

spond to CIA stations and KGB residences which too are located physically in their countries' embassies. But unlike the CIA, the DGI *Centro* chief operates with complete independence from the Cuban ambassador.[8]

The DGI also is linked to terrorist groups supported by Havana. Located within the sinister Ministry of the Interior, the DGI in the past, for example, has supported American black militants and the Puerto Rican Armed Forces of National Liberation (FALN).[9]

According to Castro's testimony, the DGI was also involved in aiding Latin American revolutionary groups in the late 1960s, by which time most, if not all, were pursuing an urban terrorist strategy for destabilizing South American governments.

> A fundamental task of the Intelligence Center in Paris was to provide support for the various guerrilla movements the Cuban government was attempting to spawn in Latin America. . . . With no direct means of commercial transportation existing between Cuba and the other Latin American countries, it was difficult for Cuba to move men back and forth. Latin Americans received guerrilla training in Cuba and then Cuba would utilize its fleet of Lamda-type fishing boats to smuggle the men, together with weapons, back into their home countries. To get those people . . . to Cuba— for training or other purposes was more difficult.[10]

Which, of course, is where the DGI's Paris *Centro* played its part. As Castro Hidalgo says:

> Persons traveling to Cuba from Latin America would fly to Paris on any of the several commercial air routes operating in Europe. They would remain in Paris while the *Centro* obtained the necessary documentation for further travel, either Russian or Czech visas. From Paris, the men would fly to Moscow or Prague, and from there to Havana on Soviet TU–114 airliners.[11]

The DGI also took a more direct hand in promoting terrorism. According to Castro Hidalgo, his service ran training camps, beginning in the early 1960s, which provided instruction in guerrilla and terrorist techniques to as many as 1,500 men a year.

The DGI defector also added these details about the camps in those days.

> Once in Havana, the trainees were grouped by nationality. Usually there were fifteen to twenty-five men in each group, although there might be as

few as three. The various nationalities were generally kept apart, for security reasons as well as because the courses given to the different groups
varied.[12]

The training camps, however, were not kept solely under the jurisdic-
tion of the DGI. In February 1967, according to Castro Hidalgo, the *es-
cuelas especiales* ("special schools") were transferred to the Armed Forces
Ministry with its considerable resources, and the training of subversives
has been a joint endeavor since.

A far more important development for the DGI, however, occurred two
years later. In 1969, the DGI, in effect, became "colonized" by the Soviet
Union. The Cuban service, like other East European intelligence arms,
was effectively put under the direction, if not control, of the Soviet KGB.

Castro Hidalgo learned of the change when his Paris chief, Armando
Lopez, informed the men of his *Centro* that: "*Somos mas sovieticos.*"[13]

According to the DGI defector, the terms of the new arrangement were
the following:

> [N]ew advisers would be assigned to the DGI. They would also serve as
> liaison officers between DGI and the Soviet intelligence service. . . . For,
> under terms of the agreement, the operations of the DGI would thereafter
> be more closely coordinated with those of the KGB. DGI virtually became
> an arm of Soviet Intelligence—a fact of special value to Russia in regard
> to operations in the United States, where DGI had been utilizing the stream
> of Cuban refugees as a cover for the infiltration of agents.[14]

Although Cuba, by the late 1960s, had thus taken on the look of a
Soviet satellite, Fidel Castro never did quite turn into a Walter Ulbricht.

Typically, when the Soviets put the DGI under its wing, Castro created
another intelligence arm, the *Departamento de America*—the America
Department in 1974.

Unlike any other of Cuba's five intelligence services, the AD, is directly under Castro's immediate control. It is located not within a government ministry but the Cuban Communist Party's Central Committee
(PCC) and, nominally, at least part of the PCC's *Departamento General
de Relaciones Exteriores* (DGRE). It has always been led by Manuel Pineiro Losada, a close confidante of Fidel's since the Sierra Maestre days.
Pineiro also has a reputation for being anti-Soviet. (His previous position
had been chief of the DGI, and, upon his appointment to head the AD,
Pineiro took his best people with him.)[15]

If the DGI, in many ways, has the appearance of a conventional secret service bureaucracy, the AD is manifestly not. Thus, while the DGI relies on numbers operating worldwide often within Cuban embassies, the AD is an elite with fewer than 300 working in relatively few countries nearly exclusively within the Western Hemisphere.[16]

The AD reflects directly the wishes of only one man: Fidel Castro. Its highly trained and experienced personnel take on only those assignments that have the Cuban leader's maximum priority.

Like those of the DGI, AD agents are assigned to Cuban embassies and missions in the Western Hemisphere, although a few may have assignments in Europe.

One estimate is that two or three AD members can be found in each— including Washington, D.C., and New York—although, where the mission is especially important, up to a half-dozen agents may be found, in Panama, for example, where operations into Colombia, including support for the M–19 terrorist organization, are mounted.[17]

Like Officers of the DGI, AD personnel do not have to report to their ambassadors *unless* the ambassador is a member of the *Departamento*. Unlike the DGI, at least four Cuban chiefs of mission, past and present, have been identified as AD agents, including Ulises Estrada in Jamaica, Julian Enrique Rizo in Grenada, Osvaldo Cardenas in Suriname, and, currently, Julian Lopez Diaz in Nicaragua.[18]

According to Mallin:

> A major responsibility of the AD is to facilitate military and sabotage training for pro-fidelista clandestine and guerrilla groups.
>
> The AD brings members of these organizations to Cuba and then gets them back home. It provides them with weapons, explosives and other materials. Actual transportation and training may not be done by the AD but by troops of the Special Operations Directorate [DOE, located within the Ministry of the Interior].[19]

The AD's star has continued to rise, primarily because it was instrumental in giving Fidel his one revolutionary victory after two long decades of effort.

Thus, it was AD agents who brought the quarrelling Sandinista factions together, and it was the *Departamento* that set up the arms network that would eventually lead to the overthrow of Somoza.

Since then Central America has become something of an AD oyster. Operating principally out of Panama and Managua, AD personnel have helped bring together disparate factions of Salvadoran, Guatemalan, and Honduran rebels. And as in the case of Nicaragua, the AD has constructed a complicated set of supply networks destined for these three countries. At the height of the effort, in the early 1980s, at least, Pineiro and Castro are said to have reviewed the progress of these activities on a daily basis.

Castro, thus, has a number of rival agencies and departments to choose from in preparing others for terrorist or guerrilla operations. They have evolved gradually over the years, and, despite long years of experience, they yet remain in the shadows.

Notes to Introduction

1. This is not to say there is no public documentation of various aspects of Cuban involvement in terrorism. They are, however, usually scattered about in larger works devoted to the subject of international terrorism. Perhaps the best and a recent account of such Cuban activities can be found in Claire Sterling, *The Terror Network: The Secret War of International Terrorism* (New York: Holt, Rinehart and Winston, 1985), especially chapter 13, 247–257. Although Castro is only one of many actors in the book, the scope of his involvement is indicated by Miss Sterling's work.

2. One exception can be found in Ramon L. Bonachea and Marta San Martin, *The Cuban Insurrection, 1952–1959* (New Brunswick, N.J.: Transaction Books, 1974).

3. The theory's high theologian, Regis Debray, would be sentenced by a Bolivian court to 30 years in jail, but owing to his family's political influence would serve only a fraction of the term.

4. Quoted in Chalmers Johnson, "Perspectives on Terrorism," in *The Terrorism Reader: A Historical Anthology,* ed. Walter Laquer (New York: New American Library, 1978) 267–268.

5. Christopher Dobson, and Ronald Payne, *The Terrorists: Their Weapons, Leaders and Tactics,* (New York: Facts on File, 1979) 8.

6. Nothing better illustrates that point than the less than heroic death of Guatemalan revolutionary Luis Augusto Turcios Lima. Nine months after being lionized at the Tricontinental Conference for being a model *guerrillero,* Turcios was killed with his girl friend in an automobile crash on the outskirts of Guatemala City as he headed for the capital for both rest and recreation.

7. Sterling, 253.

8. For details of the day-to-day operations of the DGI *Centro* in Paris in 1969, see Orlando Castro Hidalgo, *Spy for Fidel* (Miami: E.A. Seemann Publishing, Inc., 1971), especially 39–40. Castro Hidalgo was a DGI agent in Paris

until he defected, carrying with him hundreds of documents. He put together the most complete picture of the DGI that has been made public to date.

9. *Christian Science Monitor,* 6 January 1986.

10. Castro Hidalgo, 46–47.

11. Ibid., 47. Among those specifically identified were groups from Argentina, Bolivia, and Venezuela. Castro Hidalgo was responsible for the latter who were in 1969 at the bitter end of their attempts at destroying Venezuelan democracy.

12. Ibid., 94–95.

13. Ibid., 61.

14. Ibid., 63.

15. *The Washington Times,* 25 October 1983. Information on Cuba's intelligence arms, the AD, in particular, is found in a five-part series titled "Castro's Spies," written by Jay Mallin.

16. *The Washington Times,* 25 October 1983. Unlike the DGI, the AD, so far as is known, has never had a defector.

17. Ibid.

18. Ibid.

19. Ibid.

Chapter 1

Genesis

Antecedents

Although Fidel Castro imported his Marxist–Leninist ideology from abroad, he did not have to rely on foreign theory and practice when it came to terrorism.

For one thing, Cuban history is richly embroidered with acts of terrorism to achieve political ends. Terrorism as such became entangled in the island's long struggle for independence from Spain. And unlike other countries where political terrorism was practiced, in Cuba it often achieved results.

That was the case a half-century ago, for example, with the ABC— no one knows precisely what the letters stood for—a secret organization modeled after a prototype in a Victor Hugo novel. Its members were well-meaning university students who founded the ABC in late 1931. They were dedicated to overthrowing the dictator General Gerardo Machado.

The ABC was created after an older generation of soldiers and politicians—the men who made the 1895 revolution against Spain–had failed repeatedly to dislodge Machado from power. The last attempt, a landing of 40 volunteers in northern Oriente province, ended in the revolutionaries being tortured and shot by Machado's elite force that summer of 1931.

The ABC, whose members were all urban and middle class, agreed that Machado could not be defeated by conventional military means or through invasions of the island by a handful of would-be guerrillas.

The Machado regime, they felt, would have to be destroyed in the streets of Havana, and the instrument of his undoing would be carefully selected acts of terrorism.

For the most part, the target was Machado's efficient police, the ABC's favorite weapon, the bomb. But mere killing of policemen was not an end in itself. The ABC was perfectly aware that Machado's main line of

17

defense was the powerful, relatively well trained, and loyal army. A frontal assault on it was deemed suicidal.

Therefore, in the judgment of British historian Hugh Thomas, the ABC's strategy "was the deliberate creation of terror to cause a breakdown in governmental activities, so they assumed, making action of some sort by Washington inevitable."[1]

Although using terror to induce the intervention of the United States now sounds odd, if not absurd, the leaders of the ABC knew what they were about. They fully appreciated the very special relationship that existed between the United States and Cuba–a relationship that long preceded the Platt Amendment or the Spanish–American War of 1898.

The ABC rebels were certain that they could prove Machado incapable of maintaining order; the disorder would inevitably provoke the Americans to take action. Nevertheless, the young men of the ABC would be denounced at home, most vociferously by the Cuban communists who, from their start, were completely loyal to Moscow.

Still, the ABC's strategy worked, although it would not seize power for itself. It did succeed, however, in driving (literally) Machado from power after the Roosevelt administration demonstrated through its special ambassador Sumner Welles an utter lack of confidence in the 62-year-old general.

The very fact that the young revolutionaries in the ABC did not, for the most part, enjoy the fruits of victory shaped the attitudes and beliefs of the next generation of Cuban activists, among them Fidel Castro. Both he and they were convinced that the 1933 revolution was betrayed by, first, the army, soon to be led by a non-commissioned officer, Sergeant Fulgencio Batista, and, second, by the United States government.

Still, terrorism as a revolutionary weapon was by no means discredited. In fact, in the mid-1940s when the young Castro entered Havana University at the age of 19, it was still being practiced on a wide scale–within the university itself—and that would have a profound effect on the Cuban body politic.

Fidel's First Taste of Terrorism

Fidel Castro is the illegitimate son of a self-made, Spanish-born millionaire who himself was a large landholder from Oriente province whose property was located at the extreme eastern end of the island. As such, Angel Castro could afford the best for Fidel. Consequently, the young Castro, after graduating from an elite, Jesuit preparatory school in Havana, entered the University of Havana in 1945.

In a climate of violence that no North American university would come close to duplicating in the 1960s, the future ruler of Cuba became almost immediately involved in "the politics" of the school.

Politics at Havana in the mid-and late-1940s meant a near ceaseless struggle for domination among armed student groups. Killings and counter-killings between them was the norm.

According to Ronaldo Bonachea and Nelson Valdes:

> Gunmen lurked around every corner, and their games were deadly. Students and faculty alike were terrorized by a few groups of power-hungry gangsters, mostly nonstudents. In fact, Fidel remarked in 1959 that his four years at the University of Havana were much more dangerous than all the time he fought against Batista from the Sierra Maestra.[2]

Although the student gunmen were quick to hand out "revolutionary justice" with the help of the pistol and the bomb, the fighting had little to do with political ideologies.

> Their politics [Bonachea and Valdes explain] were a strange mixture of anti-imperialism, a trigger-happy sort of anarchism, and anticommunism. Their anti-imperialism was passionate, yet they lacked any understanding of the real influence of the United States over the island. Their anticommunism stemmed from their low education level, aversion to serious thinking, and distrust of those who discussed theoretical issues without acting— which was generally the case of the communists. Although their vision of a new world may have been limited, action delighted them.[3]

The gunmen, moreover, achieved considerable influence. The weak, corrupt, albeit elected government of President Ramon Grau San Martin rewarded the *bonches* with jobs. Rival gangs were soon taking over ministries with many of the *pistoleros* now wearing police uniforms. In return, the gunmen killed communist cadres, which allowed Grau to retain control of the labor unions.

Fidel Castro himself has often been accused of being involved in the mayhem, and indeed, he was once arrested for the murder of a leader of an opposing student group but was later released "for lack of evidence."

Sympathetic biographers of Castro rather casually dismiss the Cuban leader's university activities as youthful adventures, but, with evidence long suppressed and the key player, Fidel Castro himself, silent on the subject, the best verdict is "not proven" rather than "not guilty." Moreover, even if Castro never actually killed anyone, no one can deny he lived for years in a climate of violence and terror. No one, including Castro, has denied, for example, that he carried a gun. Nor is it any great leap of imagination to conclude that the atmosphere of violence was among his first political experiences, which most students of politics accept as primary and important in the shaping of a person's political values and beliefs.[4]

As for the charge of murder and its dismissal, it should be remembered too that, as in all societies where law and order have vanished, the courts no longer render verdicts when judges live in fear of their lives, a common occurence in today's El Salvador and Colombia.[5]

Meanwhile, Castro accused his enemies of the crime but, having done so, infuriated others. Prudence thus being the better part of valor, Fidel Castro skipped town for Bogota, Colombia.

Acting as an agent for the anti-American regime of Argentina's Juan Peron, Castro in April 1948 was assigned the task of helping set up a student congress at the same time and in the same city as the Ninth Inter-American Conference–a meeting that would draft the charter creating the Organization of American States (OAS).

But Bogota would be the scene of far more than two international gatherings. The assassination of a popular politician, Jorge E. Gaitan, on April 9 led to mass rioting, which nearly destroyed the Colombian capital. In that wave of violence known ever since as the *bogotazo*, Fidel Castro participated in the revolt by, among other things, leading an attack on a police station and distributing arms to the rioters.[6]

Soon, the Colombian police were on his trail, and Castro took refuge in the Cuban embassy from whence he was spirited away to Havana on a Cuban government chartered plane.

But the violence of university politics continued unabated back home, and Castro was again accused of murder, this time that of a campus policeman. Castro, in turn, became the target of repeated assassination attempts throughout the rest of 1948 and 1949.

It would leave a mark on him, the first and, some argue, his most profound political experience, an experience that taught him that small groups of men bent on violence could paralyze a government and society. In short, political violence (really terror) became "as Cuban as the palm trees," in the apt phrase of Bonachea and Valdes.[7]

Fidel Castro's preference for action was something he also urged on the political party of his choice, the *Partido del Pueblo* better known as the *Ortodoxos*, who had formed in opposition to the corrupt politics of the Grau government and its successor led by Carlos Prio Socarras.

Typically, Castro organized a splinter group within the *Ortodoxos* that would exert pressure on the party leadership to go to the streets. In that, however, the young insurrectionist was not successful, only frustrated.

Nevertheless, when Castro had left Havana University with his law degree in 1950, the preference for action, especially violent action, to achieve political goals, no matter how vaguely defined, was deeply implanted. And he had developed a band of followers.

Whether Castro was directly implicated in any particular act of terrorism is not material. How the climate of violence shaped his beliefs and attitudes is.

"He developed," Bonachea and Valdes conclude, "in an environment of turbulent political conflict with little relation to theoretical or ideological models borrowed from abroad."[8]

That would come later. Meanwhile, Castro had not only learned that direct action got results under certain circumstances, but he also discovered a larger world outside Cuba, even at this early date.

By 1950, he had already participated in two foreign adventures. Thus, not only did he acquire a taste for urban insurrection in Colombia, but he also participated in a failed attempt at invading the Dominican Republic, via the aborted Cayo Confites expedition two years earlier.

Castro's First Views on Terrorism

For Castro and many of his companions and enemies in the student action groups, the deed came before the word.

Nevertheless, Fidel even in his student days was no mere inarticulate thug. His powers of persuasion through the spoken word were already well-developed by the time he entered the University.

The event that finally forced Castro to define his revolutionary tactics would also lay the basis for his eventual seizure of power. That event was the return to power by Fulgencio Batista in March 1952. In fact, the

coup was carried out by a handful of junior officers disgusted at the disorder surrounding them. Batista did not conspire to seize the reins of
power; he merely accepted what had been given to him by the rebel officers.

More importantly for Castro, it was the end of a brief flirtation with
electoral politics. With Batista once more in the National Palace, Fidel
turned his attention to insurrection. But how?

After the March 10 coup, Castro displayed another of his talents, that
of organization. Instead of wielding a pistol or throwing a bomb, Fidel
began to coordinate all the groups of young men and women who wanted
to end quickly another period of Batista rule.[9]

Castro proceeded carefully but made clear that he intended eventually
to use force.

> The fight will not be easy, [Castro told his followers in September 1952],
> and the road to be traveled will be long and arduous. We are going to take
> up arms against the regime.[10]

Castro was, if not prescient, at least accurate. His war against Batista
beginning with the attack on the Moncada army barracks in Santiago on
July 26, 1953, initiated a five-and-a-half year struggle against the dictatorship.

But although terrorism was employed by rebel groups in the cities (and
by Batista's police in return), Castro himself chose (for the most part after
Moncada) another strategy: rural guerrilla warfare.

This choice of strategy was dictated by a set of (often) painful experiences. In the first place, the bloody fiasco at Moncada where most of
his ill-equipped little army was either killed or captured (and subsequently
murdered) taught Castro one lesson.[11]

The regime could not be destroyed with one dramatic stroke, especially
in an urban setting. That conclusion was reinforced for Castro after the
failure of urban student revolutionaries to assassinate Batista in his palace
on March 13, 1957. Again, copying the tactics of the earlier ABC, the
young men of the *Directorio Revolucionario* sacrificed their lives for
nothing.

Castro, secure by this time in the Sierra Maestre, criticized the attempt.
To a CBS newsman, the guerrilla leader said:

> [The attack] was a useless spilling of blood. The life of the dictator does
> not matter. . . . I am against terrorism. I condemn those procedures. Nothing

is solved by them. Here in the Sierra Maestre is where they should come to fight.[12]

As is usually the case with Fidel Castro, his ringing denunciation of terrorism, in fact, served several purposes. First, the *Directorio* was independent from his 26 of July movement. The attack was carried out without his prior knowledge or approval. Thus, his condemnation of the assault underlined his impatience with and opposition to any action that was not directly controlled by him.

But Castro's condemnation of the March 13 attack on the National Palace was not entirely self-serving. It also reflected Castro's own thinking about how to make a revolution.

Until the Moncada failure, Castro was hardly more than a conventional Cuban-style insurrectionary. His focus was urban with an emphasis on a single dramatic stroke that would unleash a general uprising. The preference was for action first and action second: the rest was talk, the province of the despised conventional politicians.

The failure at Moncada and his subsequent jailing on the Isle of Pines, however, forced Castro to re-think or, more accurately, to think seriously for the first time precisely how he and his followers would and should achieve power.

The disaster at Moncada and Bayamo first discredited in his own mind the insurrectionary thesis. Action could not be just a blind leap into the unknown supported only by the facile notion that his fellow Cubans really felt as he did and would follow him in battle once a heroic example was set.

At the same time, Castro had increasing doubts about the traditional Cuban revolutionary belief that the main battle was in the cities, principally Havana. By the summer of 1955, nevertheless, anti-Batista elements were setting off bombs in all the large cities on the island. The objective was not to seize power through a well-organized movement with a clear program for government, but simply to create a climate of terror and its consequence, chaos.

Fidel Castro, for his part, not only objected to the wave of bombings and assassinations but publicly denounced it. In an essay titled *Against Terror and Crime*, he said:

[A] man in his right mind cannot conceive of hurting the regime by blowing up a Chinese store outside Havana with a few little bombs. The greatest

service that can be performed for a dictatorship that stresses order is to use
the barbaric and inhumane method of dynamite, because the oppressors are
then given the justification for terrorism.[13]

For Fidel, the urban terrorists were "scoundrels" whom he "would not
hesitate to publicly denounce" because, while posing as revolutionaries,
they were, in fact, rendering "a formidable service to Batista."[14]

Terrorism may be morally repugnant, but, in Castro's view, it was,
more importantly, counter-productive and, even more so, not under his
control. During the term in prison, he also realized that a revolution as
opposed to a mere change in rulers would need to confront and then destroy the armed forces.[15]

In Cuba, Castro believed that was possible because the Cuban army
itself, although large, was weak. Favoritism and corruption had softened
it, and, moreover, it was bitterly divided. More than a handful of junior
officers wished to be rid of Batista and his clique.

But after the Moncada experience, Castro was also aware that the army
could not be defeated with one blow. Victory, he felt, could only come
through a prolonged and rurally based guerrilla war that would eventually
crumble the army's morale.

At the same time, Castro realized that, while the army was weak, Batista's police were efficient and ruthless. Since their writ extended to Havana's city limits, rural guerrillas would be relatively safe, particularly
if they operated in remote Oriente province.

His analysis based on pragmatic considerations of survival and success
proved fairly accurate and laid the foundation for Castro's later insistence
that revolutions elsewhere in Latin America would have to come from
the countryside led by a band of *guerrilleros* who made up with enthusiasm and courage what they lacked in ideological sophistication.

But he would also underestimate the importance of the cities—a mistake that would plague him for nearly a decade after he achieved power.
In fact, the urban groups were capable of bombings and killings, and,
although they did not directly threaten the regime, they did undermine it
and thus helped prepare for Castro's eventual victory. The urban groups
also suffered by far most of the casualties during the 1956–58 Cuban
revolution.[16]

According to Jay Mallin, a newsman who witnessed much of the war
in Havana:

> Bombs exploded in stores, theaters, and night clubs and on the streets. The
> bombs served several purposes: loud blasts demonstrated to one and all,

friend and foe, that the rebel underground existed and was highly active. The bombs encouraged the population, which was largely anti-government, and helped to demoralize the regime's forces, which were aware that the enemy was present and dangerous.[17]

The first peak of the bombing campaign was in November 1957 when 40 coordinated explosions were set off within a 15-minute period. That campaign, according to Mallin, succeeded in slowing business, encouraging capital flight, and reducing tourism—all of which led to further uncertainty and economic stagnation.[18]

Still many of the urban fighters, their leaders in particular, had been eliminated by the middle of 1958, although new recruits were always available, and the terror went on until the arrival of Castro in Havana.[19]

Meanwhile, Castro's rebel army, assisted inadvertently by the foreign press, established, first, his credibility by surviving, and, second, his legitimacy by attacking military outposts and then defeating Batista's elite units.[20]

As rural guerrillas, the Rebel Army itself committed only one well-publicized act of terrorism in the Sierra Maestre—kidnapping a group of U.S. and Canadian citizens in June 1958. The tactic was used to stall an army offensive and, most of all, to keep the Cuban air force from bombing rebel positions. Under American pressure, Batista called off the offensive for three weeks, which allowed the guerrillas to rest and recuperate.[21]

But Castro's pragmatism regarding the use of terrorism surfaced near the end of the struggle. As Batista's power crumbled (a process hastened by the withdrawal of U.S. support in the form of an arms embargo), the guerrilla leader outlined a new strategy in July 1958, less than six months before the victory.

The plan called for the complete occupation of the countryside by guerrilla forces, leaving the government in control only of the cities. But even there the regime's forces were to be further weakened through a campaign of urban terror, a softening up process that would make the *guerrilleros'* final drive all the easier.[22]

According to Bonachea and San Martin:

There were approximately 32 guerrilla operations during November [1958], mainly shootings at police precincts in Havana. Public utilities were constantly attacked: there were seven such attacks on the night of November 25. Bombs exploded every night, and on the evening of December 7 over

100 bombs exploded in the capital. No policeman could feel safe in the streets of any town.[23]

The coordinated attack came a few months later, beginning in late October. By the end of December, Batista and his closest followers had enough and flew to safety in the United States on New Year's Eve. Fidel Castro, the former student gunmen turned rural guerrilla, would soon arrive in Havana to take advantage of "his" revolution—a personal reign of unchallenged and uninterrupted power, unique in Cuba's turbulent history.

Notes to Chapter 1

1. Hugh Thomas, *Cuba: The Pursuit of Freedom* (New York: Harper and Row, 1971), 594–595.

2. Rolando E. Bonachea and Nelson P. Valdes, eds. *Revolutionary Struggle: The Selected Works of Fidel Castro*, vol. I, (Cambridge, Mass.: The MIT Press, 1972), 16.

3. Ibid., 17.

4. Herbert Matthews, for example, dismissed the accounts of Fidel's gunman activities as simply a black legend created by his enemies. The extent of Matthew's naiveté on this can be judged by accepting at face value Fidel's generally excellent grades based on records shown to him by his brother Raul. Assuming the records are legitimate, Matthews hopelessly confuses the University of Havana's grading standards of 1945 with, say, Harvard's. Herbert L. Matthews, *Fidel Castro* (New York: Simon and Schuster, 1969), 24–26. A more recent account by Tad Szulc also attempts to airbrush his university days by distancing Castro from the armed student groups, especially the Insurrectional Revolutionary Union (UIR). Tad Szulc, *Fidel: A Critical Portrait* (New York: William Morrow and Company, 1986), 142–143; 167; 182; and 189.

5. Bonachea and Valdes, 16; 24.

6. Ibid., 25. The most detailed account of Castro's activities, albeit from a sympathetic point of view drawn largely from the Cuban leader's version of events is found in Szulc, 173–181.

7. Bonachea and Valdes, 27.

8. Ibid., 27.

9. Szulc, 213–231.

10. Bonachea and Valdes, 40.

11. The famous attack on Moncada led personally by Fidel Castro was supplemented by a lesser known assault on the army barracks at Bayamo. Like Mon-

cada, Bayamo was also a bloody failure. See Bonachea and Valdes, 41; 47–55. Also, Thomas, 835–844, and Szulc, 248–281.

12. Quoted in Bonachea and Valdes, 95.

13. "Against Terrorism and Crime" in *La Calle*, 11 June 1955, found in Bonachea and Valdes, 252–254.

14. Ibid., 253. In a speech given to Cuban exiles in New York in November 1955, Castro was "radically opposed to terrorism and personal assault." Quoted in Bonachea and Valdes, 283. It is also cited by Ramon L. Bonachea and Marta San Martin, *The Cuban Insurrection, 1952–1959* (New Brunswick, N.J.: Transaction Books, 1974, 37.

15. On other occasions, Castro would make quite clear that the morality of terrorism was relative. In a November 1956 interview with the newspaper *Alerta*, he criticized the killing of policemen by the *Directorio Revolucionario (DR)* but very carefully qualified his criticism. "I do not condemn [such] attempts as a revolutionary weapon if the circumstances require it. But such attempts cannot be indiscriminately perpetrated." Quoted in Bonachea and Valdes, 86.

16. For details of the urban insurrection and its importance in the ultimate defeat of Batista, see Bonachea and San Martin, especially pp. 73–76. The DRs unsuccessful attack on the National Palace (unsupported by Castro's urban 26th of July) was a boon to Fidel. As a result of the assault, nearly the whole of the DR leadership was eliminated, leaving few if any rivals to claim power in early 1959.

17. Mallin, Jay, ed. *Terror and Urban Guerrillas* (Coral Gables, FL: University of Miami Press, 1971), 6.

18. Ibid. The Cuban terror of 1957–58, however, bore little resemblance to its descendants. Casualties were low because the bombs were often not packed with metal.

19. Bonachea and San Martin, 129. The failure of the April 1958 general strike also became a deathtrap for the Havana underground. Still, the numbers of the urban fighters actually *grew* from 1,500 to as many as 6,000 just before the Batista exodus. But as Bonachea and San Martin point out, the new recruits were often "easy victims of the police." More importantly, the experienced leadership had all been but eliminated as well. See ibid., 264.

20. Bonachea and Valdes, 107.

21. Ibid., 109. See also Mallin, 7. One other kidnapping, this time carried out by Castro's urban 26th of July cadre, however, did take place. In February 1958, Juan Manuel Fangio, the celebrated race car driver, was abducted from his Havana hotel and released unharmed several days later. Many analysts suspect it was a put-up job done in cooperation with Fangio. The city arm of the 26th of July Movement also pioneered yet one other by now commonplace act of terrorism: aerial hijacking. Several domestic and one international airflights were seized in the course of the revolution. See Mallin, 7.

22. The strategy was disclosed in part in the so-called *Unity Manifesto of the Sierra Maestre*, otherwise known as the Caracas Pact. It was dated 20 July 1958 and signed by the principal members of the opposition with Fidel Castro at the head of the list. Bonachea and Valdes, 386–389.

23. Bonachea and San Martin, 265.

Chapter 2

The Break with America, the Romance with Russia

But what kind of revolution? The hopes and expectations varied among Cubans, although the large majority wished an end to dictatorship and violence and wanted clean, effective, and democratic government in its place.

These aspirations are not merely a pious guess made by latter-day analysts. It is precisely what the anti-Batista opposition—including Fidel Castro—promised the Cuban people in the so-called Declaration of Caracas issued in July 1958.

The Declaration provided for a provisional government which would "establish full constitutional and democratic rights, " while it also guaranteed "fulfillment of international agreements, public order, peace, freedom, as well as economic, social, and political progress of the Cuban people."[1]

Castro, of course, had other ideas but kept them to himself. He had not risked his life for 15 years or nurtured a larger ambition merely to help found a tame, humdrum democratic regime where the usual run of politicans would engage in the kind of political game Cuban politicians had always played when given the chance.

Breaking the old mold, not repeating "the mistakes" of the 1933 revolution—the revolution betrayed in the minds of Castro and his fellow student radicals—was foremost in the new leader's mind.

But a true revolution, a literal break from the past, imposed special requirements. The first was a solution to the American problem. Castro was convinced that Washington would never accept a radical revolutionary regime in Havana so close to the United States, any more than it was perceived willing to do so in 1933.

And although Castro's public statements about the U.S. before the defeat of Batista were relatively mild, his private thoughts were not so.

In a brief note to a supporter, Celia Sanchez, written in June 1958, Castro promised:

When I saw rockets firing at Mario's house, I swore to myself that the North Americans were going to pay dearly for what they are doing. When this war is over, a much wider and bigger war will commence for me: the war that I am going to wage against them. I am aware that is my true destiny.[2]

The primary elements of Fidel Castro's world view—his penchant for action, his belief in revolution as a solution to the nation's problem, and his anti-Americanism—were all in place by the time he had reached power in January 1959.

A fourth element in Fidel's political makeup was and is his penchant for international adventure.

In truth, the revolution he had in mind could not be contained to one Caribbean island. Ego and self-survival played their part. But so did a belief, derived from Cuban patriot Jose Marti and later Karl Marx and V.I. Lenin, that a revolution was part of an inevitable historical process that was initially regional and then world-wide in scope.

But the grand revolution Fidel Castro dreamed of was, as he knew, wildly impractical without protection from a powerful benefactor. And it would take a super-power to shield him from the other super-power; the United States, the Cuban leader was convinced, would never accept that kind of revolution so close to its own shores.

Through an easy process of elimination, that left the Soviet Union, which, after the launching of Sputnik in October 1957, had taken on at least the appearance of military and technological equality with the United States.

Even so, Castro's "conversion" to Soviet-style communism was carefully paced. There were at least three audiences that had to be prepared: the Cuban people, the Soviet leaders, and the *yanquis*.

Although he quarrelled early and often with the Eisenhower administration (who, in turn, had sent a liberal and conciliatory new ambassador—one Castro refused to see for four months), Washington did not respond to his provocations for 18 months. When President Eisenhower finally did, he suspended the sugar quota in June 1960, and Cuban–American relations have never been the same since.

While Castro quarrelled with Washington, he steadily courted Moscow. More than three months before the rupture with the Americans, he managed to lure the First Deputy Premier of the Soviet Union, Anastas Mikoyan, fresh from a stopover in Mexico City, for a ten-day visit. In the end, Castro would pocket Cuba's first trade agreement with the Soviet Union.[3]

The courtship, however, took longer than the quarrel. Even after the Bay of Pigs fiasco, when Castro declared his revolution to be a socialist one, the Kremlin remained skeptical.

The lack of a strong, positive, and supporting action on the part of the Soviets prompted Castro's next pronouncement made at the end of 1961 when he said for the first time that he was a Marxist–Leninist. Even then, it was not until the following May that Moscow acknowledged for the first time in its set of May Day slogans that the "heroic people of Cuba" were "embarked on the path of building socialism."[4]

Revolution for Export

Early Years

Before Fidel Castro became a communist, he was a man of action. Within the broad church of Marxism–Lininism, not surprisingly, he would prefer Lenin to Marx as a theologian and prophet. And as a Leninist, his instincts were and have always been, ultra-voluntarist. He was and is uncomfortable with the comfortable, high church Marxist notion of inevitability and letting history take care of the problem. Revolutions, for him, were always created by flesh-and-blood revolutionaries, acting in the here and now with whatever they have at hand and using whatever means that suit the circumstances—including eventually terrorism.

The relatively easy win over Batista further inspired Castro to believe similar revolutions were possible elsewhere in Latin America. If anything, he was encouraged in that belief by similar analyses from non-communists about the region that were common in the United States in the early 1960s.

In a series of speeches by Castro and in two small books by his Argentine-born companion-in-arms Ernesto "Che" Guevara, the case for revolution throughout Latin America was laid out.

In Guevara's *Guerrilla Warfare,* the Argentine physician argued that the Cuban revolution demonstrated that a Latin American army could be defeated (in contrast to Guatemala in 1954 where a government composed of radicals and communists was overthrown by a military coup). It also showed that it could be done even if all the proper conditions for revolution did not exist. All that was needed was a *foco,* a vanguard, of disciplined and dedicated revolutionaries operating from the relative safety of the *campo.* Political organization, particularly in the cities, while helpful, was not decisive. Above all, beginning the war did not depend on that organization being in place.[5]

They were to be themes repeated endlessly in the 1960s, but words from Fidel Castro and his colleagues always had consequences—usually violent ones. The first attempts at making revolution in the region, however, were not only failures, but ludicrous ones at that.

The first, within weeks of Castro's triumphal procession into Havana, featured a boatload of *barbudos,* fresh and unshorn from their field days in the Sierra Maestre, attempting an invasion of Panama at the behest of local radical politicians. The would-be guerrillas never made it off the beach, and no blood was shed. An embarrassed Castro had to disavow their efforts.

A month later an attempt at bringing down Luis Somoza in Nicaragua was attempted by two plane loads of Nicaraguan exiles led by Pedro Juaquin Chamorro. The "invasion" was a failure, and Cuba denied all involvement, although a second group of Nicaraguans based on the island were prepared to follow up if the first wave had succeeded in establishing a beachhead.[6]

A third attempt was not so nearly lighthearted as the Panamanian and Nicaraguan ventures proved to be. In June, an expedition of Dominicans led by a Cuban Rebel Army officer invaded the Dominican Republic. That country's dictator, Rafael Trujillo, had been an old enemy of Castro's, and the quest to topple him on the part of Fidel had begun in 1947 when he joined the Cayo Confites expedition. Unlike that fiasco, the Cuban-led Dominican band made it ashore, but little else. Trujillo, long aware of the attempt, had his security forces there in strength, and the small band was wiped out.[7]

These early failures, including a mid-August assault on Haiti's Duvalier regime, however, did not discourage Castro. But straight-on amphibious and airborne assaults were to be avoided. Revolutions had to be carried out from the beginning from the inside by home-grown revolutionaries.[8]

Although Castro held out hopes that revolutions would and could break out in much of the hemisphere—he firmly ruled out—any peaceful road to power for real revolutionaries—relatively few countries even experienced guerrilla warfare in the early 1960s. Fewer had much success beyond survival of the cadre for a few fitful years. And while they all received the general blessing from Havana, only a handful got serious attention from Castro, much less material help. The revolution at home—no matter how much Stalin's dictum of "socialism in one country" was despised—still came first, as it wrestled with overwhelming domestic problems and foreign, principally American, hostility.[9]

Controversy within the Camp

Castro's favorite revolution in the 1960s was fought in Venezuela. It would also cause the largest rupture within the communist world. Even Chinese communist leaders, who despised the caution of their Kremlin counterparts, at first believed revolution was possible only in a handful of Latin American states, notably the Dominican Republic, Haiti, Nicaragua, and Paraguay—all featuring traditional, military-backed dictatorships. That formula, of course, excluded Venezuela.[10]

For the Cubans, the road to power in Venezuela lay through a guerrilla army operating in the Venezuelan countryside. But the question of strategy only followed an earlier decision to support a war against the democratically elected government of President Romulo Betancourt.[11] In striking parallel to the El Salvador of the early 1980s—a parallel that did not escape the Venezuelan government at that time, though it did escape most U.S. analysts—Venezuela had recently emerged from years of dictatorship with a military of uncertain loyalties.

To Castro that scarcely made a difference. The regime was at best "reformist" and "bourgeoise democratic," not properly revolutionary. Moreover, the country with its proximity to Cuba, its 1,400 miles of shoreline and its vast, underpopulated interior provided ideal conditions for guerrilla warfare. Also, Castro had come to dislike intensely Betancourt (himself a former communist) who had spurned the Cuban leader's request for $300 million in January 1959. Worse, the older man had treated Fidel (or so Castro thought) in a patronizing manner.[12]

The revolutionary vehicles chosen by Castro—the National Liberation Front (FLN) and its military arm, the Armed Forces of National Liberation (FALN)—were, in fact, a coalition of groups including a breakaway faction of President Betancourt's own party and the Venezuelan Communist Party. By 1961, armed actions began, but until 1964, they were carried out almost exclusively in the cities, principally in the capital Caracas. Urban terrorism, in its most basic forms, wracked that city for over three years. According to Robert Moss, in his book *Urban Guerrillas*:

> The terrorist tactics included sabotage of vital services and oil pipelines and installations. . . .; a program of selective assassination that the terrorists themselves described as a policy of 'kill a cop a day'; and a series of spectacular exploits designed to gain easy publicity. They included the hijacking of the Venezuelan freighter *Anzoatequi* (February 1963), the kidnapping of an Argentine football star, Alfredo di Stefano, . . . and the abduction of Colonel Chenault, a member of the American military mission (August and November 1963).[13]

In a preview of coming attractions, the FALN (and not the later Uruguayan Tupamaros) invented the Robin Hood-style gesture to attract favorable publicity. In this case, FALN terrorists were to steal (and then return) a collection of French impressionist paintings in early 1963.[14]

But the fun and games stage of the revolution ended quickly. The real climax of the FALN's campaign of terror was to be its attempt at destroying the December 1963 presidential elections in a direct bid for power. As in the case in El Salvador in March 1982, voters were threatened with death if they showed up at the polls. And, as in El Salvador, the vast majority of the people, over 90 percent, ignored the threat from their self-styled benefactors and exercised their hard won rights instead.[15]

Havana's attempt to destroy Venezuelan democracy, in fact, was more than just another assault on a liberal regime. The 1963 election (and a subsequent peaceful transfer of power to Betancourt's elected successor) was the first of its kind in 16 years, and only the second in modern Venezuelan history. Castro, in short, hoped to destroy democracy before it became implanted, an identical strategy he would follow in El Salvador in 1982, nearly 20 years later.

Nor did the FALN's liberal use of terrorism (including an attack on an excursion train) disturb Fidel Castro in the least. His private and public polemics regarding Venezuela were directed entirely at those in the communist world who believed armed action was inappropriate in Venezuela. At no point was there ever a word of criticism aimed at any terrorist actions taken by the FALN.

Castro's contempt for the traditional pro-Soviet communist parties of Latin America, fueled by Nikita Khrushchev's abrupt withdrawal of medium-range ballistic missiles from Cuba in November 1962, became nearly unlimited that following year. To a French journalist, he said the region's communists (Venezuelans excepted) were not "revolutionaries, they are bureaucrats, they are satellites." [16]

On several occasions, the Soviets sought to moderate Castro's public outbursts, if not his policies, between 1962 and 1964. Those attacked by Castro, namely, the Latin American communists, however, were far more adamant. For their part, the Cubans pointedly ignored any such "agreements."

Only in November 1964 were the Soviets able to put together a conference in Havana, a meeting that was attended by their subordinate Latin American communist parties and, of course, the Cubans. For the first time at this still secret gathering, the Soviet-led camp hammered out a general agreement in which Fidel Castro had to acknowledge that armed action was not always appropriate and that the local communist parties, not the Cuban leader, were best able to judge the proper moment for action in their own countries.

Despite that restriction, however, Castro still preserved for himself a free hand in six Latin American countries, including Venezuela, where armed action, including terrorism, of course, was deemed appropriate. [17]

At first, it seemed to work. Castro muted his statements about guerrilla warfare, and the Latin American communists allowed the Cuban leader a free hand in the revolutionary half-dozen. And in fact, in Colombia, Guatemala, and Venezuela, violence was stepped up in early 1965 although next to nothing of a "revolutionary" nature occurred in the other three. The Chinese, to Moscow's delight and Havana's naive surprise, were not pleased. [18]

Outwardly, the agreement forged in Havana was adhered to for nearly a year, but tensions continued owing to the failure of the groups that were on the approved list. In addition, the inability of the Dominican communists and their allies to seize power against a weak, post-Trujillo government in April and May 1965 strained matters even more. It was true that the Dominican Republic was not one of the six; nevertheless the spectacle of American troops snuffing out a "people's revolution" in a country Castro had identified with since his student days made his relations with the orthodox communists even more difficult to bear.

Still worse, in Venezuela there were ominous developments. Not only had the FLN–FALN attempt to sabotage the 1963 elections proved a spectacular failure, elements within the coalition, principally the Venezuelan Communist Party, were having second thoughts about the armed revolutionary line. In the PCVs April 1965 plenum, a communique stressing the need for a "democratic peace" was issued, and that caused eyebrows to be raised in Havana.

Typically, Fidel Castro smelled betrayal. Two years later, in his 13 March 1967, speech he explained in public.

> At bottom, behind those explanations, lay deceit. They did not say that democratic peace was a maneuver, but that the struggle, that guerrilla warfare, would be stepped up. However this was a lie. At the bottom the intention was to abandon the armed struggle, and the way was just being prepared.[19]

Worse still, for Castro, what the PCV had hinted at in April, it would state explicitly by November, namely, the war was being lost and further armed action for the moment would hurt the revolution's long-term prospects.[20]

One American analyst has described the effect on the Cuban leader:

> As the summer and fall of 1965 passed, [Castro's] unease grew until by late in the year Castro must have felt an almost unbearable psychological need to demonstrate his independence from Moscow and regain the respect of the insurrectionist groups in Latin America which had always provided his most ardent support.[21]

As a consequence, the mold that Moscow and its servants had fashioned for the Cuban leader was soon broken, and it was shattered, characteristically, in spectacular fashion. It would take the form of another conference, but unlike those dreary gatherings of Soviet-style *aparatchiki*, this one would be under the control of Fidel Castro.[22]

The Tricontinent Conference

Castro's rebellion against the Soviet party line and his renewed declaration of war against nearly all the governments of Latin America took place at the Tricontinent Conference in Havana in early January 1966.

The First Conference of Solidarity of the Peoples of Africa, Asia, and Latin America (OSPAAAL), as it was officially called, would also be Castro's formal entry on a world, rather than merely a regional, stage.

Delegates from Asia, Africa, and Latin America gathered together over 12 days for speeches, corridor politicking, and resolutions of an ultra-revolutionary nature.

For the Soviets, the Tricontinent was supposed to be another opportunity to show themselves as an Asian country and leader of the world communist movement—as opposed to their arch-rivals, the Chinese communists.

At the same time, they had reason to believe that Fidel Castro would continue to live up to the November 1964 agreement since the Cubans had not shown their hand during the preparatory meetings.

In fact, Castro prepared his ground well. The Tricontinent's opening speech delivered by Cuban President Oswaldo Dorticos was relatively mild in tone. Castro's first speech, to the delight of the Soviets, contained a stinging attack on Peking for cutting back on promised rice shipments to Havana—an otherwise odd topic to keynote a conference dedicated to anti-imperialism.[23]

But while the resentment against Communist China was real enough, it also served as a smokescreen. Castro's leverage over the proceedings did not come simply from being the host. His real power came from having the right to decide who would be on the delegations.[24]

That power was handed to him as a result of the Sino-Soviet struggle with the confident Soviets and its allies proposing "a compromise" on the question.

Castro, of course, used that power for his own purposes, and, instead of inviting a preponderance of Soviet-style communist parties, he flooded the conference with delegations from revolutionary groups of an ultra-radical nature—many of whom openly looked upon the Cubans and not the Soviets or even the Chinese as their ideological mentors.

The result, according to one analyst, made for Soviet nightmares.

> Now at the Tricontinental Conference he and the rifle-wielding guerrillas from Venezuela, Guatemala, and Portuguese Guinea were setting the tone, and in this context the old-line communists were the ones out of place. They were aging, cautious and pale in contrast to such guerrilla commanders as Luis Turcios of Guatemala, and their obvious discomfort at some of the ultraradical themes of the conference bespoke years of bureaucratic subservience to Moscow.[25]

As for Castro, his thoughts on revolution were made crystal clear in his closing speech to the delegates—a fire-eating polemic that could scarcely hide his contempt for the old men serving Moscow.

> If . . . it is understood once and for all that sooner or later all or almost all peoples will have to take up arms to liberate themselves, then the hour of liberation for this continent will be advanced. What with the ones who theorize, and the ones who criticize those who theorize while beginning to rhetorize themselves, much energy and time is unfortunately lost; we believe that on this continent, in the case of all or almost all peoples, the battle will take on the most violent forms.[26]

A majority of the delegates agreed, resulting in 100 pages of resolutions that stressed the primacy of armed action over other forms of "revolutionary" activity. The Conference also passed resolutions that called for outside aid to be given to those groups fighting for "liberation." Providing that aid from revolutionaries in power, that is, the Soviets, was also considered a solemn duty by the Tricontinental delegates.[27]

The Tricontinent concluded on that activist and contentious note, and, while the Soviet delegation voted for the resolutions, Moscow, in some embarrassment, began almost immediately to back off under heavy pressure from Latin American governments who pressed their case at the United Nations. The Soviets' first step was to disavow, in effect, their delegation in Havana. Lamely, Moscow explained to the outraged Latins that the Russian delegation had acted as representatives of a Soviet social organization, and not the government.[28]

But a Soviet retreat from the radical resolutions at the Tricontinent Conference did not deter Fidel Castro from sticking to his old pose of world revolutionary leader, *par excellence*—at least for awhile.

The call for violence by Castro continued through the next two years, climaxing in the July–August 1967 meeting of the OLAS—a spinoff of the Tricontinental Conference—in which a similar band of unorthodox rebels declared verbal war once again on U.S. imperialism and stick-in-the-mud, Soviet-style communist parties.

For his part, Castro bitterly criticized the Soviets and their protégés for standing in the way of the revolution, and the delegates at OLAS reaffirmed all the themes propounded by the Tricontinental.[29]

The OLAS conference, in fact, was the high water mark of Cuba's revolutionary voluntarism—at least in public. But despite that gathering's rhetorical ultra-radicalness (whose featured speaker was Stokely Carmichael), it was increasingly difficult to hide the fact, even from sympathetic observers, that most of the delegates who supported Castro's line were themselves obscure troublemakers who had miniscule followings in their own countries.[30]

Although Castro himself said in his August 10 speech that "no one could be so sectarian, so dogmatic, as to say that everywhere, one has to go out and grab a rifle tomorrow," the actual state of affairs in most of Latin America led the small bands of malcontents little choice in the matter. Either they did precisely that or it would be politics as usual.[31]

That point is amply demonstrated by the fate of "Che" Guevara in Bolivia. Armed with a few rifles and accompanied by a handful of followers (a number of them Cuban), Guevara spent his brief and unhappy experience in that Andean country mostly avoiding Bolivian army rangers. His death, in October 1967, shook Castro's earlier confidence in the possibility of a continental revolution, even after the insurrections in Guatemala, Peru, and Venezuela had all but sputtered out.[32]

Nor were the Soviets unwilling to reinforce the point even though they responded to the OLAS with complete silence. The Kremlin's real attitude is best summarized in a special edition of Moscow's version of "Che" Guevara's Bolivian diary.

In the introduction, the Soviet editors declared: "We do not need hysterical outbursts. We need the measured tread of iron battalions of the proletariat."[33]

Turning toward Moscow

The Soviets by 1968, however, were *willing* to back up their warning words with tough actions when it came to Castro's ultra-revolutionary behavior. Knowing full well the extent of Havana's economic dependency, the Soviets began cutting assistance to Cuba, especially in the delivery of oil and industrial raw materials. The bloc states soon followed suit.

Therefore, in that Castro-proclaimed "Year of the Heroic Guerrilla," 1968, the Cuban leader was forced to temper his words and actions and follow more closely the Soviet line on revolution. The tip-off that Castro had been brought to heel was his August 23 speech endorsing the Soviet invasion of Czechoslovakia.[34]

The romantic phase of the Cuban revolution on the international front thus was over. By itself, Havana, with its relatively few resources, did not have the means for a serious attempt at continental, much less world-wide revolution. That was a simple fact of life the Soviets had long recognized, but one that Fidel Castro only understood after nearly a decade in power.

But making Castro toe the line on Czechoslovakia and taming his revolutionary rhetoric were only part of the new arrangement. To keep a still firmer grip on Castro, the Soviets insisted (and got) Castro's cooperation on a wide variety of other fronts.

As one analyst summarized it:

> [Castro] made concession after concession to the Russians, purging the intelligence service of cadres considered undesirable in Moscow, cooperating with the traditional pro-Moscow parties, refraining from criticism of the Soviet Union, cutting back on his support for revolutionary violence, rationalizing economic management, and supporting Moscow's policies in the United Nations and throughout the Third World.[35]

It was a lot to swallow, but swallow it Castro did. In the words of Maurice Halperin:

> There was now no alternative but to completely abandon his dream of achieving instant prosperity, pure communism, and effective national independence. And with unaccustomed humility, he accepted the conditions of survival offered by the Kremlin: basic conformity with the economic, political, and ideological postulates of the Soviet model of socialism in domestic affairs, and with Soviet foreign policy in international affairs.[36]

Castro's abject surrender to the Soviets, however, hardly ended his career as a revolutionary and supporter of terrorism. Indeed, it can be said that his serious career had just begun. The turn toward Moscow, in fact, would make Havana a far more disciplined, dependable, and efficient tool for fostering violence, including terrorism, and this time on a wider and larger scale.

The Early Years: The Tally Sheet on Terrorism

Although the first decade of Cuban-style "internationalism" had produced no outright successes, it was, if nothing else, a proving ground for future adventures. The actual results, as opposed to the rhetoric, showed that Castro's path to power could not be easily followed. The special circumstances that gave Fidel a relatively easy victory in Cuba—circumstances including a divided and corrupt army that had lost its will to fight—were not to be duplicated, even in Nicaragua in the late 1970s on the brink of the Sandinista victory.

Nevertheless, despite repeated failures and limited resources, Havana not only learned through its mistakes, but it began to build the apparatus that would make Cuba a valued member of the terrorist international network. And while Castro publicly asserted that rural guerrillas could alone seize power, even in the early 1960s, he prepared men and women for urban-based terrorism as well.[37]

As has been seen already, this was most certainly the case with the Venezuelan FLN–FALN which was forced into rural guerrilla action only after it was defeated in Caracas.

Moreover, in the long and usually tedious argument between Castro and the pro-Soviet communist parties, the question usually debated did not concern the proper strategy, that is, rural guerrilla versus urban terror, much less either's morality, but whether or not armed force was the best means to achieve power.[38]

In fact, despite Castro's theoretical assumption that a rural guerrilla army alone could win, few of his followers actually chose that route in the first phase. Because of their small numbers and their isolation (and quite probably a preference for city living), Castro's would-be imitators in Latin America often ended up as urban terrorists in their often abbreviated careers in insurrection.

The Venezuelan case has been noted. But one facet of that experience needs further elaboration. It concerns a pure act of terrorism that involved Fidel Castro himself. In early March 1967, an urban unit of the Venezuelan FALN kidnapped and murdered Julio Iribarren Borges, a brother of the then Venezuelan foreign minister. The FALN soon publicly claimed "credit" for the killing in *Granma,* the Cuban Communist Party daily newspaper.

The Venezuelan government immediately went on the offensive, linking Cuba with the crime, and called for additional international sanctions to be placed on the Castro regime.

Caracas' swift action also placed pressure on the Venezuelan Communist party to clarify its position on the crime. The PCV did so by denouncing the murder and sending condolences to the family. The PCV made no attempt to defend Cuba or its relations with the FLN-FALN.

In turn, less than a week after the kidnapping, *Granma,* the official newspaper of the newly organized Cuban Communist party, printed the Venezuelan guerrilla statement, *which was signed and dated in Havana,* excusing the crime.

Having associated Cuba with the crime by indirect approval, the Maximum Leader himself in his March 13 speech justified the murder by placing the "main responsibility for the death" on Caracas because that democratic government "had unleashed repression . . . and violence . . . in the service of its imperialist master."[39] He then went on to attack the Venezuelan communists.

It was, as an analyst D. Bruce Jackson later wrote, "one of the more extraordinary denunciations of a 'fraternal' communist party in the turbulent history of the world communist movement."

And unlike earlier *pronunciamientos* on terrorism, Castro this time did not bother to weigh seriously the merits of such actions. The killing itself was merely a side issue. For Castro, it would be a turning point. In the next two decades, the Cuban leader would never again address the morality of revolutionary terrorism in public.[40]

But revolutions and revolutionaries, no matter how defined, do not live by words alone—a fact of which the Castro regime was more than aware, even in the early and heady days of its own triumph. And despite the limited assistance to the struggling Latin American revolutionaries of the 1960s, the Cubans were already putting in place the guerrilla and terrorist infrastructure that would make a return on investment in the 1970s.

According to analyst William Ratliff:

> Guerrilla training camps were set up in Cuba during the early 1960s, the main center being at Minas del Frío in the Sierra Maestre. The U.S. Central Intelligence Agency reported in April 1965 that the Cuban General Directorate of Intelligence (DGI), with Soviet advisors, had provided more than $1 million to Venezuelan guerrillas during the period from 1960 to 1964 [years in which the FLN–FALN favored urban-based terrorism]; at the time of the OLAS conference in 1967, the *Washington Post* reported that the DGI "is now spending $1.1 a month to support stepped-up guerrilla warfare in Latin America," adding that "most of the money [is used] to train insurgents, with some 3,000 latinos already trained in Havana and returned to their native countries since Castro came to power.[41]

It should be noted that the CIA estimate on numbers was, as usual, a cautious one. Other estimates range from 6,000–9,000 men trained in that period.[42] Moreover, there is another report that the Soviets under the direction of a senior KGB officer assisted in the construction of additional training camps in Cuba, putting them on a more professional footing shortly after the January 1966 Tricontinent Conference.[43]

What the prospective terrorists and guerrillas received from Havana, aside from military and intelligence training, was money, false documents, travel arrangements, and contacts.[44]

But as has been seen, the revolutionary pay-off in the first ten years was meager despite the time, effort, and capital invested in the enterprise.

Thus, as a consequence of both failure and Soviet pressure, a painful reassessment of what had gone wrong was made. Castro concluded, according to DGI defector Castro Hidalgo, that more care and caution had to be exercised. In the first place, Cuban officers, as was the case in Bolivia and Venezuela, should not be sent into the field unless the revolution was already well-advanced and there was a genuine invitation from the insurgents.

Moreover, it was decided that Havana would be far more scrupulous in selecting potential trainees. Not every self-professed revolutionary would be welcome, as Castro himself said in an April 1970 speech. Cuban support, he said, would not be given "for just any faker [or for] destroyers of revolution, men who had the opportunity to wage a revolutionary war, [but] instead sabotaged it and destroyed it. . . ."[45]

And efforts would be made to do as much of the training outside of Cuba as possible. In the early 1970s, the principal base for such training was located in Chile, thanks to the cooperation of the Salvador Allende government. Later, with the downfall of Allende in 1973, and after the Sandinista triumph in Nicaragua in 1979, a new off-island site was secured.[46]

Above all, Castro toned down his rhetoric—at least to some degree. In the early 1970s, for example, his officials began making a distinction between aiding deserving revolutionaries (which was proper) and "exporting" revolution (which was not).

In January 1975, for example, the No. 3 man in Havana's hierarchy, Carlos Rafael Rodriguez, in an interview with a left-wing Mexico City daily, said somewhat piously that Cuba had "always" spoken of "aiding revolution, never about exporting it." Fidel Castro picked up the theme a year later in a speech by announcing that "nobody can export revolution or impose it by means of war." He added, however, that "nobody can prevent its peoples from making it, either. . . ."[47]

Eventually, this formula found a place in the Cuban constitution issued with great fanfare in 1976. Article 12 states that for Cuba "its help to those under attack and to the peoples for their liberation constitute its internationalist right and duty."[48]

But these glib distinctions offered by the Cuban leadership (and often accepted at face value) tell us little. Nowhere do they say what distinguishes "aiding" from "exporting" revolution. Apparently, the criteria are whatever Havana finds convenient at the moment. Nevertheless, the formula served to make Fidel Castro seem to many more restrained, more responsible than in the past.

Revolution Revisited: The New Wave of Violence in Latin America

Castro's re-thinking and reorganization paid off—up to a point—as other groups in Latin America became active in the late 1960s and early 1970s. For the most part, the violence occurred in a new area, southern South America, primarily—Argentina, Brazil, Chile, and Uruguay—although Guatemala was a significant exception.

But unlike the earlier efforts, there was little pretense at launching a rural-based guerrilla insurrection. Instead, the weapon was urban terrorism in its rawest form. The new wave even had its own prophet. "Che" Guevara, the Argentine patron saint of the rural guerrilla, was replaced by a Brazilian, Carlos Marighella, who authored a handbook on urban terrorism in June 1969, entitled *Minimanual of the Urban Guerrilla*. And like Guevara, Marighella would enjoy his own brief vogue.[49]

But unlike Guevara or his student Regis Debray with their bloodless and abstract analysis, Marighella reveled in the prospect of shedding blood.

A characteristic quote from the manual follows:

> Experience has shown that the basic arm of the urban guerrilla is the light machine gun . . . The urban guerrilla's reason for existence, the basic condition in which he acts and survives, is to shoot.[50]

And unlike some of his companions-in-arms, Marighella was not the least bit squeamish in discussing terrorism. That, he said, was "an arm the revolutionary can never relinquish" which must be used "with the greatest coldbloodedness, calmness, and decision." And by "terrorism," he also characteristically was explicit: acts committed by urban guerrillas which included kidnapping, sabotage, robberies, and murder.[51]

Although Marighella paid lip service (and then only in passing) to rural guerrilla warfare, that strategy of the Cuban revolution was only a second stage for the Brazilian after the urban war was well-established. In fact, he made a half-hearted attempt at rural insurgency before organizing his campaign of terror in Brazil's major cities. But like the Venezuelans before him, the cities proved more attractive. In fact, Marighella's never came close to reaching the theoretical second step.[52]

But before Marighella himself was killed in November 1969, his group, the National Liberation Action (ALN), had succeeded in kidnapping the American ambassador (he was later released in exchange for "political prisoners" who took refuge in Cuba) in the course of a four-year campaign of urban terror. Despite Marighella's theoretical precepts that such armed actions would be aimed at the "physical liquidation of the chiefs and assistants of the armed forces and of the police," most of the casualties were civilians.[53]

The ALN's gun-toting style of terrorism, a true reflection of the *Minimanual,* did not, however, alienate Havana in any way. In fact, Marighella enjoyed close ties with Fidel Castro until the former's death. The Brazilian was an honored guest at the 1967 OLAS conference where he unreservedly endorsed the revolutionary pronouncements of the Cuban leader (and thus underlined Marighella's break with the pro-Soviet Brazilian communists.) And his terrorist *Minimanual* with its minimalist approach to politics was done the honor of being reproduced in its entirety in *Granma* six years after the death of its author.

If the Cubans had any reservations about Marighella's terror tactics, they kept them to themselves. The Brazilian's *Minimanual* was also published in a number of editions in several languages in Havana and was enthusiastically promoted throughout the world—a unique service performed within the Socialist camp.[54]

As a result, the ALN's greatest "contribution" to the revival of insurrection in Latin America after the death of "Che" Guevara became Marighella's *Minimanual.* It would certainly affect the style and methods of the new wave as Guevara and Debray had done a few years earlier when young men took to the mountains instead of the streets. But the ALN as urban terrorists in Rio de Janeiro and Sao Paulo enjoyed far less success than their predecessors did in Havana during the 1950s.[55]

Far better known, and better adept at urban terrorism, were the Uruguayan Tupamaros. This group, whose official name was the National Liberation Movement (MLN), began operations in 1963, but it was not until 1969 that the Tupamaros attracted much attention outside of Montevideo.

The scope of their efforts was almost entirely urban–and since nearly half of Uruguay's population lived in metropolitan Montevideo—the strategy made some sense.[56]

At first, the Tupamaros cultivated popular approval in a society that had grown politically and economically stagnant. But the Robin Hood phase passed quickly. Nevertheless, it was a technique that other urban groups would copy in the initial stages of their insurrections, and was probably the Tupamaros' unique contribution to the theory and practice of waging urban warfare, although, as we have seen, the Venezuelan FALN was the first Latin American group to achieve publicity through a bloodless caper.[57]

The Tupamaros quickly escalated from kidnapping foreign (American, British, and Brazilian) diplomats in 1970 to random killing of low-ranking soldiers (because they were easy targets) in 1971.[58] That switch in tactics proved costly. As a result, the military took a direct hand, and, by the summer of 1973, the Tupamaros were admitting defeat, albeit, a "temporary" one.

As in the case of Marighella and the ALN, the Tupamaros insisted they were aiming their "armed actions" at "undermining the foundations of the regime itself," but the killing of privates, kidnapping of civilian Uruguayans for ransom, and a string of bank robberies chastened the Tupamaro theory with a cold splash of actual practice.[59]

The Tupamaros, of course, were Marxist–Leninist in dogma and looked to Cuba for direct inspiration. Moreover, their leaders were trained in Cuba in the early 1960s, and their new leader, Mauricio Rosencoff, who took over after the arrest of Raul Sendic, is reported to have received funds and instructions from Cuban intelligence.[60]

In the end, the Tupamaros were no more successful than the Brazilian ALN, even though their terrorist tactics were more sophisticated and they demonstrated an ability to generate favorable international publicity.[61]

Their only real achievement—in contrast to the Brazilians—was to help destroy Uruguayan democracy for over a decade. The weak and divided civilian government the Tupamaros were anxious to overthrow was gradually replaced by a tough military dictatorship that waged a successful war against the MLN.

Thus, by the early 1970s, urban guerrillas had shown, despite Cuban encouragement, that their tactics could not succeed in a large, dynamic country with a tough military-backed government such as Brazil or in a small and stagnant country with a weak democratic system like Uruguay.

Could a Latin American Castroite group with a penchant for urban terrorism ever come to power—even with a sympathetic and socialist government to help? Chile would provide the answer to that question.

It was made possible by Salvador Allende's coming to power. Although he was not "elected" in the usual sense of the word, his coalition government of socialists, communists, and dissident Christian Democrats and Radicals was intent on creating revolution from above, thus disproving the need for armed force from below in order to achieve power—a favorite thesis of Fidel Castro that had long put him at odds with the region's more orthodox communist parties, including the Chilean Communist Party.[62]

Allende, however, hardly had a monopoly on undemocratic procedures. Other groups in Chile were impatient with the new president's gradualism in dismantling the "capitalist state."

The most important of the groups was the Movement of the Revolutionary Left, organized in 1965, and dedicated to installing a Marxist–Leninist regime in Chile by force.

The MIR, unlike Allende and his socialist and communist backers, did not believe that merely forming a government was the same as seizing power. As a consequence, the MIR developed its own strategy for winning the revolution—a plan that involved both urban terrorism and rural guerrilla warfare.

But unlike the Brazilian ALN and the Uruguayan Tupamaros, the MIR combined theoretical sophistication and practical organizational skill that made the *miristas* a serious force that received both attention and support from Havana in the 1970s.

The MIR, however, did not begin that way. In the early years of its existence, it tended to resemble its insurrectionary counterparts that dotted the Latin American landscape. At first, the MIR was devoted to promoting university unrest. But inspired by the resolutions coming from the 1967 OLAS conference in Havana, it soon turned to bank robberies and weapons' theft to lay the basis for a future armed revolt. By 1969, the

Christian Democratic government of Eduardo Frei had had enough of MIR's largely urban "armed actions" and drove it underground; as a result, many *miristas* spent two years in hiding or in jail.[63]

That experience seems to have toughened them intellectually and physically. After 1970, they no longer resembled the romantic, middle class "revolutionaries" they once were and which many of their Latin American *companeros* would always remain. Like Castro emerging from his own stint on the Isle of Pines, the MIR leaders had formed a serious plan to seize power.

Unlike the members of Allende's governing coalition, the *miristas* were never under the illusion that Allende was the last step in the revolutionary process or that a Marxist–Leninist dictatorship could be established without a fight—at some point.[64]

They openly compared Allende to the Kerensky government of 1917, and more immediately, the Arbenz regime in Guatemala in 1954. Allende, by definition, was transitional, but whether the Leninists would seize power as in Russia or the army would as in Guatemala depended on what the MIR and its allies did with the time at their disposal.

The MIR's fundamental thesis was that, during the Allende years, it would have to build "alternate power" structures in order to wage simultaneously urban and rural warfare.

The emphasis, nevertheless, was placed on preparation for urban-based combat, and the model for seizing power was the Bolshevik one under Lenin, not Castro's 26th of July.[65]

Specifically, the MIR built up its strength in a series of industrial parks and encampments that surrounded the capital of Santiago. As Robert Moss, one of the few writers on Chile who actually visited the MIR strongholds in the early 1970s, observed:

> They pointed like long knives towards the heart of Santiago [threatening] . . . the administrative center and the affluent *barrio alto*. They contained the key industries and nearly all the important targets for a group that intended to paralyze the city's vital services: light, power, gas, water, etc.[66]

According to Robert Moss, in some state-run industries, MIR militias were formed, capable, among other things, of attacking opposing demonstrators and seizing factories when ordered.

But the MIR's grand objective far surpassed the tactics of the street fighter. It was:

[to] create the forces that they hoped would be able to take on and defeat the armed forces in the event of a civil war and crush the opposition if it attempted a second "national strike". . . . [The] committees set up in the workers' suburbs were intended as the Soviets of the new Chile.[67]

If the army had not intervened in September 1973, the MIR might have succeeded. As it was, the *miristas* were quickly, once again, driven underground. Despite promises of "spectacular action," however, the MIR was only capable of scattered shows of force: a bank robbery a year after the coup and bombings in 1977 and 1979.[68]

Still, the MIR did have a serious plan, unlike its contemporaries, and it did go about the hard business of implementing its strategy. The work involved far more than picking up a rifle and shooting it, which virtually was the *reductio ad absurdum* style of a Marighella.[69]

Not surprisingly, the MIR's seriousness of purpose impressed the Cubans. In contrast to their rather sparse support of the Brazilian ALN and the Uruguayan Tupamaros, there is ample evidence the Cubans were deeply and heavily involved in aiding the MIR and its associates.

Thus, while Fidel Castro demonstrated a close and friendly relationship with Salvador Allende, the Cuban leader had long expressed his doubts about any revolutionary strategy which suggested the peaceful road to power was possible. These doubts would not go away even after 1968 when Castro was forced to make his peace with Moscow.

Still, it was a different Fidel who visited Chile in November 1971. Instead of openly and blatantly issuing orders for an armed revolt, Castro pursued a far more subtle dual-track strategy.

Publicly, he affected a modesty in offering advice to his audiences in that extraordinary 24-day state visit. On two occassions, he even offered a formula allowing exceptions to his iron rule of revolution. "And we certainly could not have been thinking of," he insisted, "or referring to the case of Chile or even the case of Uruguay—to name examples which, in reality, were exceptional and in a minority." Castro then added by way of explanation that workers in the two countries had an important role which allowed the Chilean communists to pursue their broad front strategy with a chance of success.[70]

Privately, he was taking no chances. Proof of that is the close support Havana gave the MIR in the Allende years. Cuba not only then had its largest embassy in Santiago, but, from that station, its intelligence officers directed a major effort to help Chile's armed action groups-in-being.

The Cubans supplied the MIR with arms, which accounts for the large stockpile of weapons found in the *mirista* strongholds. And along with the North Koreans, they provided military instructors.[71]

Havana also trained the MIR top cadre. That training, said a December 1981 State Department white paper, ranged from:

> . . . political indoctrination and instruction in small arms use to sophisticated courses in document fabrication, explosives, code writing, photography, and disguise. In addition, Cuban instructors trained MIR activists in the Mideast and Africa.[72]

Another facet of the Cuban effort in Chile would serve as a model for later. The Cubans, for the first time, worked closely with other communist countries as well as some 14,000 "internationalists" that flocked to Chile after Allende took office. It was, in fact, a striking forerunner of what is happening in Nicaragua today, although now it is on a larger and vastly more successful scale.[73]

Argentina

The defeat in Chile did not discourage Havana or lead it to any known reassessment of using urban terrorism as a weapon against Latin American governments. As a consequence, at least one more major effort at creating a city-based insurgency was made with Cuban support after 1973— this time in Argentina.

What became known as the "dirty war" bore a striking resemblance to terrorist efforts in Brazil, Chile, and Uruguay. But Argentina was also far more complex. For one thing, a number of groups were involved in the mayhem, and the most important of them were purely Marxist–Leninist in the conventional use of that term, even by the somewhat loose standards of Fidel Castro.

The first, the Popular Revolutionary Army (ERP), was Trotskyite in origin—a variant of communism that Castro himself had bitterly criticized beginning in 1966.[74]

The ERP, although it proclaimed the need to follow a rural guerrilla strategy, conducted most of its operations in the cities—Buenos Aires, the capital, in particular. There, the ERP established the familiar pattern of urban terrorists: robbery, kidnapping, and murder.

But kidnapping (particularly that of foreign business executives) became a highly refined technique with the Popular Army.[75] By 1974, the ERP demanded (and received) no less than $14.2 million in ransom for the release of an Exxon executive. Still, even the ERP could be topped. The following year, another urban action group, the Montoneros, who came from the left wing of the Peronist movement, got $60 million for three executives from the Argentine firm of Bunge and Born.[76]

And once again the urban terrorists proclaimed war on the military but largely confined themselves to hitting "soft" targets. As one analyst observed about the Argentine groups:

> [I]t is a peculiarity of urban guerrilla warfare that terrorist operations undertaken by a small number of personnel, and thus at relatively low cost and risk, are particularly effective. On the other hand, operations of a military nature, that is, direct confrontations with the armed forces, require numerous personnel, with considerable likelihood of failure, heavy casualties, and loss of prisoners who may be tortured into betraying vital secrets.[77]

Although the ERP made a stab at rural guerrilla warfare in the north of Argentina in 1975, it and the Montoneros never really moved beyond the city limits, despite the fact that it took no less than seven Argentine governments (four military, three civilian) to crush them. The cost to the country's political civility, in addition, was higher than in any other internal conflict in the hemisphere up to that time.

The Cuban support of the ERP and the Montoneros was relatively low key. But the top leaders of the ERP especially were given training in Cuba beginning in 1962 in urban and rural warfare. They were also provided with the follow-up support and protection necessary for survival after military defeat.[78]

But the Argentine experience demonstrated something much more fundamental for the Cubans, and it would sow the needs for future trouble—namely that, even in defeat, the "revolution" could still win, at least, eventually.

Havana learned that a highly developed and politically sophisticated country like Argentina can, when faced with urban terrorism, conduct the war in such a way that its own security forces become discredited at home and abroad. So damaged are they, it is hoped, that in the future, the insurgents (many of the leaders are alive in comfortable exile) will be in a far better position to wage a successful war. For Castro, at least, losing in Argentina was a moral victory, and it came, for him, at a cheap price.

The South American Southern Cone in the early 1970s, therefore, was no total loss for Havana. At a low cost, it helped support a few thousand terrorists who helped destroy two long-standing democracies and poison the political wells of another, Argentina. Only in Brazil did the machine-gun-happy followers of Carlos Marighella have nothing to show for their efforts.

From their failures, the Cubans also relearned what "Che" Guevara had called for in his letter to the Tricontinental Conference. To be successful, he said, the revolution must be carried out on a continental scale. For the Argentine physician, that was not merely romantic anti-Americanism. It was literally the road to power for would-be communist governments in the region. But it was only in the Southern Cone that the first operational attempt to make that a reality was carried out long after Guevara's death in Bolivia.

It was baptized the Junta of Revolutionary Coordination (JCR) and was formed at a secret meeting in the Argentine north-western provincial city of Mendoza in February 1974. At that meeting were representatives from the Argentine ERP, the Chilean MIR, the Uruguayan MLN, and the Bolivian ELN founded by "Che" Guevara.[79]

The JCR's manifesto predictably claimed that armed struggle was the proper tactic in destroying U.S. imperialism in Latin America and that only simultaneously waged insurgencies would insure success. As for the right way to take power, the JCR ruled out no form of violence and added a single caveat, namely, the nature of the armed and unarmed struggle would be determined by "the peculiarities of each region and country."[80]

Although its individual members were hardpressed in 1974 and 1975, the JCR did not provide help to Colombian action groups and a Paraguayan unit, *Frepalina,* which needed a start-up boost.[81]

The Junta was headquartered in Buenos Aires, and the ERP was its primary source of funds. Not surprisingly, the JCR became largely the creature of the Argentine terrorists.

While in operation in Argentina, however, its members received training and arms from the Cubans (as well as the Libyans and Iraqis), and it ran a clandestine training school, a weapons factory, and a center for forging false documents—the critical infrastructure for any terrorist group. These facilities were all within Buenos Aires until the ERP was shut down by the Argentine government (then led by Mrs. Peron) in 1975.[82]

That the concept found favor with the Cubans is demonstrated, according to one analyst, by their providing two training sites in Cuba for the JCR. The camps offered courses typically given only to special forces.[83]

After its defeat in Argentina, the JCR first relocated in Lisbon (Portugal was friendly to revolutionaries in the mid-1970s) and eventually Paris in 1976, where, at least until late in that decade, it continued to supply Latin American "revolutionaries" with money and false documents as well as recruit Europeans for the Cuban-run training camps.[84]

At the moment, the JCR remains an organization potentially capable of carrying out coordinated and multinational urban-based terrorism that could be revived, when and if opportunities present themselves. At a minimum, it provided Havana the first extensive experience in managing a coordinated, international effort to advance communist revolutions, in this case, primarily through the use of terrorism.

Notes to Chapter 2

1. Bonachea and Valdes, *Revolutionary Struggle* . . ., 388. In an interview with Andrew St. George of *Look* magazine in February 1958, Castro promised respect for private investment and weighed in against nationalization of property. He also promised "a truly honest election" within a year. Quoted in Bonachea and Valdes, 370.

2. Quoted in ibid., 379. His public remarks about the United States were mild; witness responses to questions by reporter Andrew St. George in ibid., 371, and in Castro's article, "Why We Fight," in the February 1958 *Coronet* magazine. Also in Bonachea and Valdes, 364–367. Earlier, in his famous *History Will Absolve Me* pamphlet, "he made no major attack on the U.S.—indeed, Castro spoke less violently of the 'colossus of the north' than most Cuban nationalist politicians of the previous fifty years," according to Hugh Thomas, 851. The full text is in Bonachea and Valdes, 164–221.

3. Theodore Draper, *Castroism, Theory and Practice* (New York: Praeger, 1965), 142.

4. *Pravda,* 15 April 1962 and reprinted in the *Current Digest of the Soviet Press,* 9 May 1962. The slogan on Cuba followed that of orthodox communist Czechoslovakia and preceded Yugoslavia who, although heterodox, was then on good terms with the Soviet Union thanks to Nikita Khrushchev's attempts at detente with Tito. Moreover, Cuba ranked well above other Kremlin favorites, including Algeria, India, and Indonesia.

5. William E. Ratliff, *Castroism and Communism in Latin America, 1959– 1976* (Washington, D.C.: American Enterprise Institute, 1976), 28. See also D.

Bruce Jackson, *Castro, The Kremlin, and Communism in Latin America* (Baltimore: The Johns Hopkins Press, 1969) *passim* for a discussion of the theoretical disputes between early Castroism and the more cautious and orthodox Marxist–Leninists of the Soviet camp. For a more elaborated version of the early Guevara–Castro thesis on revolution, see the work of their then protégé Regis Debray, in his *Revolution within the Revolution* (New York: Grove Press, 1967) and its analysis in Jackson, 122–134.

6. According to Chamorro, he did request aid from the Cubans (Castro and Guevara specifically), but he was refused because of differing political views. Shirley Christian reports that another (unnamed) Nicaraguan told her that Guevara would have sent arms if Chamorro had succeeded in establishing a base inside the country. Shirley Christian, *Nicaragua: Revolution in the Family* (New York: Random House, 1985), 26.

7. For an account of the Panama adventure, see John C. Dreier, *The Organization of American States and the Hemisphere Crisis* (New York: Harper and Row, 1962), 68. For the Dominican invasion, see Thomas, *Cuba: The Pursuit of Freedom*, 1228, and Andres Suarez, *Cuba: Castroism and Communism, 1959–1966* (Cambridge, MA: MIT Press, 1967), 63–68. Castro's two principal speeches outlining his theory on revolution are "The Second Declaration of Havana" made on 4 February 1962 and a restatement of his thesis in the face of more orthodox communists criticism on 13 March 1967 and 10 August 1967. For a latter day and skeptical view, see Carla Anne Robbins. *The Cuban Threat* (New York: McGraw-Hill, 1983), 9–12.

8. Havana's response to Port–au–Prince's charges that the attack was planned by "Che" Guevara and manned entirely by Cubans was silence. Robbins, 11–12.

9. Those countries that experienced guerrilla warfare included Colombia, Guatemala, Nicaragua, Peru, and Venezuela. The first phase is generally considered to have ended with Che Guevara's death in Bolivia in October 1967. See Ratliff, especially 99–132.

10. Ratliff, 18. Later, for a few years, the Chinese would be in agreement with the Cubans that armed struggle was appropriate throughout the region. Peking's enthusiasm for Latin America cooled considerably after its 1966 quarrel with Havana—one that has not yet been resolved—and the failure of its own Maoist style revolutionaries who often amounted to little more than micro-factions. Peru's rural-based guerrilla group, the Mao-inspired *Sendero Luminoso*, is an exception, but the current leadership in Peking has rejected much of the thought of Mao Tse–tung that the Senderos still acknowledge as the shining path.

11. Jackson, 16.

12. Suarez, 48, and Thomas, 1090.

13. Robert Moss, *Urban Guerrillas* (London: Temple Smith, 1972), 168.

14. Ibid. Also Robbins, 23–27.

15. Ratliff, 68: 71. Also Jackson, 23, and Moss, 169–170. Castro's material commitment to destroying the Venezuelan elections was a four-ton arms shipment that he sent a month before voting day, December 1. For the details, see President

Romulo Betancourt's recounting of the weapons and their capture in "The Venezuelan Miracle," *The Reporter,* 13 August 1964, pp. 37–42.

16. Quoted in Jackson, 21. The articles, based on the interview with Castro, were written by Claude Julien and were published in *Le Monde,* 22 and 23 March, 1963.

17. The other five were Colombia, Guatemala, Haiti, Honduras, and Paraguay. Jackson, 28–31.

18. Ibid., 30–31.

19. Quoted in Jackson, 50. Castro had come a long way from his days as a rebel when he had denounced terrorism. The March 13 speech was prompted by the kidnap and murder by the FALN of Dr. Julio Iribarren Borges, a former director of Venezuela's Social Security Administration and brother of the then foreign minister. The PCV criticized the killing and that proved too much for Castro, who a week later attacked the Venezuelan party without quarter. See ibid., 112–114, and this text.

20. Jackson, 55–67.

21. Ibid., 35.

22. It was a control he did not hesitate to use. When the Cubans clashed with the Soviets over the future site of the Tricontinental secretariat (Havana was the Cuban choice; the Russians wanted Cairo), Castro closed the airport until the delegates gave him what we wanted. Jackson, 81.

23. Fourteen months later Castro would refer to Mao as "senile, barbarous and no longer competent to stay in office." Quoted in Thomas, 1477, from Castro's 13 March 1967 speech.

24. The best analysis of the Tricontinent Conference can be found in Jackson, 68–94; Suarez, 230–234; and Council of the Organization of American States, *Report on the First Afro–Asian–Latin American Peoples Solidarity Conference and Its Projections,* 2 vols., (Washington: The Pan American Union, 28 November 1966). See also Maurice Halperin, *The Taming of Fidel Castro* (Berkeley: University of California Press, 1980), 185–194. Also see Paul Bethel, "The Havana Conference," *The Reporter,* 24 March 1966, for an early and interesting interpretation of the event.

25. Jackson, 82. The delegations were approximately 30 in number from each continent. Although the focus was on Latin America, it should not be forgotten that the Cubans also invited delegations from terrorist and guerrilla organizations in Angola, Mozambique, Portuguese Guinea, Rhodesia, South Africa, and Southwest Africa. See the Organization of American States, *Report of the Special Committee to Study Resolutions II.1 and VIII of the Eighth Meeting of Consultation of Ministers of Foreign Affairs on the First Afro-Asian-Latin American Peoples Solidarity Conference and its Projections,* 9–21.

26. Quoted in Jackson, 83. The full text of the speech can be found in Council of the OAS *Report,* vol. II, 47–63.

27. Jackson, 84–87. The First Tricontinent Conference, however, would be the last. The OSPAAAL secretariat, which the Cubans fought bitterly to have headquartered in Havana, would eventually deteriorate into another publishing

house, at first putting out a glossy magazine *Tricontinental*, which, in time, would be reduced to a cut-rate, cheap paper publication. Halperin, 194.

28. Jackson, 93. Also Halperin, 189.

29. Ratliff, 33–34; 199–208. Also see James D. Theberge, *The Soviet Presence in Latin America* (New York: Crane, Russak & Company, 1974), 60–61. The Soviets sent only two observers, while guerrillas and their allies dominated the Latin American delegations. One of Castro's pet hatreds, the Venezuelan Communist Party, was also condemned by name, its policy labeled "bungling and opportunistic." Quoted in Ratliff, 208.

30. See, for example, the reporting of Marcel Niedergang in *Le Monde*, 2 August 1967, and cited in Ratliff, 201. For Carmichael's role at the OLAS conference, see Halperin, 259–260. Halperin's own judgment of OLAS is harsh. He called it "a carnival of absurd revolutionary rhetoric." Ibid., 260.

31. Quoted in Ratliff, 33.

32. The Guatemalan guerrilla leader Luis Turcios was killed a year earlier, the apparent victim of an automobile accident in the outskirts of Guatemala City, and Venezuela's Douglas Bravo, whom Fidel had championed for years, would denounce the Cuban leader in early 1970 for being a Soviet tool. Ibid., 112; 37. Also Thomas, 1479.

33. Quoted in Ratliff, 13, from *New Times* (Moscow), 18 October 1968. Also Halperin, 260. Moscow's allies, however, were more outspoken in their criticism. See, for example, *L'Humanite* (Paris), the French Communist daily, a criticism that was reproduced in the U.S. Communist Party daily, *The Worker* (New York), 20 August 1967, and quoted in ibid.

34. Theberge, 63. See also Ratliff, 45. Although Castro's defense of the Soviet destruction of a more liberal communist regime in Prague served some of his own interests, namely that the literal reading of the Brezhnev Doctrine might insure his own survival, Castro would be subjected to widespread criticism in Latin America where intervention, especially by major powers, is sacrosanct to left and right. Moreover, it did not help for some members of the much despised Venezuelan Communist Party to voice their objections to the Czech invasion. Ratliff, 55. The August speech on the Czech situation was presaged by Castro's July 26th speech. Ordinarily an ultra revolutionary address commemorating the attack on the Moncada barracks, the 1968 speech made no mention of Guevara, armed struggle, guerrilla groups in Latin America, or even the otherwise "heroic" Vietnamese. See Halperin, 306.

35. Theberge, 64.

36. Halperin, 325.

37. According to a Venezuelan FALN defector, he and other young Venezuelans were taught guerrilla and urban terrorist tactics at the Tarara training center near Havana in the fall of 1960. See Juan deDios Marin, "Inside a Castro 'Terror School'" *Reader's Digest* (December 1964) V. 85: 119–123.

38. It was only after the failure of urban terrorism, for example, that the Venezuelan communists decided in April 1964 that rural guerrilla warfare was the proper strategy. Three years later, after more failure, they decided that all forms of armed struggle were (temporarily) in error. See Ratliff, 71–72.

39. For further details of the crime, see Halperin, 233–235.

40. Jackson, 112–113, and Ratliff, 104. The real crime, according to Fidel Castro, was not the murder of a human being by the FALN, but the "treason" committed by the PCV, for among other things, criticizing acts of FALN terrorism.

41. Ratliff, 41–42. Also Thomas, 1479. Ratliff adds that by the mid-1960s serious attention was also being paid to training Africans. The CIA report referred to was its report to the House, Sub-Committee on Inter-American Affairs, *Communism in Latin America* (Washington, D.C.: Government Printing Office, 1965), 120–123. Also see the *Washington Post*, 18 June 1967, and the *New York Times*, 2 August 1967.

42. Ratliff, 42. Some of the information on the DGI's activities was provided by a DGI defector, Orlando Castro Hidalgo, in testimony before the U.S. Senate Internal Security Sub-Committee, 16 October 1969, *Communist Threat to the United States through the Caribbean*, pt. 20 (Washington, D.C.: U.S. Government Printing Office, 1969) and also Castro Hidalgo's book, *Spy for Fidel*, cited earlier.

43. The officer has been identified as Colonel Wadim Kotscherigine. Yonah Alexander and Richard Kucinski, "Latin American Insurgencies: The Terrorist International Network," (unpublished manuscript, n.d.), 12.

44. Ratliff, 42.

45. Quoted in ibid., 37. The speech, delivered on April 22 (Lenin's birthday), was published in *Granma*, 3 May 1970. Castro's bitter assault was aimed at the Venezuelan insurrectionary Douglas Bravo who earlier had accused the Cuban leader of surrendering to the Soviets—which indeed he had.

46. Ratliff, 42.

47. *El Dia* (Mexico City), 26 January 1975. Castro presented his dictum at the Soviet Communist Party's 25th Congress and was printed in *Granma*, 7 March 1976. Both quotations can be found in Ratliff, 39.

48. Quoted in ibid., 41. For the full text see *Granma*, 7 March 1976.

49. Marighella's *Minimanual* can be found in Mallin, Ed., *Terror and Urban Guerrillas*, 67–115. See documents. Although Guevara, as noted above was an advocate of the rural guerrilla, he did not rule out entirely the use of urban-based terrorism as he makes clear in his text on guerrilla warfare where he devotes a short section to "suburban warfare." See "Che" Guevara, *Guerrilla Warfare*, trans. J. P. Mornay (New York: Vintage Books, 1961), 29–31. Guevara was much more explicit in the uses of terrorism in his "Instructions for Cadres Who Work in Urban Areas." These instructions were aimed at his Bolivian city "comrades" who were to murder "informers, notorious torturers, and high officials of the regime," as well as kidnap for ransom and engage in economic sabotage. The text can be found in Rolando E. Bonachea and Nelson P. Valdes, *Che: Selected Worlds of Ernesto Guevara* (Cambridge, MA: MIT Press, 1969), 189. Written in 1967, these "guidelines" were first published in *Granma*, 14 July 1968.

50. Quoted in Ernst Halperin, *Terrorism in Latin America* Beverly Hills, (California: Sage Publications, 1976), 10.

51. Quoted in Ratliff, 142–143.

52. E. Halperin, 10, and Ratliff, 140–141. Marighella was no youthful rebel. He had been a member of the pro-Soviet Brazilian Communist Party (PCB) for decades until he broke with the PCB in December 1966. Ratliff, 138–140. See also Samuel T. Francis, "Latin American Terrorism: The Cuban Connection," *Heritage Foundation Backgrounder,* 9 November 1979, 7–8.

53. E. Halperin, 10. From Marighella's *Minimanual,* quoted in Ratliff, 141–142. The ALN and another smaller urban terrorist group, the Revolutionary Movement–8 (MR–8) sputtered on for several more years after Marighella's death, until, in early 1973, the ALN announced that it had no popular support. In *Le Monde,* 15 February 1973, and cited in Ratliff, 139.

54. Ratliff, 140–141. The November 1970 issue of *Tricontinental* was devoted to the *Minimanual,* and it was prefaced by a laudatory essay on Marighella by the Cuban editors. "On this occasion, no homage to his memory seems more appropriate than to dedicate this complete issue of his Mini-Manual to the urban guerrilla as *the best contribution for those who may accept the challenge he offered . . .*" (emphasis mine). Quoted in Herbert Romerstein. *Soviet Support for International Terrorism,* Washington, D.C.: (The Foundation for Democratic Education, Inc., 1981), 14. *Tricontinental* also published other examples of his work. One, gushing prologue written by comrade-in-arms J. Camara Ferreira, preceded the Marighella articles. *Carlos Marighella* (Havana: Tricontinental, Colleccion/los hombres, [1970]), 9–20. That was followed by an equally adoring (but unsigned) "biography" of Marighella. Ibid., 21–31.

55. For a Marxist, even a dissident one, Marighella showed remarkably little interest in the history of urban terrorism, including the actual experience of the Cuban revolution.

56. Even "Che" Guevara had entertained the possibility of a largely urban effort in countries dominated by its major cities, including Argentina. "Che" Guevara "Mensaje a los Argentinos," in *Cristianismo y Revolucion,* [Buenos Aires] (October 1968): 22. For a sympathetic commentary, see Michael Lowy, *The Marxism of Che Guevara,* Trans. Brian Pearce (New York: Monthly Review Press, 1973), 103.

57. Other Tupamaro spectaculars included a raid on the Naval Training Center (May 1970) where they captured 350 rifles and machineguns, and what has been called "a spectacular tunnelling operation" which freed 106 failed terrorists. Richard Clutterbuck, *Protest and the Urban Guerrilla,* (New York: Abelard–Schuman, 1973), 252–253.

58. One of them, an American, Dan Mitrione, a security adviser at the U.S. embassy, was murdered, or "executed" in Tupamaro parlance, on 9 August 1970. Ratliff, 134. The Cuban Communist Party newspaper *Granma* printed the Tupamaro "conversations" with Mitrione in full sympathy with the Uruguayan terrorists. Romerstein, 21.

59. Ratliff, 134–137. Also E. Halperin, 10–14.

60. Francis, 10.

61. E. Halperin, 10–11. Unlike the Venezuelan FLN–FALN in 1963 and the Salvadoran FMLN in 1982 and 1984, the Tupamaros did not attempt to wreck

the November 1971 national elections. Voting was too well-established a habit in Uruguay for the Tupamaros to challenge frontally.

62. Allende, in fact, received a smaller percentage of the vote in the 1970 election than he did in 1964. Since he had not achieved a majority vote, the decision was thrown to the Chilean Congress where his supporters hammered out an agreement with the Christian Democrats, whose votes gave him the presidency. In turn, Allende promised to respect Chile's democratic institutions, a pledge he had no intention of keeping. See Robert Moss, *Chile's Marxist Experiment* (New York: Halsted Press, 1973), 7–51. Allende told Regis Debray that the so-called Statute of Guarantees with the Christian Democrats was "a tactical necessity." For Allende, the real purpose of power was to destroy "the bourgeois State." He continued: "at the present moment, we are seeking to overcome it. To overthrow it!" Quoted in Regis DeBray, *The Chilean Revolution: Conversations with Allende* (New York: Vintage Books, 1971), 82; 119.

63. Moss, 107, and Ratliff, 169.

64. For a detailed account of the MIR strategy and its implementation, see Ratliff, 169–176, and Moss, 99–122. For a detailed look at the antecedents of the MIR and the nature of "revolutionary politics" in Chile in the 1950s and 1960s, see Ernst Halperin *Nationalism and Communism in Chile* (Cambridge, MA: MIT Press, 1965).

65. But even here the MIR did not pay merely lip service to rural guerrilla warfare, as the ALN and the Tupamaros had. The MIR not only believed a simulaneous effort was required, they had, through land seizures, especially in the southern provinces, established the physical bases for conducting such a campaign. Nor did they overlook the possibilities of stirring up the Mapuche Indians, among the most exploited and neglected groups in Chilean society. See Moss, 115–117; 119–120.

66. Ibid., 100.

67. Ibid., 103.

68. Ratliff, 176, and Francis, 8.

69. For another critique of Marighella and his methods, see Anthony M. Burton, *Urban Terrorism: Theory, Practice and Response* (New York: The Free Press, 1975), 80–83.

70. From a question-and-answer session held at the Chilean Communist Party's Central Organization of Workers (CUTCh), 23 November 1971 *Fidel in Chile* (New York: International Publishers, 1972), 116, and quoted in Leon Goure and Morris Rothenberg, *Soviet Penetration of Latin America* (Miami: Center for Advanced International Studies, University of Miami, 1975), 26. On an earlier occasion in Chile, Castro implied to students at the University of Concepcion on November 18 that Chile and Uruguay were exceptions to the revolutionary rule because as in the case of Uruguay "all the left is participating in [the elections], all the forces of the left are participating in this Broad Front." In fact, the Tupamaros did endorse the elections (in which the extreme left fared poorly), while refusing to lay down their weapons. *Fidel in Chile,* 79.

71. Moss, iv; 101–102. As for Allende, Castro's 1971 trip was a net loss for

the hardpressed Chilean president. Fidel's branding the entire opposition as "fascist" enraged even left wing Christian Democrats. Ibid., 123. Also Theberge, 39–40, and Ratliff, 42. Ratliff cites a defecting Cuban intelligence officer who reported in late 1971 that "Chile was the new base for Cuban support of Latin American revolutionaries." Ibid. James Theberge reports, however, that the Cubans and the North Koreans disagreed on strategy, with Havana favoring a more "cautious" policy of bombings and assasinations but avoiding direct clashes with the armed forces, while Pyong–yang wanted a more aggressive policy of large-scale sabotage that would force the army to move too soon. Theberge, 41.

72. "Cuba's Renewed Support for Violence in Latin America," United States Department of State, Special Report No. 90, 14 December 1981: 11. Unlike an earlier State Department white paper released in February 1981 in which minor errors were seized on by the Soviet bloc propaganda apparatus and others in the Western press who sought to discredit it, the December paper was never challenged. In fact, its unprecedented release of classified information provoked sharp exchanges within the administration between those who wished to have the information made public and those who wished to protect sources and methods.

73. The Cuban DGI also helped train the Bolivian National Liberation Army (ELN) in Chile with apparent Soviet approval. Ibid., 39.

74. The ERP would break with the Trotskyite Fourth International in early 1973. Subsequently, the latter publicly criticized its estranged Argentine brothers. It was a position that Castro would never emulate. Francis, 4. Also Roger W. Fontaine "Communist Revolutionaries in Argentina," in *Argentina, OAS and Hemispheric Security* (Washington, D.C.: American Foreign Policy Institute, 1979), 44–55.

75. There were 178 kidnappings in 1973 alone. See E. Halperin, *Terrorism in Latin America,* 17.

76. E. Halperin, *Terrorism,* 17. The "Juan Jose Valle" Montoneros were founded in early 1970, and their most famous terrorist act was kidnapping and killing former Argentine President Aramburu. J. Bowyer Bell, *Transnational Terror* (Washington, D.C.: American Enterprise Institute, 1975), 51–52.

77. E. Halperin, *Terrorism,* 18.

78. Francis, 6. Also Theberge, 45 and the State Department's Special Report, no. 90, 11. Among the leaders were Joe Baxter, who a few years before was a member of an Argentine neo-fascist movement called the Tacuara. Walter Lacquer, *Terrorism* (Boston: Little, Brown, and Company, 1977), 203. See also Romerstein, 21. Romerstein documents the Cuban assistance given to this originally Trotskyite group from internal documents of the movement, specifically, *International Internal Discussion Bulletin* of the Fourth International XIV, no. 8 (September 1977): 14–15. The IIDB was available only to members.

79. Yonah Alexander and Robert A. Kilmarx, eds. *Political Terrorism and Business* (New York: Praeger, 1979), 36–37. Also Francis, 5, and Ratliff, 40. The ill-starred ELN, unlike its brothers in the Southern Cone, barely ever existed. It never quite escaped the failure of its beginning under Guevara or its manifestly non-Bolivian origins. Guevara's "army" at its greatest strength had 51, 17 of whom were Cuban and 29 were Bolivian. Ratliff, 123. Three months later in

June 1967, according to Guevara's diary, the ELN had dwindled to 25 with 17 Cubans. Ibid., 40.

80. The manifesto was first published in the leftwing Mexican magazine *Por Que?* [Mexico City], 20 June 1974. The English translation is available in its entirety in Ratliff, 209–215.

81. Francis, 5.

82. Ibid.

83. Ibid.

84. Ibid. Meanwhile, both the Argentine Montoneros and the Uruguayan Tupamaros have relocated in Havana on call for special assignments. State Department's Special Report No. 90, 11–12. Also see Claire Sterling, "The Terrorist Network," in *The Atlantic Monthly* (November 1978) v. 242: 43. A Montonero base was also uncovered in Rome in the summer of 1977, and it included weapons and false papers. Vittofranco S. Pisano, "The Red Brigades: A Challenge to Italian Democracy," in *Contemporary Terrorism*, Ed. William Gutteridge (New York: Facts on File, 1986), 192.

Chapter 3

Terrorism in Full Flower

By the mid-1970s, most observers were prepared to write off Fidel Castro's penchant for making trouble as just that—an inclination to do so, but without much evidence of success.[1]

The rural guerrilla efforts in countries as diverse as Venezuela and Bolivia had failed, with the defeat of "Che" Guevara being both ignominious and pathetic.

Urban terrorist groups too had no better luck at seizing power. The cities of the Southern Cone proved to be their graveyards just as much as Havana and Santiago de Cuba had become the cemeteries of an earlier generation of Cuban insurgents.[2]

Moreover, Castro missed an opportunity to exploit one serious and near spontaneous insurrection that broke out in Santo Domingo in the spring of 1965. But the bitterest pill of all was the fall of Salvador Allende in Chile. Although Castro had tried to cover his bets by supporting the regime on the one hand and preparing the ultra-left to seize power on the other, in the end nothing worked, and General Augusto Pinochet Ugarte assumed power.

Despite these setbacks, however, Fidel Castro never abandoned his hopes for communist revolutions throughout the hemisphere. Castro's mistakes as well as his perserverance have led to more success in the last decade than in his first fifteen as Cuba's Maximum Leader. And although the Soviets helped trim his rhetoric, if not his actions, after the Tricontinent Conference, Fidel also gained by having a firmer basis for cooperating with the Soviet Union and then later with other radical (and violently anti-American) regimes and movements.

Characteristically, Castro's rebounding from failure and frustration in the mid-1970s was anticipated by few, if anyone, in the West. Not only did the Cuban leader refuse to play the game of only normalizing relations with Latin America, his next major effort was not aimed at Latin America at all. Nor was it another attempt at unconventional warfare, either rural or urban based.

Instead, Castro decided to rescue a floundering Marxist guerrilla movement in Angola and help it secure power after the departure of the Portuguese. That decision, made in the summer of 1975, led to the intervention of Cuban special forces which put iron in the Angolan and Marxist MPLA (Revolutionary Movement of the People) forces in their battle against two other Angolan guerrilla groups. These, in turn, were assisted by South African forces.

It was this bold gamble, the sudden movement of thousands of Cuban troops to a remote African nation, that propelled Castro from revolutionary has-been to hero once again. His sending more troops into Ethiopia and their role in defeating the armed forces of neighboring Somalia a little more than two years later only reinforced the belief that Cuba was at the cutting edge of the American decline.[3]

But despite his military successes in Africa, Fidel Castro had far from given up on Latin America. From the experience he had accumulated after three decades of waging revolutions at home and abroad, Castro became an even more formidable adversary in the 1980s. And this time, one of Havana's most lethal weapons would be terrorism.

Target: Central America

Nicaragua

Eclecticism now marked Castro's new approach to armed force. No longer was rural guerrilla warfare the only road to power. The tedious debate of the 1960s about how to seize power was over. Whatever worked was right—a ruthless pragmatism of violence that is still very much in vogue in Havana.

The emphasis Castro has placed on Central America since 1978 vividly demonstrates the triumph of practice and necessity over earlier convictions. Ironically, however, the Cuban leader's first clear-cut success would come 20 years after. It occurred less than 500 miles from Cuba, in other words, in his own backyard.

The Sandinista triumph in Nicaragua in July 1979 was in many ways similar to Castro's. Both revolutions displaced unpopular, long-lived, and corrupt dictators. The United States each time at a critical moment withdrew its support for regimes which over the years had been perceived as close friends of Washington. The rebels also had the support of the middle class and democratic groups who thought they were supporting a turn toward democracy. The revolutionaries also had the sympathy of foreigners who were by no means all members of the communist world.

Thus, Cuban help for the Sandinistas was not the only factor in their victory. Havana's role was not sufficient, and it may not even have been necessary. But Castro's sponsoring of the Nicaraguan *comandantes* over a score of years guaranteed that the Sandinistas would remain close to their long-time benefactors, and later, by extension, the entire Soviet bloc.

For years, however, the Sandinistas seemed to be little more than just another inept group of Marxist insurgents who had trouble shooting straight.

Although anti-Somoza rebels had been fighting even before Castro seized power, the FSLN (Sandinist Front of National Liberation) (as it was formally named in 1962) had made little progress throughout the 1960s and well into the next decade. In 1976, for example, it probably had no more than 100 fighters and was nearly exterminated in 1965.[4]

The FSLN revived, however, after the 1967 OLAS conference in Havana—a meeting the then Sandinista chief, Carlos Fonseca Amador, would attend. Its subsequent armed actions for the most part until the middle 1970s were the familiar acts of urban terrorists: bank robberies, kidnappings, and assassinations.[5]

Despite some daring operations—like hijacking a Costa Rican airliner in 1970 and raiding a 1974 Christmas party in which a dozen Nicaraguan politicians and businessmen were kidnapped, even Eden Pastora's takeover of the National Palace in 1977—Sandinista prospects remained slim until 1978 when, at the behest of Castro, the FSLN's three factions united in July 1978. As a consequence, Cuban aid considerably increased.[6]

Until then, Havana had limited its support for the Sandinistas to training its leadership, providing sanctuary, and lending them propaganda support. Although a few weapons were sent in the heady days of the early 1960s, Cuba's support of the FSLN was nothing beyond what it had extended to dozens of such groups.[7]

After mid-1978, however, Havana would train and arm the Sandinistas militarily and this time in large numbers. By the end of the summer of 1978, Cuban intelligence agents had established a sophisticated arms-running network.

According to the State Department's December 1981 white paper:

> . . . arms were flown from Cuba to Panama, transhipped to Costa Rica on smaller planes and supplied to Nicaraguan guerrillas based in northern

Costa Rica. To monitor and assist the flow, the Americas [sic] Department established a secret operations center in San Jose. By the end of 1978, Cuban advisers were dispatched to northern Costa Rica to train and equip the FSLN forces with arms which began to arrive direct from Cuba. FSLN guerrillas trained in Cuba, however, continued to return to Nicaragua via Panama.[8]

Havana did more than run guns and supplies, however. It also provided specialists in the field to command and control the war against Somoza. According to the State Department's white paper which was based on U.S. intelligence sources:

When the insurgent's final offensive was launched in mid-1979, Cuban military advisers from the Department of Special Operations, a special military unit, were with FSLN columns and maintained direct radio communications in Havana.[9]

In Cuba, in early 1979, Castro continued to jawbone the Sandinista factions to remain unified while giving them advice on how to conduct the struggle.[10]

The Cubans also drew on their Chilean experience as well as the core of South American supporters they had recruited in the early 1970s. These so-called "internationalists," many of whom were trained terrorists were formed into an "internationalist brigade" and fought along side the FSLN regulars. They have, for the most part, remained in Nicaragua since the Sandinista victory in July 1979.[11]

As for the fighting, most of it took place in Nicaragua's cities which account for that war's high number of (mostly civilian) casualties. The Sandinistas, besides engaging in conventional fighting, were not above the use of sheer terror, primarily by setting off hundreds of bombs in Managua, the capital. In balance, however, both sides seemed contemptuous of human life, especially of innocent bystanders. The total number lost according to the Red Cross was 10,000 in the last ten months of the war alone (in a country of less than three million). Ninety percent of them were civilian.[12]

El Salvador

The effect of the Nicaraguan victory on Fidel Castro can scarcely be exaggerated. After two decades of failure, the formula for winning that had proven so elusive had at last been found. Ironically, it was similar to the one that had worked in Cuba, albeit the real one and not that of the revolution's myth makers—including Fidel himself.

To be sure, Castro had learned from past mistakes while slowly building up his assets, and he had learned to work with others. He was even prepared to be patient for once in the fight against Somoza—showing more patience than was actually needed.

His revolutionary confidence restored in July of 1979, the Cuban leader in Havana told Salvadoran rebels in December that El Salvador and Guatemala would be next, and Honduras would be turned into one huge Ho Chi Minh trail through which men and materiel would be funnelled.[13]

At the beginning of 1980, the prospects in El Salvador seemed especially promising. A succession of tough, but not especially competent, army officers in mufti had been running the country for decades. A coup in October 1979 ousting one of them promised to be only the first in a series of destabilizing power shifts a la South Vietnam after the murder of President Ngo Diem in 1963.

Nevertheless, before the Sandinista's triumphal march into Managua, communist expectations were not all that great in neighboring El Salvador.

"There were guerrillas in El Salvador," in the words of one State Department white paper, "but no guerrilla war."[14]

> Extremist forces of El Salvador's left were violent but fragmented into competing factions. They had neither a unified organization nor the heavier, more destructive modern weaponry.[15]

Until 1980, the various armed factions pursued a policy of pure urban terrorism. In the late 1970s while operating mostly in the capital, San Salvador, the extremists robbed banks, attacked American businesses, machinegunned the U.S. embassy, kidnapped Salvadoran officials, and killed others, making El Salvador one of the most violent nations on earth.

Cuba's role in this was largely confined to training members (some 200) of the oldest and most active of the extremist groups, the Popular Forces of Liberation (FPL), but Havana also had ties with the Armed Forces of National Resistance (FARN).[16]

With the Sandinistas safely installed in Managua, however, a higher priority could be given to El Salvador. The biggest problem facing the Cubans was uniting the fractured and squabbling extreme left groups who, if anything, were more deeply divided than their Sandinista *companeros*. No wonder then that at that December 1979 meeting in Havana, Castro insisted on the Salvadorans combining forces as the price of Cuba's expanded support.

As a result of his jawboning, an initial unity agreement was agreed upon among the three groups in attendance. Besides the FPL and the FARN, the Salvadoran Communist Party (PCES) also showed up. Earlier, the PCES had formed an armed group—thanks in part to Cuban and Soviet insistence. For the PCES, it was a significant departure from past practice, which, until then, had resembled most orthodox pro-Soviet communist parties in Latin America.[17]

The agreement, though not perfect, was enough for Havana. After the Salvadoran rebel groups formed a combined military command titled the United Revolutionary Directorate (DRU), the Cubans put together an arms supply network which was a virtual carbon copy of the one that had nourished the Sandinistas two years earlier.

According to U.S. intelligence:

> During this period, Cuba . . . coordinated the development of clandestine support networks in Honduras, Costa Rica, and Nicaragua sometimes using arms supply mechanisms established during the Nicaraguan civil war. . . . Cuba provided few weapons and ammunition to Salvadoran guerrillas from its own resources but played a key role in coordinating the acquisition and delivery of arms from Vietnam, Ethiopia, and Eastern Europe through Nicaragua.[18]

Havana also increased its training program for the Salvadorans in anticipation of the "final offensive" scheduled for early 1981. This time, however, the Cubans concentrated on instructing whole units (up to battalion size) rather than only cadres as they had done in the past. The program was thorough, lasting three months, and encompassed far more than the usual instruction in basic guerrilla techniques.[19]

The Cubans provided for the first time highly specialized training courses as well. According to the State Department's December 1981 white paper:

> A former FPL guerrilla who defected in fall 1981 reported that during 1980 he had received 7 months of military training in Cuba, including instruction in scuba diving and underwater demolition. Soviet scuba equipment was

used. The group trained as frogmen called themselves "combat swimmers" and were told that their mission was to destroy dams, bridges, port facilities, and boats.[20]

As for the "final offensive" to be launched just before Ronald Reagan's assuming office, the Cubans not only helped plan the attack in detail, but they also strongly urged that it be carried out—a marked contrast to Fidel Castro's earlier caution with the Sandinistas. Supplying the FMLN, however, was a strictly joint effort with Nicaraguans and Cubans managing the airlift of weapons.[21]

The failure of the Salvadoran rebel blitzkrieg, however, did not discourage Havana even though ordinary Salvadorans—many held at gunpoint—refused to join the insurrection. Cuba has remained in the center of the planning and supply effort for the Salvadoran guerrillas since. Its officers, along with others from Nicaragua and Soviet bloc countries, work out of the rebel's command and control headquarters in Managua, an activity that was only briefly slowed in the wake of the successful U.S. and Caribbean Commonwealth liberation of Grenada in the fall of 1983. The overall pattern of that effort, however, has changed little since the 1981 failure.

According to one State Department white paper:

> After the unmasking of the network, Cuba and Nicaragua reduced the flow in March [1981] and early April. Prior to a guerrilla offensive in August an upswing in deliveries occurred. The arms flow continues via clandestine surface and air routes. In addition, the Cubans over the last year [1981] have established a network of small ships to deliver arms to Salvadoran insurgents groups.[22]

Moreover, the switch from pure urban terrorism to a more rural based insurgency in the early 1980s has by no means ruled out the use of the former. In fact, immediately after the failure of the so-called final offensive, the FMLN ordered a series of terrorist attacks—seven rocket and machine gun assaults on the U.S. embassy alone in March and April 1981.[23]

The following year, the FMLN, like their Venezuelan counterparts, the FALN, attempted to destroy the March 1982 elections using their urban agents to frighten voters away from the polls by bomb throwing and machinegun fire.

And like their Venezuelan counterparts, the FMLN failed and in the process, much of their urban capabilities was destroyed in 1982. Periodically, however, the FMLN's urban terrorist arm reasserts itself, especially in San Salvador. The favorite target is off-duty American servicemen. In the smaller towns, FMLN terrorists have continued to kidnap and kill mayors and other officials in an attempt to destroy governmental infrastructure.[24]

Indeed, because of better counter-insurgency techniques, the Salvadoran armed forces have succeeded in forcing the enemy to break down into smaller combat units. As a result, small group tactics, including urban terrorism, have become once more a major part of the FMLN effort.[25]

Meanwhile, Cuban support for the Salvadoran rebels continues to the present. Moreover, although the total level of assistance has dropped as the fortunes of the Salvadoran rebels have sunk in recent years, the whole apparatus of support remains in place. If circumstances were to change— a policy shift in Washington or a final Sandinista victory over the Contras—the Cuban-supervised network could once again be working at full capacity.

In any case, most American officials believe that, although the Marxist FMLN has taken severe losses in the last four years (their numbers are said to have dropped from 14,000 to 4,000), the government's command of the situation is still believed to be fragile and subject to sudden reversals.[26]

Honduras

While Havana's subversive priority in Central America after mid-1979 has been (and continues to be) supporting the war in El Salvador, efforts have been directed at the other countries on the isthmus too.

Honduras, the poorest nation in the region, borders both El Salvador and Nicaragua. Because of its geographical position alone, it has become a target of both Havana and Managua. Cuba's interest was aroused in the early 1960s when it provided military training to a handful of Honduran radicals. But, according to U.S. intelligence, relations with the Honduran groups were strained, at best, until the late 1970s. According to one State Department report:

> Cuba then resumed military training for members of the Honduran Communist Party (PCH) and integrated them into the "internationalist brigade"

fighting in the Nicaraguan civil war. After the war, PCH members returned to Cuba for additional training.[27]

Although since 1980, Honduras is looked upon by Havana largely as a conduit of convenience for arms shipments to El Salvador, Cuba has also laid the foundation for an insurgency in Honduras beginning in 1981.

The Cubans, in familiar fashion, have insisted that the splintered Honduran left form a fighting coalition. In March 1983, the quarrelsome Hondurans finally merged into the National Unity Directorate of the Revolutionary Movement of Honduras (DNU–MRH).[28]

But practical unity seems so far to be beyond the will and capability of the Honduran extreme left. The basic split is a generational one, with younger radicals more interested in the immediate use of armed force to bring down the government—a view shared by officials in Managua and Havana, but not by their elders.[29]

Despite these problems, however, Havana (and Managua) continues to support a variety of groups with arms and training. The best known of these organizations is the People's Revolutionary Union/Popular Liberation Movement (URP/MLP), better known as the Cinchoneros.

The Cinchoneros began operations in 1981, and their actions since have been almost exclusively terrorist in nature. In March of that year, the group hijacked a Honduran airliner and forced it to fly to Managua where they demanded the release of ten arms-smuggling Salvadoran guerrillas who had been captured earlier in Honduras.

Six months later, the Cinchoneros seized control of the chamber of commerce building in Honduras's second city, San Pedro Sula. They held several cabinet ministers and over a hundred business leaders as hostages in return for their demands to free more imprisoned guerrillas and terrorists. The attempt collapsed when the terrorists received no support from the public while government security forces expertly obtained their surrender without any of the Cinchonero demands being met. They were allowed safe passage to Cuba, however.[30]

Another group, whose cadres have also been trained in Nicaragua and Cuba, the Popular Revolutionary Forces (FPR), has carried out an airplane hijacking (April 1982) and also is responsible for the repeated bombings of American-owned businesses in Honduras. The FPR's most spectacular act of terrorism, however, was the July 4, 1982, sabotaging of Tegucigalpa's main power station.[31]

Meanwhile, terrorist safehouses have been raided over the years by

Honduran authorities, netting arms caches and terrorists who prove to be either Hondurans, Nicaraguans, or Salvadorans.

Both Cuba and Nicaragua, however, have not been content to aid urban terrorists. They have also attempted to spark a rural insurgency. In 1983 and 1984, Cuban and Nicaraguan trained Hondurans attempted to infiltrate Olancho and El Paraiso provinces, so far with little success owing to the alertness of the Honduran security forces.[32]

That, however, did not discourage either the Cubans or the Nicaraguans. According to one State Department report based on U.S. intelligence:

> In April 1985, the Sandinistas were again caught trying to provide support for the Honduran guerrilla groups, but this time the operatives arrested were Nicaraguans. Between April 11–14, seven Nicaraguans were arrested in El Paraiso Department trying to infiltrate arms to Cinchoneros based in Olancho Department. One of them was a member of the Nicaraguan Directorate of State Security (DGSE) who stated that he had coordinated similar arms infiltrations since November 1984.[33]

Guatemala

Before El Salvador and Honduras, even before Nicaragua, there was Guatemala. For the Cubans, the reason is simple. Guatemala, in Havana's estimate, is the key to Central America. If the region's largest country became communist, the others would either become securely Marxist or would follow soon after. That Guatemala also borders Mexico presents other opportunities as well for Havana.

Already by the early 1960s, Fidel Castro had believed that Guatemala was the first target of choice and opportunity. The problem was that the Guatemalan extreme left was also badly split. In the mid- and late-1960s, the principal armed group, the Rebel Armed Forces (FAR), was wracked with dissension over its relationship with the Guatemalan communist party (the PGT).[34]

The cautious nature of the pro-Soviet PGT, in time, proved to be too much for those in the FAR who demanded that a greater emphasis be placed on using violence. It was a familiar strain—almost an exact duplicate of the quarrel between the Venezuelan communist PCV and the fighters that made up the FALN. And as in Venezuela, the argument led to a formal split between the FAR and the PGT, which was announced in January 1968.

That break also coincided with the FAR's decline. By the early 1970s, it had been all but tamed by a tough and aggressive Guatemalan army. Still before the eclipse, the FAR waged both a rural guerrilla war and an urban-based insurgency.

Urban terrorism, as in Venezuela, began in 1963 and continued through the rest of the decade. Until his death in October 1968, Castro's favorite Guatemalan guerrilla, Turcios Lima, was especially insistent on the use of terror.

Turcios did not carry out his group's killings and kidnappings in silence. Indeed, he boasted of their effectiveness in discrediting the government.

> [When] we intensified this type of action, the situation changed and this very bourgeosie demanded that the Government guarantee their lives and properties, and practically threatened the Government with an economic boycott if those guarantees were not granted. . . . These happenings provoke political crisis.[35]

With the defeat of the rural guerrillas by 1967, however, an even bigger emphasis was placed on urban terrorism by Turcios and his followers. According to one analyst:

> Some urban terrorism was carried out, especially in Guatemala City. Between 1968 and 1970 kidnappings and assassinations were directed against foreign nationals as well as Guatemalans, prominent among the former being the ambassadors of the United States (1968) and West Germany (1970).[36]

Thus, once again as in Venezuela, the myth held that in Guatemala the insurrection was exclusively or nearly rurally based. The reality was that terrorism was turned to early and waged with utmost savagery by men who enjoyed the support of Havana.

Terrorism, however, had netted the Guatemalan revolutionaries very little. The factional in-fighting that crippled the Guatemalan leftists of the 1960s became the focal point of a renewed Cuban effort in the 1980s. After Castro's success in uniting the Nicaraguan Sandinistas and the Salvadoran rebels, the Cuban leader stepped up his efforts to produce a fighting Guatemalan coalition.

There was, in fact, much to do. By the late 1970s, Guatemala was blessed with no less than four armed groups: the Guerrilla Army of the Poor (EGP), the Organization of People in Arms (ORPA), the remnants of the FAR, and (another) dissident faction from the PGT, called the PGT/D.

No wonder then that, throughout that watershed year 1980, Havana pressed for a united Guatemalan armed struggle. In November, representatives from each faction met in Managua at the invitation of the Sandinista *comandantes*.

At that meeting were two special representatives of Fidel Castro: Manuel Pineiro Losada, chief of the America Department of the Cuban Communist Party and Cuba's most experienced operator in foreign subversion, and Ramiro Jesus Abreu Quintana, head of the AD's Central American division. The two Cuban agents witnessed what their leader wanted most of all: a signed agreement of Guatemalan unity involving a political entity, the National Revolutionary Union (UNRG), and a military arm, the General Revolutionary Command (CGR).

Castro placed such enormous importance on this first formal union of the Guatemalan extreme left that the document was presented to him personally by representatives of the CGR in Havana.

According to the State Department's December 1981 white paper:

> After this unity agreement was concluded, Cuba agreed to increase military training and assistance. A large number of the 2,000 or more guerrillas now active have trained in Cuba. Recent military training programs have included instruction in the use of heavy weapons.[37]

The weapons came from Nicaragua and were smuggled through Honduras and have included rocket launchers, mortars, machineguns, and M–16 rifles from stocks left in Vietnam.[38]

As a result, the Guatemalan extreme left stepped up its actions in the cities and the countryside. In the cities, terrorism became the principal tactic of the EGP. Among other things, it took credit for placing a bomb in the luggage intended for a U.S. Eastern Airlines jet in July 1981. The bomb exploded, fortunately, on the ground.[39]

The Guatemalan extreme left also attempted, in a by now familiar tactic, to disrupt the Guatemalan presidential elections in March 1982. The groups failed to have much impact, although the election was widely held to be marred by extensive fraud on the part of the government—fraud so blatant, in fact, that it led to a junior officer coup. That coup set in motion the chain of events that led to the successful 1985 presidential elections that saw the Christian Democrat candidate Vinicio Cerezo emerge the decisive winner.

The urban arm of the Guatemalan extreme left proved to be the least effective, thanks to extensive raids on EGP safehouses in Guatemala City in April and July 1981. Large caches of weapons were found, and most of the U.S.-made rifles were also from stocks captured in Vietnam.[40]

In recent years, the fortunes of the guerrillas in Guatemala have declined. The coalition, the UNRG, continues to exist, but Castro, so far, has not been able to impose the kind of political and military unity in Guatemala that he did in Nicaragua and El Salvador. Nevertheless, he and his Soviet bloc allies continue to train and arm the Guatemalan extremists in the hope, ultimately, of their victory.[41]

In the meantime, the Guatemalan extreme left did succeed in its effort, particularly in the early 1980s, to provoke the Guatemalan security forces into taking extreme measures, amply documented by various human rights organizations (who nonetheless rarely assigned blame to the provocateurs.) Whether Guatemala's new and fragile democracy will be able to restore legitimacy to the regime, and thus undercut the extreme left's success in this area, remains to be seen.

Costa Rica

Democratic Costa Rica has also been a target of Cuban-sponsored terrorism in the 1980s, although the standard issue, pro-Soviet communist party, the People's Vanguard Party (PVP), struggled mainly for most of the last quarter century to achieve political legitimacy by getting on the ballot—and with limited success.[42]

Nevertheless, in 1979, the PVP joined in the fight against Somoza, and with Cuban assistance, sent several hundred Costa Ricans into Nicaragua to help the Sandinistas. According to U.S. intelligence, many of them remained in Nicaragua after the July 1979 victory to carry on further training of their fellow nationals for operations within Costa Rica. Their main task, so far, has been to conduct operations against Nicaraguan Contra forces operating along Nicaragua's southern border.[43]

The campaign of terrorism, itself, within Costa Rica did not begin until 1981, and it was carried out by a number of Costa Rican and foreign groups. The intention was to destabilize and intimidate Nicaragua's democratic neighbor, which, despite its historic policy of neutralism, was becoming increasingly critical of the Sandinistas.[44]

In the last five years, the terrorism for the most part has been carried out in San Jose, the capital, and it has included the wounding of American Marine guards, the killing of policemen, kidnappings, bombings, bank robberies, and attacks on Western embassies and ambassadors' residences. The terrorism has been carried out by both Costa Ricans and foreigners (usually Salvadorans or Nicaraguans)—all of whom have had contact with and support from Havana.[45]

Although terrorism in Costa Rica peaked in 1982, and has been reduced substantially since owing to good police work and an alert and a cooperative citizenry, the Cuban-coordinated network remains largely in place ready to be activated whenever Havana or Managua decides it is in their best interests to do so.[46]

The exact Cuban role in the destabilization of Costa Rica is only now beginning to emerge, however.[47] Much legitimate attention has been paid to the activities of the Nicaraguan Sandinistas who, to some extent, have become a convenient surrogate for Havana. Nevertheless, Fidel Castro has not delegated everything to his "Cubans."

According to U.S. intelligence, the Cubans have also supplied weapons to and training for Costa Rican terrorists. Havana has also funded a new leftist party in 1983 in an attempt to unify the fractured Costa Rican extreme left in the by-now quite familiar pattern. Success, so far, however, appears to be limited.[48]

Still, the progress the Cubans and Nicaraguans have made in a few years at building a terrorist network capable of carrying out a variety of missions is impressive. Equally impressive is Havana's ability to mix and match human resources in order to get the job done. Nothing better illustrates this point than the results of a Costa Rican police raid on a terrorist safehouse in March 1982 in the capital, San Jose.

Besides finding a large cache of weapons destined for El Salvador, the security forces netted nine agents: four Salvadorans, two Nicaraguans, a Chilean, a Costa Rican, and the group's commander, an Argentine Montonero.[49]

The Havana-directed network of "internationalists," sometimes trained and recruited more than a decade ago, was by the early 1980s beginning to show results in Central America. And Costa Rica, the region's premier open society, would have the dubious privilege of being unwillingly the first country to showcase all of the assets the Castro regime had accumulated over the years.

Notes to Chapter 3

1. In 1976, one respected analyst said of the FSLN in Nicaragua: "These actions [assassinations] and sporadic kidnappings, robberies, and other activities won them little support from the Nicaraguan people in the city or the countryside, though popular support was surely discouraged by severe measures taken against the FSLN members and even against suspected supporters of the organization." Ratliff, *Castroism and Communism . . . ,* 130.

2. Nevertheless, the South American terrorists of the 1970s would develop a coterie of intellectual admirers. Perhaps the best known is Abraham Guillen, a Spanish anarcho-syndicalist who wrote extensively in support of city-based terrorism in highly urbanized countries. He would later come to criticize Marighella and the Uruguayan Tupamaros, however, for their failure. Guillen held up another obscure Uruguayan terrorist group, the OPR–33 (Revolutionary Popular Organization), as a model. Guillen's fondness for OPR–33 can be explained because it too shared his anarcho-syndicalist ideology. Like OPR–33, he believed it was vital to combine terrorism with broadbased political work to build support for the revolution. How that can be achieved and still keep the fighting cadre secure is not explained, as Walter Lacquer has pointed out (p. 184). But it is a problem that had been anticipated even by Guevara in his *Guerrilla Warfare,* 30. A sample of Guillen's thinking can be found in Donald C. Hodges, ed., *Philosophy of the Urban Guerrilla: The Revolutionary Writings of Abraham Guillen* (New York: William Morrow and Company, 1973), especially 256–277. Also Abraham Guillen, *Estrategia de la Guerrilla Urbana* (Montevideo: Ediciones Liberacion, 1966). The book had a second edition in 1969. Both were available to the Tupamaros and other urban terrorists in the years immediately before their major effort. For a brilliant critique of Guillen, see Ratliff, 146–152.

3. For an account of the Cubans in Africa, see Thomas H. Henriksen, ed., *Communist Powers and Sub-Saharan Africa* (Stanford: Hoover Institution Press, 1981), and Carmelo Mesa–Lago ed., *Cuba in Africa* (Pittsburgh: Center for Latin American Studies, University of Pittsburgh Press, 1982). A more recent study is William E. Ratliff, *Follow the Leader in the Horn.* (Washington, D.C.: The Cuban American National Foundation, 1986).

4. Ratliff, *Castroism and Communism,* 129. Carlos Fonseca, a graduate of Patrice Lumumba University in Moscow, literally founded the FSLN in Havana where he was receiving terrorist training along with other young Nicaraguans. Romerstein, *Soviet Support,* 15.

5. Ratliff, *Castroism and Communism*, 130. Fonseca who would later be killed also spent several years in virtual exile in Havana in the early 1970s.

6. Ibid., 129–130. Also the State Department's "Special Report No. 90," 6. The other event in 1978, the January killing of *La Prensa* publisher Pedro Joaquin Chamorro allienated much of President Anastasio Somoza's remaining support at home and encouraged governments like Venezuela, Panama, and Costa Rica to help the FSLN. They provided the shield of respectability behind which Castro happily hid his own operations. As for National Palace raiders, half of them went to Cuba where they received additional training, returning later to Nicaragua. Shirley Christian, *Nicaragua*, 65.

7. State Department's Special Report, No. 90, 5.

8. Ibid., 6. A few years later, of course, anti-Sandinista rebels, many of whom had participated in the 1979 campaign against Somoza, would once more be fighting from bases in northern Costa Rica.

9. Ibid.

10. Ibid. Castro's advice was to engage in a prolonged war with Somoza, gradually wearing out the dictator's forces, and to avoid any frontal assaults on the National Guard. The counsel was ignored, and the Sandinistas were soon marching into Managua. See Shirley Christian, 103–117.

11. The State Department's "Special Report No. 90," 6. Cuban advisers who were wounded in battle were evacuated to Cuba. Also Christian, 66–68; 91–94.

12. Christian, 117.

13. "Background Paper: Central America," The Department of State and the Department of Defense, 27 May 1983: 5.

14. "Revolution Beyond Our Borders," Department of State, Special Report No. 132, September 1985: 5.

15. Ibid.

16. Francis, *Latin American Terrorism*, 12, and "Background Paper: Nicaragua's Military Build-Up and Support for Central American Subversion," Department of State and Department of Defense, 18 July 1984: 15. The purpose of the terrorism, according to U.S. intelligence, was to frighten the populace, raise funds, and lay the basis for guerrilla warfare. In contrast to the Uruguayan and Argentine terrorists, the Salvadorans did make it to the second stage. In the 1960s, however, Havana virtually ignored El Salvador since the Cuban leadership was convinced that both Guatemala and Nicaragua seemed far more promising. By the 1970s, however, Havana not only provided training and money but began introducing the somewhat provincial Salvadorans to the international communist world.

17. The participating groups besides the PCES were FARN and the FPL. The Popular Revolutionary Army (ERP) was admitted in May of 1980, eight months before the "final offensive" was to be launched. The four would form with the Central American Revolutionary Workers' Party (PRTC) the FMLN. State Department's "Special Report No. 90," 6, and "Special Report No. 132," 5.

18. State Department's "Special Report No. 90," 6–7.

19. Ibid., 7.

20. Ibid. That report would be later confirmed by defectors, one of whom,

Alejandro Montenegro, would describe the training he received prior to his special unit's successful attack on the Salvadoran air force's principal base at Ilopongo in January 1982. The unit was trained in Nicaragua under the supervision of a Cuban major. A similarly styled attack using specially trained commandos was carried out against the army's Fourth Brigade headquarters at El Paraiso in April 1987. See "Special Report No. 132," 10, and "Background Paper: Nicaragua's Military Build-Up," 25.

21. "Special Report No. 90," 6, and "Background Paper," 17. Also the State Department's "Revolution Beyond our Borders," 7.

22. "Background Paper," 7.

23. "Revolution Beyond Our Borders," 10.

24. The Cubans have even encouraged terrorism against FMLN guerrilla leaders who prove less than cooperative. According to one defector, a top FARN commander, Ernesto Jovel, was killed in Managua in 1980 or 1981 because he openly opposed the Cuban strategy. "Background Paper," 17.

25. "Revolution Beyond Our Borders," 12.

26. See, for example, the "Intelligence Information on External Support of the Guerrillas in El Salvador," Department of State and Department of Defense, August 1984. This briefing was based on a classified congressional briefing made by General Paul F. Gorman, Commander-in-Chief, U.S. Southern Command, and Thomas R. Pickering, U.S. ambassador to El Salvador. According to Ambassador Pickering, 95 percent of the material presented to the Congress was declassified for the above report. It gives a detailed presentation of U.S. and Salvadoran intelligence on the FMLN supply networks as of mid-1984. It shows that the bulk of rebel supplies from Nicaragua was coming in by small boat rather than overland through Honduras or by air as in previous years, owing to improved interdiction capabilities of the Salvadoran armed forces. See especially, pp. 7–12 and pp. 14–16. Also see "Background Paper," 18–23.

27. "Special Report No. 90," 9.

28. "Background Paper," 28.

29. "Revolution Beyond Our Borders," 14.

30. Ibid., 14.

31. Ibid.

32. Ibid., 14–15.

33. Ibid., 15.

34. A second group, the M–13 earlier broke with the communist-led coalition of guerrilla forces and continued its armed activities until May 1970 when its U.S. Army-trained leader, Yon Sosa, was killed in a clash with Mexican troops on the Mexican–Guatemalan frontier. Ratliff, *Castroism and Communism,* 112–118. For another account of Guatemala's experience with urban terrorism, see Burton, *Urban Terrorism,* 89–93.

35. Quoted in Moss, *Urban Guerrillas,* 178.

36. Ratliff, *Castroism and Communism,* 116. Other crimes included arson and the deliberate attempt to wreck the 1970 elections through an escalated campaign of killing and kidnapping mostly policemen and politicians. Moss, *Urban Guerrillas,* 182.

37. State Department's "Special Report No. 90," 7–8.

38. The story of one Guatemalan guerrilla defector is of interest. In June 1981, 28-year old Paulino Castillo, an ORPA guerrilla, told reporters that he underwent a seven-month training program in Cuba. His 23-man group who were in Cuba beginning in February of 1980—three months after the unity agreement was signed—were divided into two sections. The first was trained in rural guerrilla tactics, the second in urban terrorism. Castillo traveled to Costa Rica from Guatemala by bus. He obtained a Panamanian passport to enter Panama. In Panama, other agents supplied him with a Cuban passport and travel money to Cuba. The newly trained guerrilla returned to Guatemala via Nicaragua and then promptly surrendered to a Guatemalan army patrol. See ibid., 8.

39. Ibid., 8.

40. "Revolution Beyond Our Borders," 13.

41. "Background Paper: Central America," Department of State and the Department of Defense, 27 May 1983: 10. The released paper was a sanitized version of the intelligence available on Soviet, Cuban, and Nicaraguan activities in Central America which was presented to the Permanent Select Committee on Intelligence of the House of Representatives. The House Committee, in turn, found the administration's findings "convincing."

42. Ratliff, *Castroism and Communism,* 69. Another Marxist group, the Revolutionary Movement of the People (MRP) has referred to terrorist acts committed in Costa Rica as "well intentioned." State Department's "Special Report No. 90," 9.

43. State Department's "Special Report No. 132," 16. Costa Rica, of course, was the principal conduit through which the Cuban government shipped critically needed arms and supplies to the Sandinistas in the last year of the Somoza regime. Cuban intelligence's headquarters for this operation was in San Jose, and its impressive success was, in part, due to the cooperation of venal Costa Rican officials. A special commission of the Costa Rican legislature created in June 1980 reported in May 1981 that at least 21 flights of arms from Cuba were transshipped to the Sandinistas and, after their victory, to the Salvadoran rebels. The key figure in arranging the transport of the weapons to the El Salvador, however, was a Chilean, Fernando Carrasco, a member of the MIR. Ibid., 16–17.

44. Ibid., 17–18. The first terrorist acts, however, were committed in 1977 when an apparently Trotskyite armed group, the Revolutionary Commandos of Solidarity, attacked American-owned firms in that country. See Francis, 11.

45. State Department's "Special Report No. 132," 18–19. The attack on the U.S. Marine guards, for example, in March 1981 was the work of a Costa Rican group which, in turn, was an off-shoot of the People's Revolutionary Movement. The bombing of the Honduran airline's office in July 1982 was largely the work of Nicaraguan agents, although a Colombian M–19 terrorist who was recruited by the Nicaraguan embassy in San Jose did the actual job. In November of that year, an attempted kidnapping of a Japanese businessman was mostly the work of Salvadorans, although they were assisted by a Honduran and two Costa Ricans. Ibid., 17–18. Assassination attempts directed at Nicaraguan resistance leaders have also been attempted, instigated by the Sandinistas who used, in the case

of the attempt on Eden Pastora, a member of the Basque ETA (Basque Nation and Liberty). Ibid., 18. "Background Paper: Nicaragua's Military Build-up and Support for Central American Subversion," Department of State and the Department of Defense, 18 July 1984: 30: 33–34.

46. Costa Rica, although boasting a higher living standard than its Central American neighbors, has become increasingly vulnerable economically in the last five years. Acts of terrorism, in part, were designed to discourage critically needed foreign investors. The attempted kidnapping of a Japanese businessman, for example, led his company, the Matsushita Corporation, to withdraw all of its personnel from the country. "Background Paper: Nicaragua's Military Build-up," 30.

47. Castro's attack on a virtually unarmed, neutral, and democratic country like Costa Rica has surprised some observers. It should not. The Cuban leader has never confined himself to subverting only right wing dictatorships. Moreover, Costa Rica has never been in any Castro pronouncement giving it an exemption from attack. And even in the November 1971 formula where Castro stated that Chile and Uruguay were in no need of a violent revolution, the Cuban leader was, in fact, working quietly to promote just that with the Chilean MIR and the Uruguayan Tupamaros.

48. "Background Paper: Central America," 12.

49. "Background Paper: Nicaragua's Military Build-Up," 31. In another operation sponsored by the Sandinistas, a six-man team in July 1981 was infiltrated into Costa Rica. Their intention was to invade the Guatemalan embassy and hold the ambassador as hostage until Guatemalan terrorists were released from jail. The team, caught by Costa Rican police, consisted of two Guatemalans, two Nicaraguans, a Salvadoran, and a Mexican. Ibid., 30.

Chapter 4

Cuban-Sponsored Terrorism in the Caribbean

Even in recent years, Fidel Castro has not forgotten to fish in troubled home waters and with some (albeit temporary) success. There is no indication that failure has tempered much his enthusiasm for making trouble in the Caribbean, however.

Castro's most conspicuous achievement was helping to establish a proto-communist state on the island of Grenada, the first in the English-speaking world. Moreover, Grenada was also seen by the Cubans as a base from which the entire Eastern Caribbean could be destabilized.

Although Havana became intrigued with the potential of the English-speaking Caribbean only in the early 1970s, thanks in part to U.S.-inspired local black power movements, that interest has not entirely waned with the political demise of half-forgotten troublemakers like Stokely Carmichael and H. Rap Brown or even the sudden reversal in Grenada.

Nevertheless, the English-speaking islands have not held interest for Castro as the Spanish-speaking islands have, foremost among them the Dominican Republic.

Dominican Republic

Cuba's nearby neighbor has long fascinated and frustrated Fidel Castro. His personal attempt to invade the Dominican Republic in 1947 as a member of the Cayo Confites expedition ended in ignominious failure. His sponsoring of another invasion attempt in 1959 after the fall of Batista was a bloody fiasco. The 1965 insurrection that broke out in the capital of Santo Domingo was squelched with American troops before Castro could make himself a serious factor in the insurrection, although a number of Dominican extremists who quickly found positions of power within the so-called "constitutionalist" forces was trained in Cuba.[1]

But reversals have not daunted the Cuban leader. Nor has his subversive intention been altered by the fact that the Dominican Republic has become, after decades of dictatorship, a fully functioning and vigorous democracy in the last 20 years.

The Cubans continue to pursue a long-term strategy of building up the extreme left, but, as in other places, the chief problem remains the lack of unity among the would-be revolutionaries. Repeated attempts at bringing them together have failed, although in recent years intelligence officers from the America Department have regularly visited the island offering money and other support. The Cubans made a special effort in the months before the 1986 presidential elections by subsidizing the Dominican Liberation Party of ex-president Juan Bosch but, again, with little to show for their efforts.

Havana, however, is not playing this game alone in the Dominican Republic. According to U.S. intelligence:

> At the same time, the Soviet Union has been pressuring the [Dominican Communist Party] to unite with other extreme left organizations. The PCD and the other pro-Cuban Dominican Liberation Party receive funds from both Cuba and the Soviet Union and send significant numbers of their members and potential sympathizers for academic and political schooling as well as military training in Communist countries. Cuba has given military instruction to many members of small extremist splinter groups like the Social Workers movement and the Socialist Party.[2]

Complementing the military aspects of the Soviet bloc's long-term strategy is an extensive scholarship program for Dominican youth. In 1981, for example, the PCD announced that some 700 students were studying at Soviet universities, the bulk of them at Patrice Lumumba University, a prime recruiting ground for the KGB. Annually, some 100 young Dominicans, picked by the PCD, are funnelled in the Soviet bloc "educational" system.[3]

In the case of the Dominican Republic, the Soviets and Cubans have worked closely together and quite probably have laid the basis for armed action when the opportunity presents itself and leftwing factionalism can be overcome.

Jamaica

For more than a decade after Castro's rise to power, Havana showed little interest in its English-speaking neighbors. The first real opportunity for Fidel Castro came with Jamaica in the early 1970s.

Geographically, at least, that interest made sense. The island lies less than a 100 miles from Cuba's Oriente Province, and on clear days, Cuba is visible from the beaches on Jamaica's north coast.

Cuban interest and how that interest developed is also yet another facet of Castro's talent in fostering subversion in new and different ways. It began with the development of close relations with the leftist government of Prime Minister Michael Manley whose party, the People's National Party (PNP), ruled the island from 1973 to 1980.

Their relations, however, were far from conventional, even by communist terms. By 1975, for example, the Cubans were "training" Jamaicans in Cuba. Ostensibly the purpose was to give the young Jamaicans practical skills in construction. In fact, the majority of the 1,000 to 1,400 Jamaicans sent to Cuba was given training in urban terrorism.[4]

That program was carried out with the knowledge of at least the extreme left members of Manley's cabinet, and it became a source of controversy in both the 1976 and 1980 parliamentary elections. The details of the program, however, were largely and publicly unknown until one of the "brigadistas" told his story.

Colin Dennis, a then 25-year old self-described "socialist," was recruited in May 1980 by two members of the central committee of the Communist Party of Jamaica (CPJ).[5]

Stuck in an uninteresting job, Dennis jumped at the chance for travel to Cuba and asked no questions about the nature of the visit. Nor was he ever informed. Dennis was told, however, to make his departure a secret and follow all other instructions without question on pain of being "exterminated."

Only in Cuba, in a remote camp in Pinar del Rio province, west of Havana, did Dennis begin realizing what he had gotten himself into. The camp—even its name was withheld from the recruits—was to provide terrorist training for young Jamaicans drawn from the ranks of the PNP, the CPJ, and another Marxist–Leninist splinter group, the Workers Party of Jamaica (WPJ).

Security was tight, and the trainees were told that escape was impossible because the camp was ringed by a mine field. But even then, their ultimate mission was shrouded in secrecy.

According to Dennis:

> It was hard to pin down the moment when all the pieces fitted together and I realised just why we were all in Cuba: to study urban guerilla [sic] warfare. We were never told "You are all in Cuba to study guerilla war-

fare." The knowledge gradually seeped through during that first week. Even here in Cuba, the aura of secrecy that had surrounded the programme while we were in Jamaica had not disappeared.[6]

The course lasted eight weeks and concentrated on weapons training in light arms (pistols, rifles, and machineguns), hand grenades, Soviet rocket launchers, and explosives.[7]

Cuban instructors also taught them ambush and assault techniques useful in attacking police stations, banks, and prisons. And, of course, political indoctrination—the least successful part of the program—was included.

Only later did Dennis learn how these new skills were to be used precisely.

. . . on our return to Jamaica we would be expected to impart our newly acquired skills to the youths in our respective communities, and that this course could be regarded as a teacher-training programme. When I heard this, I found the information revolting. It was my view that any government that schooled its citizens in terrorism legitimised that terrorism and had no moral authority to put down any acts that were deemed to be anti-state. In short, it had as much moral authority as a burglar who tried to prevent his child from shoplifting.[8]

Dennis also leaves the impression that there was something hurried and disorganized about the whole process.[9] Groups arrived at odd times, and the training schedule became jumbled. At times, the program became lackadaisical, and both discipline and morale suffered as a result.

Still, at the end of the period most of the young recruits were skilled enough to engage in the kind of violence that was then wracking Jamaica, especially in Kingston, the capital.[10]

What may well account for the hurry-up atmosphere of the training was the nearness of the elections that had been scheduled for October 1980. The PNP needed gunmen. If the party had won the election, the new trainees could have formed a "popular militia" to counter the politically neutral police and defense forces. If the PNP had lost, they would have provided the manpower for an all-out campaign of urban terrorism.[11]

That intention is not based on mere speculation. According to U.S. and Jamaican intelligence, the Cubans smuggled in large amounts of arms and ammunition using as cover a business front it controlled. Subsequently, M–16 rifles began turning up in the hands of gunmen—a weapon never before seen in Jamaica—who used them to attack the opposition Jamaica Labour Party (JLP) and the security forces. Some of the weapons were later traced to stocks left in Vietnam in the early 1970s.[12]

The Cuban strategy did not work. The JLP won a landslide victory in October 1980, making an open defiance of the results through urban terrorism a difficult and failure-prone prospect. Moreover, the new government broke relations with Cuba nine days after the JLP victory.[13]

Two months later, Prime Minister Edward Seaga ended the "brigadista" program. Nevertheless, as many as 2,000 "brigadista" remain in place for possible future use.

As for the Cubans, they made little real attempt to disguise their intentions. Part of the reason was their confidence that the PNP would remain in power. They overlooked the fact that their activities could still be scrutinized by an independent opposition party and press and a professional police force.

As a result of that confidence, Cuban officials made little attempt to disguise the closeness of their relationships with their Jamaican counterparts. Top security officials were sent to Cuba for advanced training. At the same time, Havana's large embassy staff was headed by a key intelligence officer, Ulises Estrada, and little was done to conceal his background.[14] The Cuban failure in Jamaica may prove ephemeral, as in other places. Currently, the PNP is ahead in the polls after eight years of JLP rule, while many of Jamaica's economic and social problems remain unsolved. Moreover, as Havana well knows, PNP leader Michael Manley gives little indication he would do things much differently upon his return to power.

Nevertheless, the once and possibly future role of the Cubans in Jamaica is striking. They worked closely with a friendly government (as in Chile under Allende) while preparing urban terrorists to seize complete power by destroying the opposition and the security forces. If anything, the only modification of the Chilean strategy was the apparent complete agreement and collusion of key cabinet ministers in Havana's plan for turning Jamaica into a communist state.

Grenada

Castro's greatest success in the Caribbean so far, however, was helping establish a Marxist–Leninist regime in Grenada, the spice island anchoring the chain of Windward and Leeward islands in the eastern Caribbean.

That regime, headed by a former black power radical turned communist, Maurice Bishop, came to power through a coup that ousted the government of the elected, but erratic and sometimes brutal, Prime Minister Eric Gairy. Within days of that March 1979 takeover, Bishop had suspended the 1974 Constitution and ruled instead through "People's Laws," that is, by fiat.

From the beginning of the regime, the intention of Bishop and his closest collaborators was to establish a full-fledged communist state as rapidly as possible while engaging in deception as to the new regime's real intent.

Bishop's party, the New Jewel Movement (NJM), was thus turned away from its black power and populist roots, which idealized the Tanzania of Julius Nyere, and headed toward a Soviet-style system complete with a party politburo, central committee, mass organizations, and secret police that would dominate the state.[15]

Havana, of course, was not deceived and quickly moved to support the new regime. Less than a month after Bishop's men had seized the defense force barracks, Castro delivered 3,400 U.S. and Soviet rifles, three million rounds of ammunition, 200 sub-machineguns, 100 rocket launchers, a dozen each 82 mm mortars, 75 mm cannon, and anti-aircraft guns to a country of less than 100,000 population whose lightly armed security forces had once amounted to a few hundred men.[16]

Also, Castro almost immediately dispatched an intelligence officer (again from the America Department) to coordinate Cuban activities. As ambassador, Julian Torres Rizo became intimately involved in the business of turning Grenada into a communist police state.[17]

The Cubans not only introduced the farm fresh Grenadians to the tangled web of Soviet bloc and allied groups, but they also gave them guidelines on what to say and do at international conferences.[18]

In the critical military-security area, Havana became especially active. In addition to the first shipment of arms, the Cubans also provided "specialists" to the newly formed Grenadian armed forces, the People's Revolutionary Army headed by General Hudson Austin, by profession a prison guard, as well as twenty officers assigned to train and advise field units. Grenadians were also to be trained in Cuba.[19]

In all, Grenada would sign at least five secret military agreements with communist states including Cuba, North Korea, and the Soviet Union, and possibly Bulgaria and Czechoslovakia. The Soviet bloc would provide, over a six-year span, enough weapons and supplies to outfit 10,000 men, several thousand beyond the inflated hopes of the NJM for an army of 7,200. Even at that, the lower figure would have made Grenada one of the most heavily militarized countries on earth.[20]

The arms and training, of course, were only two parts of the Soviet bloc strategy. In addition, the socialist camp, led by the Cubans, would construct a new airport with a 9,000 foot landing strip capable of landing anything in the Soviet air inventory. And the Grenadians, despite their awareness of the need to deceive, did little to hide Point Salines airport's real purpose.

Selwyn Strachan, the Grenadian Minister of Mobilization, for example, said publicly that Cuba would use the facility to help transport troops to Africa and that the Soviets would find it useful because of its "strategic location" along side major sea lines of transportation, petroleum in particular.[21]

Maurice Bishop also stated in an interview with *Newsweek* that, when the airport was completed, he assumed it would be used by the Cubans.

> Suppose there's a war next door in Trinidad, where the forces of Fascism are about to take control, and the Trinidadians need external assistance, why should we oppose anybody passing through Grenada to assist them?[22]

But power projection was not to be confined to Soviet-bloc forces, at least not if the ambitious Bishop regime could help it. The military build-up also helped to intimidate Grenada's neighbors, the small island-states of the Eastern Caribbean. The extra weapons and supplies would be available for extreme leftist groups that could be found on most of those islands. Properly equipped, they, in turn, could instigate the type of terrorism that would shake the region's fragile economies and vulnerable democratic institutions, laying the basis for another Grenada-style coup.[23]

That Bishop (and Castro) harbored regional ambitions is clear enough from the captured documents. But before the military build-up could be completed, Bishop also believed his chief contribution to expanding Soviet bloc influence in the area would be to establish a special relationship with Suriname's leftist leader, Desire Bouterse. Prospects also looked good to him in Belize.

But the desire to play a larger revolutionary role as a loyal member of the Soviet bloc was inspired by more than ambition. That was made clear in a secret memorandum written by the Grenadian ambassador to the Soviet Union, W. Richard Jacobs, and sent to the Minister for External Relations, Unison Whiteman.

Ambassador Jacobs wrote in July 1983:

> Our revolution has to be viewed as a world-wide process with its original roots in the Great October Revolution. For Grenada to assume a position of increasingly greater importance, we have to be seen as influencing at least regional events. We have to establish ourselves as the authority on events in at least the English-speaking Caribbean, and be the sponsor of revolutionary activity and progressive developments in this region at least.[24]

As for Suriname, the Grenadian envoy hoped that "if we can be an overwhelming influence on Suriname's international behaviour, then our importance in the Soviet scheme of things will be greatly enhanced [sic]."[25]

In fact, the effort with Suriname was made, although Fidel Castro could not resist being involved in that effort as well. In the Eastern Caribbean, however, Grenada did attempt to carve out a separate role for itself by having twice yearly meetings of the region's leftists held on the island. As the Soviet Union's self-appointed agent for the area, the Grenadians had no compunctions in asking Moscow for financial aid to help write off the costs.[26]

The murder of Maurice Bishop by his own colleagues in October 1983 and the subsequent rescue operation mounted by American and Caribbean forces cut those ambitions short.

The loss of Grenada for Castro equalled, if not surpassed, in importance the defeat of "Che" Guevara in Bolivia 16 years earlier. It had a profoundly demoralizing effect on the Cubans, and Castro's harsh reprisals on those who surrendered on Grenada sowed the first seeds of dissatisfaction within the Cuban military regarding his rule in decades.

Moreover, the Reagan administration's decisive action sent a powerful message to the Sandinista regime in Nicaragua. No longer were the Salvadoran high command of the FMLN welcome in Managua and many, in late October 1983, were ordered out of town. The effect, albeit temporary, was to throw the Salvadoran insurgency into low gear, if not stall it altogether.

But what the end of the New Jewel regime in Grenada also meant was that the prospects for terrorism in the Eastern Caribbean had been radically reduced—at least for the next few years.

Notes to Chapter 4

1. The orthodox communist party of the Dominican Republic, the PSP, in a post-crisis analysis, candidly confessed that the split in the armed forces that sparked the uprising had caught the party unawares and "consequently [we] proved incapable of taking the right decisions at the crucial moments. This lost us the possibility of directing things." Quoted from J. I. Quello and N. Isa Conde, "Revolutionary Struggle in the Dominican Republic and its Lessons," *World Marxist Review*[9] (January 1966): 55. For a balanced and contemporary account of the Dominican crisis and communist involvement, see Selden Rodman, "A Close View of Santo Domingo," *The Reporter*, 15 July 1965, 20–27. Also see John Bartlow Martin, *Overtaken by Events* (Garden City, New York: Doubleday, 1966), 672–676. Martin, a skeptical liberal, had been ambassador to the Dominican Republic during the brief and interrupted term of President Juan Bosch in 1963. Martin later returned as a special emissary of President Johnson's after the 1965 revolt broke out. His conclusion from studying it first hand was: ". . . the U.S. Marines had originally come here to protect U.S. lives but that in my opinion their purpose now was or should be to prevent a Castro/Communist takeover, because what began as a PRD (Juan Bosch's Dominican Revolutionary Party) revolt had in the last few days fallen under the domination of Castro/Communists and other violent extremists." Ibid., 676. For direct evidence of their involvement, see ibid., 673.

2. State Department's "Special Report No. 90," 10. It should be noted that the PCD is nearly unique in Latin America. Unlike most pro-Soviet communist parties in the region, it was attracted by Fidel Castro's more adventurous approach to revolution. In later years, this small party's refusal to take sides in the 1960s would eventually earn it support from both Havana *and* Moscow. Ratliff, *Castroism and Communism*, 54.

3. "Special Report No. 90," 10. In 1981, 75 other Dominican students were parceled out to Bulgaria, Cuba, East Germany, Hungary, and Romania. Ibid.

4. Ibid., 9, and the *Daily Gleaner* [Kingston], 3 December 1980. The *Gleaner's* estimate was that at best only about ten percent had been given civilian training.

5. Colin Dennis, *The Road Not Taken: Memoirs of a Reluctant Guerilla* (Kingston: Kingston Publishers Ltd, 1985).

6. Ibid., 38. Dennis' story tracks with the account previously cited of a Venezuelan trained in a similar camp 20 years earlier. The deception in both their recruitments is striking. In the Venezuelan's case, he was promised a good technician's job in Cuba by the director of the local Cuban friendship society. See Juan DeDios Marin, 121.

7. The weapons included the M–16 and the Kalashnikov, according to Dennis, 216.

8. Ibid., 38. Deception as in this case is not an isolated example. Honduran guerrilla defectors, for example, told interviewers in 1983 that they were lured into Nicaragua two years earlier with promises that they would receive agricul-

tural and mechanical training. Instead, they were shipped to Cuba for nine months of military training at Camp P–30 in Pinar del Rio run by the Cuban Ministry of Interior's Department of Special Operations. "Background Paper: *Nicaragua's Military Build-Up*," 27.

9. At one point, Dennis was informed by a Cuban instructor that his course of training was originally set for six months, but it had been compressed to twelve weeks and then finally eight because of low morale. Dennis, 88.

10. As for Dennis, on his own admission, he had the makings of a poor terrorist. In the graduation training exercise, he notes, "I had run in the wrong direction during the action, and when I finally arrived at the prison I did not know what to do. I hadn't even fired a shot. It was when the action had almost died down that I discharged my cartridges." Ibid., 101.

11. Ibid., 149.

12. State Department's "Special Report No. 90," 9. The Cuban front, the Moonex International, was registered in Lichtenstein with subsidiaries in Panama and Jamaica. One shipment that was discovered by authorities in May 1980 included 200,000 shotgun shells and .38 caliber pistol ammunition purchased in Miami and shipped without licence to Kingston. Moonex's local manager was later apprehended by police when he attempted to leave the country by private plane despite police instructions. He was arrested in the company of Jamaica's Minister of National Security and the Cuban ambassador. Ibid. and the *Gleaner,* 19 June 1980.

13. "Special Report No. 90," 9.

14. Estrada later was withdrawn from Jamaica only after the 1980 election. Before his posting in Kingston, the Cuban had been a deputy of the elite America Department for five years and also played a major role in the Sandinista victory in Nicaragua. Ibid.

15. "Grenada, A Preliminary Report," Department of State and Department of Defense, 16 December 1983: 8–9. Maurice Bishop made his intentions clear in his 13 September 1982 "Line of March for the Party" secret speech given to the NJM cadre. After a standard Marxist analysis of Grenada's class structure, Bishop told the faithful the purpose of the revolution is to build socialism "led by a Marxist–Leninist vanguard Party." But to do so successfully, deception must be employed. Hence, he said, the need to form initial alliances with non-communists. Appointing respectable "bourgeois" names to the original ruling council (a tactic used by the Sandinistas), Bishop said, was done "so that imperialism won't get too excited and would say 'well they have some nice fellas in that thing; everything alright [sic].'" As a pointed reminder to his audience regarding the need for deception, Bishop cited the example of the then-recent failed coup in Gambia where the insurgents immediately proclaimed themselves Marxist–Leninists. According to Bishop: "The same day they overthrow them— same day, they didn't even give them three days. So fortunately, NJM had a little more sense than that." The speech can be found in Michael Ledeen and Herbert Romerstein, eds., *Grenada Documents: An Overview and Selection*, Department of State and Department of Defense, September 1984: 13–14; 18–19. The documents selected by Ledeen and Romerstein were part of some 35,000 pounds of material that were swept up by the U.S. and Caribbean forces that

landed on the island in October 1983. As such, it is the first, intact, and complete communist archive ever to fall into Western hands.

16. "Grenada, A Preliminary Report," 22. The Soviets were pleased as well. In a meeting with a Grenadian Major Einstein Louison, Marshall of the Soviet Union N.V., Ogarkov said that 20 years ago there was only Cuba in Latin America, but "today there are Nicaragua, Grenada and a serious battle is going on in El Salvador." Quoted in a Grenadian embassy memorandum, 10 March 1983, and available in Ledeen and Romerstein, Document 24–1.

17. State Department's "Special Report, No. 90," 10. In his work, Torres Rizo was assisted by his wife, Gail Reed Rizo, an American-born radical of the 1960s who first visited Cuba as a member of a Venceremos Brigade, the U.S. equivalent of the Jamaican "brigadistas." Reed Rizo, in one of the captured documents, gave Bishop advice in a handwritten "Dear Maurice" memo outlining how the Grenadian premier could influence the American media during his trip to the United States. See Ledeen and Romerstein, Document 31–1.

18. "Grenada, A Preliminary Report," 10; 22. Before a meeting of a Libyan-sponsored "General Congress of the World Center for the Resistance of Imperialism, Racism, and Zionism, held in June 1982, the NJM delegate received prior instructions from the Cubans on how to act. Specifically, he was told to "avoid giving support for the idea of Libya being the center of the World anti-imperialist struggle." Quoted from the NJM delegate's report to the NJM Central Committee, dated 26 June 1982 and found in Ledeen and Romerstein, Document 34–1. The "instructor" was Manuel Pinheiro Losada, chief of the AD.

19. "Grenada, A Preliminary Report," 22–23.

20. Ibid., 18–21 and Ledeen and Romerstein, 6. Paul Seabury and Walter A. McDougall estimate that, when the arms transfers were completed, 15–25 percent of the Grenadian population would have been under arms. Paul Seabury and Walter A. McDougall, eds., *The Grenada Papers* (San Francisco: ICS Press, 1984), 18.

21. "Grenada, A Preliminary Report," 30.

22. *Newsweek,* 31 March 1980, and quoted in the State Department's "Special Report, No. 90," 10. In private, Bishop told Soviet foreign minister Andrei Gromyko in April 1983: "There is also the strategic factor which is well known." Quoted in "The Soviet–Cuban Connection in Central America and the Caribbean," Department of State and Department of Defense, March 1985: 13.

23. But that would be reserved for the future. Until the regime was felt secure, the directive was to be "discreet and cautious with left opposition states" in the Eastern Caribbean, according to the July 1983 plenary meeting of the NJM central committee. Quoted in Seabury and McDougall, 274.

24. Quoted in Ledeen and Romerstein, Document 26–6. Grenadian foreign policy, although widely advertised as "non-aligned," was almost slavishly pro-Soviet. It had, for example, voted against a UN resolution condemning the Soviet invasion of Afghanistan. Even Sandinista Nicaragua had chosen to abstain. See the State Department's "Special Report, No. 90," 10.

25. From Ledeen and Romerstein, Document 26–6.

26. The 1983 meetings cost $500,000. See "The Soviet–Cuban Connection," 17.

Chapter 5

South America: The Prospects for Terrorism in the 1980s

Despite the failures in Venezuela, Peru, and Bolivia in the 1960s and the defeat of urban terrorist groups in Argentina, Brazil, Chile, and Uruguay in the 1970s, Fidel Castro has not forgotten about South America.

Although Havana's priority is still Central America, the huge continental land mass below the Darien gap continues to intrigue the Cubans. Moreover, as a result of Washington's preoccupation with Central America, Havana finds such opportunities in South America both tempting and timely. Once more, the principal troublemakers will be urban-based terrorist groups.

Four countries are currently targeted—Colombia, Ecuador, Peru, and Chile—a chain of western Andean countries that Castro hopes will somehow spark a continental anti-American revolt envisioned by Ernesto Guevara more than 20 years ago.

Colombia

Violence in Colombia is nothing new. In fact, it long pre-dates the rise of Fidel Castro. The Cuban leader himself was both witness to and participant in the event that set off Colombia's modern era of turmoil. It would be called *la violencia*, and it constitutes one of the most long-lived and brutal periods of history in any Latin American nation.

The catalyst that touched off the violence was the *bogotazo,* an urban insurrection in the capital city that nearly destroyed the regime of President Ospina Perez. But the restoration of order in Bogota in May 1948 did not end the violence. It merely moved to the countryside where bands of guerrillas, often pledging loyalty to one of the principal parties (Liberal and Conservative), carried out a war of utter savagery for the next five years.

Until the Cuban revolution, these roving groups of guerrillas had no serious purpose other than murder and robbery, especially in the mid-1950s.[1] By the mid-1960s, however, two rural guerrilla organizations were in the field. The National Liberation Army (ELN) was specifically oriented toward Cuba, and the Colombian Revolutionary Armed Forces (FARC) was a merger of several previous groups and was directed, if not controlled, by the Colombian Communist Party (PCC).[2]

For nearly a decade, the ELN and the FARC roamed at will through a half-dozen Colombian provinces, acting independently from each other and receiving only a small amount of assistance from Havana, mostly in the form of propaganda support and training for some of the leaders.[3]

Castro's decision to aid the guerrillas then and now was not influenced by the fact that Colombians had rid themselves of their last military dictator two years before Batista fled to Florida, however.

Since 1957, Colombia has been a flawed, but working democracy. In fact, steadily declining voter participation which critics had pointed to in the 1960s and 1970s as some fatal mark of illegitimacy has been halted and reversed.[4]

The Colombian insurgents' early strategy revolved around rural guerrilla warfare which ELN commander Fabio Vasquez categorically said must be adopted because the Colombian proletariat was too weak and the security forces too strong. Only in the last stages of the revolt could effective action be taken in the cities, Vasquez argues.[5]

By 1973–74, however, the Colombian military was proving to be effective in the countryside as well, so effective, in fact, that the ELN and the FARC were forced to agree to a division of labor. The FARC would continue in the countryside, and the more clearly Castroite ELN would commence urban operations.[6]

The agreement did not prosper nor did the two extreme leftist groups. Urban action came to nothing, and the Castro-backed ELN was successful only in sponsoring scattered university strikes. The strikes were largely due to the popularity of Camilo Torres, an upper-class priest turned guerrilla, and for awhile a favorite of Fidel Castro.[7]

By 1976, most of the ELN and FARC leaders were dead, including Torres, and their followers scattered as the army first turned on the ELN and then the FARC.[8]

As in the case of other South American insurrections, the mid-1970s were a lowpoint in guerrilla warfare and terrorism in Colombia. Those years of comparative quiet, however, were brief, particularly in Colombia.

But the second round of Colombian revolutionary violence (which continues today) differs from the first. For one thing, the Cubans played a far greater role in promoting the overthrow of the Colombian government. Also, the strategy shifted from an emphasis on the rural guerrilla to the urban terrorist as a new insurgent group became prominent and dominant, the April 19 Movement, the M–19. Moreover the Cuban-supported insurgency in Colombia has also gone "international," after it joined the growing network of mutually supportive terrorist groups. Finally, the Colombian groups have added a new twist, undreamed of by Comandante Guevara: namely, they have forged an alliance with narcotics traffickers in order to improve profits, purchase more arms, and thus advance "the revolution."

Few of these developments, however, would have taken place if it had not been for the 1979 Sandinista victory in Nicaragua. In fact, the Colombian insurgency's revival began the following year.

That renaissance was sparked by a relative newcomer to the Colombian scene, the April 19 Movement, better known as M–19. The group itself was an outgrowth of a vaguely populist, nationalist, and authoritarian movement led by the deposed dictator General Gustavo Rojas Pinilla.[9]

The catalyst was the wildly competitive and bitterly contested 1970 presidential election in which Rojas lost by a small margin to the "establishment" candidate, Misael Pastrana Borrero. ANAPO (National Popular Alliance), naturally, claimed the victory, and Bogota, for days, teetered on the brink of another *bogotazo*. But the ANAPO protest fizzled out.

Although the short term explosion was avoided, a frustrated and radicalized element within ANAPO went underground to form the M–19 in 1973.[10]

In their first actions, M–19 resembled the Uruguayan Tupamaros by affecting a Robin Hood pose.[11] Among other things, the group stole the sword and spurs of Simon Bolivar. But the M–19 became far more serious when it kidnapped and murdered a popular trade union figure in 1976. From then on, it dropped the romantic outlaw disguise and went on a year long urban campaign of terror which included kidnappings, bank robberies, and assassinations aimed at Colombians and foreigners (principally Americans) alike.[12]

But in a country as torn by violence as Colombia, these exploits of the M–19 tended to be viewed as only one part of a passing scene and of no great note. The group changed all that, however, in February 1980 when it committed its first international media "spectacular."

It was an operation that would set them apart from all other insurgent groups in Colombia's history, and it was the first step in M–19's internationalization. The operation involved the M–19's invasion in broad daylight of the Dominican Embassy where a number of diplomats, including the American ambassador, was held hostage in exchange for jailed terrorists. The negotiations lasted over two months and ended with the M–19 terrorists being flown to Cuba for asylum.[13]

Within weeks of that operation's conclusion, Cuban intelligence agents arranged a meeting between the M–19 and the much battered FARC and ELN. According to U.S. intelligence sources, they discussed joining forces and coordinating strategy and tactics along lines similar to the abortive 1974 agreement between the FARC and the ELN.

That meeting, according to these same sources, was preceded by an earlier contact of the M–19 with the Nicaraguan FSLN, itself only a few months in power. Neither set of talks apparently succeeded in its clearly Cuban-inspired aims, but a rough sort of cooperation did begin among the Colombian rebel groups.[14]

Havana's most blatant involvement in Bogota's affairs came, however, at the end of 1980. Clearly not satisfied with M–19's reliance on urban terrorism, the Cubans trained, equipped, and arranged transportation for a shipload of M–19 guerrillas to invade their home land and operate in the *campo*.

According to the State Department's December 1981 white paper:

> In November [1980], the M–19 sent guerrillas to Cuba via Panama to begin training for the operation. The group included new recruits as well as members who had received no prior political or military training. In Cuba the guerrillas were given 3 months of military instruction from Cuban army instructors, including training in the use of explosives, automatic weapons, hand-to-hand combat, military tactics, and communications. A course in politics and ideology was taught as well. Members of the M–19 group given asylum in Cuba after the take-over of the Dominican Republic Embassy also participated in the training program.[15]

In February 1981, up to 200 M–19 guerrillas landed on Colombia's Pacific Coast after transitting Panama with no difficulty. The effort to establish another rural guerrilla army, however, proved to be disastrous. The combat-hardened Colombian army relentlessly pursued the would-be *guerrilleros* through the jungle until their surrender. Among those nabbed was the leader of the Dominican embassy takeover, Rosenberg Pabon Pabon.[16]

The M–19 received a second, possibly worse setback when its commander, Jaime Bateman, was killed in April 1983 in a somewhat mysterious plane crash in Panama. As a result, its activities in Colombia went into decline while FARC picked up the pace with a series of kidnappings of U.S. citizens.[17]

But, as in most guerrilla and terrorist setbacks, the M–19 was far from crushed. In recent years, it has continued to dabble in rural warfare, usually with highly unsatisfactory results, while concentrating on urban terrorism.

And unlike FARC and the remnants of the ELN, it refused to accept a truce offered by President Belisario Betancur after he assumed office in 1982.[18]

The M–19 and the Narcotraficantes

The M–19's greatest innovation in subversion (and one in which the Cubans have played a leading role) is its forming an alliance with Colombia's drug trafficers, the *narcotraficantes*.

The M–19 (and to a lesser extent, the FARC) has developed an odd, but logically symbiotic relationship with Colombian exporters of marijuana and cocaine, the bulk of which is shipped to the lucrative North American market.

In testimony before U.S. congressional committes, officials from the State Department, the Drug Enforcement Agency, and the state of Florida have laid out the M–19–Cuban–drug trafficker connection in stark detail.

In March 1982, then Assistant Secretary of State for Inter-American Affairs Thomas O. Enders told members of the Senate Subcommittee on Security and Terrorism that American intelligence from a variety of sources had uncovered a drug and terrorist organization that was aided and abetted by Havana.

According to Enders:

> Since 1980, the Castro regime has been using a Colombian narcotics ring to funnel arms as well as funds to Colombian M–19 guerrillas. This narcotics ring was led by Jaime Guillot Lara, a Colombia drug-trafficker now in custody in Mexico. He has admitted to working for Havana in pur-

chasing arms for the M–19. We have information that Guillot traveled
twice to Cuba since October 1981 and that on the second visit he received
$700,000 from the Cuban Government to purchase arms for the M–19
guerrillas.[19]

Enders then detailed how Guillot played the leading role in transferring
the weapons he bought from a ship to a Colombian plane that the M–19
had already hijacked. Providing security at the airstrip were five armed
M–19 terrorists.[20] Guillot also supplied the M–19 with money by means
of a Panamanian bank. All of this, moreover, was coordinated with the
Cuban embassy in Bogota.[21]

The Cuban involvement, however, went deeper than that. According
to Enders:

> In return for Guillot's services, the Cubans facilitated the ring's trafficking
> by permitting mother ships carrying marihuana [sic] to take sanctuary in
> Cuban waters while awaiting feeder boats from the Bahamas and Florida.
> According to a relative of Guillot, one such mother ship detained by Cuban
> authorities was released when Guillot protested to the Cuban Ambassador
> in Bogota.[22]

Since the drug and terrorist network has been uncovered, four senior
Cuban officials have been indicted for drug smuggling into the United
States by a federal grand jury in November 1982. They were convicted
along with Jaime Guillot on February 25 the following year.[23]

This particular episode throws light on several aspects of Cuban support
of terrorism. First, Havana's relationship with the M–19 is far more intimate than Cuban officials have been willing to admit. The M–19 has
not only been provided training and arms, but it has also had its drug
shipments to the United States protected in transit by Cuba.

Moreover, the Castro regime rarely does favors for ideological reasons
alone. Acting as a shield for drug traffickers earns Havana hard currency.
But the exposé of Guillot–Lara has merely been the opening round. *U.S.
News*, quoting a classified U.S. government report, says that the case "is
only the tip of the iceberg of Cuba's ultrasecret involvement in the drug
trade."

The document citing DEA intelligence sources adds that there are more
than 50 instances of Cuban involvement in drug trafficking since 1982,
and one Colombian drug merchant is said to have fled to Cuba for sanctuary.

The magazine further reports:

> Castro's officials not only provided equipment and chemicals to refine the cocaine, but the operation was set up on an unnamed military base, affording maximum security.[24]

Nor is that the end of the matter. The same report charges that the Castro regime has its own cocaine labs near Havana and that trafficker aircraft is also permitted safe flight through Cuban air space.[25]

Moreover, the relative success of the Colombian guns for the drugs' network has led other terrorist groups connected with the Soviet bloc to engage in similar activities to finance their operations, according to U.S. officials.

Francis M. Mullen, then head of the DEA, testified in 1984 that "terrorist and insurgent groups worldwide are becoming directly or indirectly involved in the drug traffic." And in the same hearings, William Von Raab, U.S. Customs Commissioner, charged Bulgaria, Cuba, and Nicaragua specifically with fostering drug trafficking and terrorism as "part of their national policy" through "financing, organization, and use of sovereign territory."[26]

The Cuban-supported M–19 continues to believe that maintaining its drug habit is a vital part of its strategy to take power in Colombia. That is clear from the thrust of the group's terrorist activities in the last few years.

According to U.S. intelligence:

> Reacting to an all-out drug campaign by the Colombian government, the Colombian drug criminals have murdered Colombian government officials, bombed the U.S. embassy, and issued death threats against U.S. diplomats and their families, Colombian President Betancur and his cabinet, and members of the Colombian supreme court.[27]

That the M–19's participation in this campaign of terror and intimidation is of high priority was confirmed by the group's attack on the Colombian Palace of Justice in 1985. The assault killed 11 members of Colombia's Supreme Court and destroyed thousands of records, making prosecution of 200 key drug traffickers next to impossible.[28]

Since the raid, other judges have been killed or have died from the stress or had death threats made against them and their families. As a result, in the last year, no Colombian judge has become involved in any extradition hearing despite pressure placed on them by Colombia's new president Virgilio Barco.[29]

In effect, the M–19–drug trafficker alliance has been preserved, giving that Cuban-supported terrorist group renewed life.

Ecuador

The Andean republic has never been high on Fidel Castro's list. Indeed, for most of the 1960s and 1970s, Ecuador apparently appeared on no one's list at all. Although an Ecuadoran version of the Revolutionary Leftist Movement (MIR) appeared in the 1960s as in Chile and Peru, the organization engaged in little violence and none of a terrorist nature. In March 1962, a pro-Castro student guerrilla group did take to the sierra and lasted two days.[30]

As in other countries, Ecuador's relative calm came to an end after the Sandinista victory in Nicaragua and the emergence of the M–19 in Colombia.

Early in 1981, a new group appeared in Ecuador calling itself the *Alfaro Vive Carajo!* (AVC). Named after a turn-of-the century anti-clerical revolutionary politician, Eloy Alfaro, the AVC first attracted attention by carrying out Robin Hood exploits similar to those of the M–19 and the Tupamaros in their early stages of activity.[31]

But as with its Colombian and Uruguayan counterparts, the AVC soon turned to violence, mostly urban terrorism in the form of assassinations, robberies, and kidnappings. Although in the last two years, the Ecuadoran security forces have hit the AVC hard, it remains active, albeit on a reduced scale.[32]

Estimates on its size range from the official Ecuadoran government's 500–600 to 3,000 advanced by some U.S. analysts.[33]

The relationship between the AVC and the M–19 appears to be intimate. "They are the same thing," Ecuador's President Leon Febres Cordero charged in early 1986.[34]

In fact, when four terrorists were killed after police rescued a prominent banker they had kidnapped, three of the dead abductors were members of the Colombian M–19. Ecuadoran officials have also charged that the M–19 helped plan and execute the kidnapping which was carried out in August 1985.[35]

According to U.S. intelligence, the AVC cadre received its training in Nicaragua and in El Salvador where members were integrated into FMLN combat units for "live fire training." Moreover, on at least one occasion, a top AVC officer traveled to Managua in 1984 in search of additional funding. It is uncertain whether the money was provided or if the Sandinistas told the AVC that it had to become a credible threat before winning any additional help.

Peru

Guerrilla and terrorist violence has a longer history in Peru than in Ecuador, although so far it has had little success, despite the lives lost and property damaged.

The first attempted insurgency in Peru after the Castro revolution was initiated in late 1962. It lasted six months. But Leon Trotsky and not Fidel Castro inspired Hugo Blanco's revolt. His Left Revolutionary Front (FIR) began a rural and peasant-based insurrection north of his birthplace, Cuzco; but, by May of the following year, the army had smashed Blanco's tiny band, and he was later captured and imprisoned.[36]

Three years later, in 1965, a specifically pro-Castro group, the Revolutionary Left Movement (MIR), led by Luis de la Puente, also made a stab at rural-based warfare, but the MIR was no more successful than the FIR, although it did manage to establish several fronts.[37]

A third effort in the 1960s made by another pro-Castro group, the National Liberation Army (ELN), under the command of Hector Bejar, enjoyed even less success than the previous two. The ELN lasted less than three months in the field.[38]

Although the MIR and the ELN had signed a document affirming their intention to coordinate their actions, their rhetoric never, in fact, was translated into operational reality. Thus, by January 1966, the month of Fidel Castro's Tricontinent Conference, the revolution in Peru, orthodoxly rural in nature, was dead.[39]

Fifteen years would pass before another insurgency broke out in Peru, and when it did, it took a bizarre and bloody twist. The continent's best known guerrilla group, the *Sendero Luminoso* (Shining Path), began operations, perhaps coincidentally, in 1980—again shortly after the defeat of Somoza in Nicaragua.

From the beginning, the Senderos have waged a brutal, largely rural war, in the Indian-dominated highlands. Conventionally described as Maoist in doctrine, the Senderos, in fact, have said next to nothing about their ideology. Their leaders are also equally mysterious, although the guiding force is said to be Abimael Guzman, a Marxist professor who taught at the University of Ayacucho. Guzman is known to have maintained close ties with the Argentine Montoneros.

The Senderos probably number about 2,000 militants and are drawn from provincial school teachers and students. They are financed by bank robberies and drug sales, U.S. intelligence sources report. Some observers believe they receive funding from sympathizers in Europe and South America, but little hard evidence exists on this question. Most analysts contend that the Senderos have not been given Cuban or Soviet assistance, but top Peruvian officials in the government of President Fernando Belaunde Terry have accused Havana of doing so.[40]

A second group, the Tupac Amaru Revolutionary Movement, is both more recent and more clearly pro-Castro. It sprang to life in 1984 and has since received a clear propaganda endorsement from Havana, and it may have already received limited amounts of training and other forms of support.

The Tupac is also almost entirely devoted to acts of urban terrorism, committed mostly in Lima, the capital. Specifically, Tupac has engaged in sabotage, assassination of political figures and policemen, bank robberies, and kidnapping.[41]

There are intelligence reports that indicate Tupac Amaru leaders have visited Nicaragua, suggesting that Peruvian terrorists have established links with at least the Sandinista regime.

In the meantime, the government of President Alan Garcia is far from controlling either the *Sendero Luminoso* or the Tupac Amaru. If either begins to make serious headway, Havana's interest in supporting insurgency, including urban terrorism, will likely increase.

Chile

Although the Chilean MIR, which had once shown so much promise, was nearly under control by the late 1970s, insurgency, terrorism in particular, is far from over. Indeed, a largely urban-based terrorist group, the Manuel Rodriguez Patriotic Front, is active and playing a large role in shaping the future of Chilean politics—win or lose.

The Cuban tie to contemporary Chilean terrorism is clear, strong, and unchallenged by Havana. After the fall of Allende, in revenge, Fidel Castro promised Chilean extremists every bit of help his regime could muster. He has kept that promise.

At first, the prime beneficiary continued to be the MIR. Throughout the 1970s, the MIR in exile received training in all the insurgent's arts, including document fabrication and photography. In addition, Cubans trained MIR agents in the Middle East and Africa.

But the Cubans increased their aid to the MIR significantly after victory in Nicaragua seemed assured. According to the State Department's December 1981 white paper:

> By mid-1979, the MIR had recruited several hundred Chilean exiles and sent them to Cuba for training and eventual infiltration into Chile. At the same time, members of the MIR who have been living and working in Cuba since Allende's overthrow began to receive training in urban guerrilla warfare techniques. The training in some cases lasted as long as 7 months and included organization and political strategy, small unit tactics, security, and communications.[42]

After the completion of the training, Havana aided the *miristas* to enter Chile surreptitiously with false passports and identification cards. As a result, MIR actions, including bombings and bank robberies, were on the upswing through 1980, with the official Cuban newspaper *Granma* claiming 100 "armed actions" had been carried out by their proteges in that year.[43]

The new MIR drive had its effect on other would-be Chilean revolutionaries as well. Fearful that the MIR would once more upstage every other group on the extreme left, the exiled leadership of the Chilean Communist Party moved quickly to adjust its revolutionary line. Previously (including throughout the Allende period), the Chilean communists had condemned violence as an inappropriate way to seize power.

Now that was all to change. At the end of 1980, the long-time leader of the PCCh, Luis Corvalan, held talks with Fidel Castro in Havana where the Cuban leader lobbied for a united Chilean extreme left. Corvalan apparently agreed because, in his speech at the Cuban Communist Party Congress in December of that year, he openly endorsed armed struggle for the first time. The next month, the Chilean communist specifically characterized the MIR's campaign of terrorism as "helpful," and he indicated his willingness to enter discussions with his old opponents on the extreme left. The new look ended in a unity agreement being signed in the Central American fashion.[44]

In subsequent years, the MIR continued its policy of urban terrorism, but *mirista* activity seems to have peaked in 1981, after which it went into another period of decline. But the suppression of the MIR was countered by the appearance of the PCCh's own armed wing, the Manuel Rodriguez Patriotic Front (FMR).

The FMR has employed precisely the same tactics as the MIR, operating largely in the country's population and industrial centers of Santiago and Valparaiso. Robberies, killings, bombings, and sabotage have increased in the last several years, which has further polarized the Chilean political scene, making a transition from the rule of President Augusto Pinochet to representative and elective democracy extremely difficult.

Indeed, the Front's most spectacular action, the nearly successful assassination of Pinochet in September 1986, succeeded in the sense that the stubborn Chilean strongman will be made even more inflexible. That most likely was the FMR's long-term hope. The short-term one anticipated a massive increase in repression following the attempted killing, a goal that terrorist groups have generally pursued.[45]

Meanwhile, the reconciliation between those ancient rivals, the Chilean communists and Fidel Castro, a process that began in Havana at the end of 1980, seems to have fully flowered into a genuine entente, if not an outright alliance.

In terms of strategy, the Chilean communist party and its armed wing, the FMR, have now embraced the MIR strategy of the 1970s. Their intention is to foster the continued polarization of the country until a civil war is unleashed. At that point, the PCCh, with its allies, hopes to be then strong enough to emerge the winner after the war has exhausted the country.

Still as both Havana and the PCCh knew in 1985, the amount of training and armament provided had only allowed the FMR, the remnants of the MIR, and a few other miniscule terrorist organizations enough striking power to carry out a limited number of terrorist acts.

That situation changed, however, when Havana dramatically increased its aid to the FMR in a bold and risky operation the following year. In July 1986, Cuban fishing boats off-loaded some 50 tons of arms in the sparsely populated desert country of Chile's northern coast. The weapons were destined for the FMR in Santiago, and, indeed, captured photographs of the operation showed the Front's armed gunmen overseeing the project.

Chilean police discovered the main cache and subsequently other smaller caches the following month. It was by far the largest arsenal found since the overthrow of Allende in 1973. The weapons included 3,100 M–16 rifles, 100 Belgian-made FAL rifles, 1,800 Soviet-made RPG–7s, and a variety of other equipment, including boots, uniforms, and Japanese communications sets. They were enough to supply an army of 5,000 men, both American and Chilean officials estimate.[46]

As another result, some U.S. analysts believe that Havana is now convinced that the right conditions exist in Chile for a successful insurgency.

In 1985, the same analysts argue, Fidel Castro was faced with at least a stalemate in Central America. The Salvadoran war was not going well, and the Sandinistas were being pressured by the Contras. Consequently, Castro shifted his attention further south, and of all the prospects in South America, Chile seemed the most promising. The country's increasingly unpopular military ruler, who would hold office at least until 1989, and the society's rapid fragmentation nearly guaranteed serious trouble. A newly united extreme left added another element to an explosive mixture. Moreover, Pinochet had little support elsewhere in the world, quite aside from the unremitting enmity of the Soviet bloc. Even the Reagan administration was visibly distancing itself from the ageing military president.

All of this seemed to fit a familiar pattern in Havana's view, one that duplicated the last years of Batista and Somoza. Given that, it is more than probable that Castro moved Chile much higher on his list of priorities and, in doing so, ran little risk. After all, the Cuban leader has never made his hatred for those who overthrew Allende a secret. And as Somoza found out, a sense of personal revenge on the part of its leader plays no small part in the forming of Cuban foreign policy since 1959.

If this analysis proves correct, then terrorism conducted by the FMR and the remnants of the MIR should increase through the remainder of this decade, with the 1989 presidential plebiscite serving as the political target of convenience. In short, Central America will not be the only focus for Cuban-sponsored terrorism in the hemisphere.

Notes to Chapter 5

1. J. Mark Ruhl, "The Military," in *Politics of Compromise: Coalition Government in Colombia*, ed. R. Albert Berry, Ronald G. Hellman, and Mauricio Solaun (New Brunswick, New Jersey: Transaction Books, 1980), 195.

2. Ibid., 196, and Francis, *Latin American Terrorism*, 9. Also Ratliff, *Castroism and Communism*, 118–121, and Peter Janke, *Guerrilla and Terrorist Organisations: A World Directory and Bibliography* (New York: Macmillan, 1983), 452–457.

3. State Department's "Special Report, No. 90," 10.

4. That curious argument is suggested by, among others, Richard Gott, *Guerrilla Movements in Latin America* (New York: Doubleday, 1971), 223–224.

5. Ratliff, *Castroism and Communism*, 119.

6. Francis, 9. Also Janke, 454.

7. Ruhl, 196; 198. Also Gott, 268–300. Torres, whom Gott clearly admires, was killed in 1966.

8. Ruhl, 196–197.

9. The closest Latin American counterpart to ANAPO is the Peronist movement in Argentina. Both were led by military strongmen whose followers fell along a spectrum from extreme left to extreme right. Their chief difference is that Peron held power while building his mass following. Rojas did so after being removed from the national palace in 1957. Robert H. Dix, "Political Oppositions under the National Front," in *Politics of Compromise*, 131–179.

10. Janke, 450–451.

11. It was not all that M–19 borrowed from the Tupamaros. Its organization of city-based columns divided into independent cells was a copy of the Uruguayan original. Ibid., 451.

12. Ibid., 451–452.

13. State Department's "Special Report, No. 90," 10. Havana has denied involvement in that M–19 operation or any another of the Colombian group. Nevertheless, several M–19 terrorists told their hostage, U.S. Ambassador Diego Asencio, that they had been trained in Cuba. Cited in Pamela S. Falk, *Cuban Foreign Policy: Caribbean Tempest* (Lexington, MA: Lexington Books, D.C. Heath and Co., 1986), 68.

14. State Department's "Special Report, No. 90. "The meeting in Managua, however, would be the start of a long and continuing close relationship between the Sandinistas and the M–19.

15. Ibid. As can be seen, Havana rarely wastes assets, and that practice could have serious implications for Argentina and Uruguay as well as Jamaica.

16. Ibid., 11. The Cubans piously denied involvement in the M–19 invasion reminiscent of early Cuban expeditions against Panama and the Dominican Republic. But one top Cuban leader, Carlos Rafael Rodriguez, said in an interview (with *Der Spiegel* on 26 September 1981) that Havana did train members of the M–19, (and while he was at it, he admitted the Salvadoran FMLN as well), but nothing else. Rodriguez explained: "We did not deny this because in the past few years many people came to our country for various reasons to ask for training. We did not deny this desire. If a revolutionary for Latin America wishes to learn the technique and organization of resistance for his own self-defense, we cannot refuse in view of the brutal oppression. This also holds true for the Salvadorans." Rodriguez could have mentioned Cuban propaganda support for the M–19 as well. While that is not surprising, the support included one revealing

element. When the M–19 kidnapped and then brutally murdered an American religious worker in February 1981, Havana's propaganda machine falsely accused Chester Bitterman and the Summer Institute of Linguistics of being CIA agents. The Institute, in fact, translates the Bible into obscure South American Indian languages. Nevertheless, Havana's repeating that old chestnut and endorsing the M–19's action were at best an indirect blessing of urban terrorism. See the State Department's "Special Report, No. 90," 11.

17. *Patterns of Global Terrorism: 1983*, Department of State, September 1984: 17. The three Americans were held for ransom (which was paid) and then released.

18. Although the much battered ELN has been in eclipse since the old pro-Castro group discovered that Havana loved another, the M–19, more, it still proved capable of pulling off an occasional spectacular of its own. In November 1983, the ELN kidnapped, and then released the following month, President Betancur's brother. Despite the truce, however, which has seen FARC agents involved in electoral politics, the war does go on. According to one estimate, in the first quarter of 1987, 24 soldiers, 48 policemen, 70 guerrillas, 100 government informants, and 14 politicians were killed. *The Economist*, 18 April 1987, 39.

19. From the Hearings before the Senate Subcommittee on Security and Terrorism of the Committee on the Judiciary, *The Role of Cuba in International Terrorism*, 97th Congress, 2d sess., 1982, and quoted in *Castro and the Narcotics Connection* (Washington, D.C.; Cuban American National Foundation, 1983), 23. Guillot subsequently was released by the Mexican goverment in September 1982 because of Mexico's special relationship with Cuba, many analysts believe. Since 1983, the Colombian has been reported seen in Spain, Cuba, and Nicaragua. See ibid., 9, and Michael Ledeen, "K.G.B. Connections," *The New Republic*, 28 February 1983 which can be found in *Castro and the Narcotics Connection*, 70. For additional details of Cuban involvement, see also the hearings before the House Foreign Affairs Committee on February 21 and 23, 1984, entitled "U.S. Response to Cuban Involvement in Narcotics Trafficking and Review of Worldwide Illicit Narcotics Situation," 1984. The testimony of Deputy Assistant Secretary of State for Inter-American Affairs James Michel and DEA Administrator Francis M. Mullen, Jr., 20–48, are especially relevant.

20. Ledeen, "K.G.B. Connections," 70.

21. Ibid, 23. According to Enders, Guillot also arranged for an arms shipment to be sent to Bolivia. Other estimates suggest the Cuban–Colombian drug connection began in 1975. See *U.S. News and World Report*, 4 May 1987, 35.

22. *Castro and the Narcotics Connection*, 23. There are two versions of how the deal was struck. DEA officials believe the arrangement was worked out in 1981 between Guillot and Raul Castro in Managua. Colombian military intelligence believes the agreement was made in 1979 when Guillot met M–19 leaders at the Cuban embassy in Bogota. *Foreign Report*, 4 March 1982. It was on that same trip to Nicaragua that Raul Castro introduced the idea of drug smuggling to Sandinista officials, according to a Sandinista defector in testimony to the Senate's Labor and Human Resources Subcommittee in August 1984. In July of

that year, Federico Vaughn, a close aide to Nicaragua's Minister of the Interior Tomas Borge Martinez, was indicted by a federal grand jury in Miami for cocaine trafficking. "The Soviet-Cuban Connection," *Washington Post*, 3 August 1984.

23. Those four Cuban officials include one senior DGI officer, a vice-admiral of the Cuban navy, and the two top-ranking diplomats in the Cuban embassy in Bogota at the time. In response to a direct question from Florida's Republican Senator Paula Hawkins as to whether or not Fidel Castro could have been un-involved in the narcotics effort, U.S. Ambassador to Colombia Thomas Boyatt replied: "No, ma'am." Quoted in *The Washington Post*, 3 August 1984. From hearings before the Senate Drug Enforcement Caucus, the Senate Judiciary Sub-committee on Security and Terrorism and the Senate Foreign Relations Subcom-mittee on Western Hemisphere Affairs, 30 April 1983.

24. *U.S. News and World Report*, 4 May 1987, 36.

25. Ibid.

26. *Washington Post*, 3 August 1984.

27. "The Soviet Cuban Connection" 38. The M–19, however, has not had a monopoly on the drug connection. According to a joint State and Defense white paper: "When the Colombian armed forces and National Police entered the town of Calamar in February 1984, they discovered that the guerrilla Revolutionary Armed Forces of Colombia had *campesinos* cultivating hundreds of hectares of coca plants." Ibid.

28. *The Economist*, 18 April 1987, 38–39. Also *U.S. News and World Report*, 36. The arms used by the M–19 were traced to stocks given the Sandinistas by the Venezuelan government during their fight against Somoza. See *U.S. News and World Report*, 4 May 1987.

29. *The Economist*, 18 April 1987, 39.

30. Gott, 9.

31. "Carajo" is an Ecuadoran expletive. See *The Washington Times*, 14 Jan-uary 1986.

32. The AVC lost its commander, Fausto Basamtes Borja, in a shootout near the Quito airport in early January 1986. Ibid.

33. The State Department estimate, disclosed by Assistant Secretary of State for Inter–American Affairs Elliot Abrams in a January 1986 press conference was 1,000 members. Ibid.

34. Ibid. Why would Ecuadoran terrorists choose a Colombian group rather than, say, a Peruvian? Ecuador has long had relatively friendly ties with Colom-bia and was once part of Simon Bolivar's Gran Colombia. Peru, on the other hand, is a longstanding enemy, and the two countries fought a brief but bitter war in 1942 whose legacy, an unresolved border dispute, continues to hamper good relations.

35. Ibid. According to Ecuadoran officials, raided AVC safehouses have also included large caches of drugs used to finance operations.

36. For a sympathetic account of Blanco's efforts, see Gott, 314–329. Blan-co's insurgency was supposed to have been financed by a bank robbery in Lima, but the funds were intercepted by the police. He would get some sympathetic

recognition from "Che" Guevara, and later Cuban propaganda would extol the exploits of Hugo Blanco. Ibid., 314.

37. Ibid., 336–371. Also Ratliff, *Castroism and Communism*, 121–123. De la Puente, who broke from the leftwing American Popular Revolutionary Alliance (APRA), probably sealed his fate by issuing a bombastic manifesto outlining his intentions before carrying out his first guerrilla action. It was a mistake that his successors would not repeat.

38. Rafliff, 123, and Gott, *Castroism and Communism* 372–380.

39. Gott, 372–373, and Ratliff, *Castroism and Communism*, 123.

40. *The Washington Times*, 31 July 1985. Although the bulk of their activity is in the countryside, the Senderos do engage in urban terrorism too. They have bombed public utilities, government ministries, businesses, and the U.S. embassy. See *Patterns of Global Terrorism*, 17.

41. The 200 tons of East German arms of Soviet design on board the Danish freighter the *Pia Vesta* that lingered off the coast of Peru in June 1986 may have been intended for the Tupac Amaru, according to U.S. officials. There were enough rifles and rocket launchers to equip 1,500 men. But since the freighter was unable to dispose of the arms and returned instead to Panama where the crew and cargo were interned, the precise recipient of those arms may never be known. See *The Washington Times*, 20 June 1986.

42. State Department's "Special Report, No. 90," 11.

43. Ibid.

44. Ibid. The victory of a united Sandinista movement in Nicaragua and the growing threat of the FMLN coalition in El Salvador are events likely to have impressed the ageing Corvalan whose "peaceful" tactics had netted the Chilean Communist Party next to nothing after seven years of exile. Moreover, Corvalan must have sensed in 1980—a feeling no doubt reinforced by his Soviet sponsors—that the cutting edge of the revolution would be, once again, the armed rebels and not the politicians in the gray suits. Hence, his decision not to be left behind—again.

45. For a reconstruction of the attempted assassination of Pinochet, see *El Mercurio* [Santiago], 27 November 1986.

46. Ibid., and statement of the Chilean ambassador to the Permanent Council of the OAS, August 27, 1986. The Chilean government subsequently asked for technical assistance from the United States in identifying the origin of the M–16s. U.S. intelligence sources later confirmed that at least some of the rifles that retained their serial markings could be traced to stocks left in Vietnam. As for the FMR, its members documented the landing with numerous photographs, which were later captured by the Chilean police.

Chapter 6

Cuba in the Middle East

Fidel Castro's support of revolution, including the use of terrorism, is by no means confined to the New World. Even his deceased colleague Ernesto Guevara, who so profoundly believed in a continental revolution, attempted an insurrection in the former Belgian Congo in 1965.

Thus, the Cuban leader who could not be confined to his island-country as he pursued regional ambitions in the early 1960s would not restrict himself to one hemisphere either.

In the last two decades, Havana has helped foster revolution in distant places in league with a variety of unsavory governments and organizations who, with the Cubans, have not hesitated in using terrorist methods to achieve their goals.

As a result, that network of interlocking relationships has also had its impact on Latin America, Central America in particular.

Cuba and the PLO

The close ties between Fidel Castro and Palestinian leaders like Yasir Arafat are by now common knowledge. Yet that relationship was not inevitable, and it took years before the two cooperated with each other against their perceived mutual enemies, principally the United States and Israel.

Both Havana's big plunge into the Middle Eastern cauldron and its connection to the PLO (Palestine Liberation Organization) came at the same time. As with much else that shaped Castro's ambition to be a world figure, the two came together at the 1966 Tricontinent Conference.

A large Palestinian contingent was in attendance, and not surprisingly, the resolution accepted by more than 500 delegates called for the breaking of all treaties with Israel, the expulsion of the Jewish state from all international organizations, and the imposing of a world-wide cultural and economic boycott.[1]

Still, despite that radical set of proposals, the Castro regime was not yet prepared to sever ties with Israel or openly embrace the PLO. It did not play an active role in formulating the resolutions on the Middle East at the Tricontinent, and, when challenged as to the meaning of Cuba's support for the resolution, Castro later used the excuse the Soviets managed in dealing with outraged Latin American countries. Cuba, Castro told an Israeli diplomat, does not consider itself bound by the Tricontinent resolution because the conference was attended by representatives from parties and groups rather than states.[2]

Nevertheless, this one step backward only barely concealed the two forward steps taken in the Cuba–PLO relationship. In 1968, Cuban military and intelligence officers were sent to North African and Iraqi camps to aid the PLO. The following year Cuban and PLO officers were subsequently trained together in the Soviet Union, after which they were dispatched to the Sinai to mount raids on Israeli outposts.

In May 1972, the collaboration became closer. At a meeting in Algeria, Castro and PLO leaders worked out a joint program in which the two sides would train Latin American terrorists with specialized instruction to be given in camps located in Lebanon, Libya, and South Yemen.[3]

The secret alliance that developed in the late 1960s and early 1970s, however, would not become publicly apparent until the 1973 conference of non-aligned nations held in Algiers.

It was the first Fidel Castro had ever attended, and the networking that he did at the meeting was greatly advanced by the PLO. Indeed, the Palestinian connection was a major factor in Castro's quick rise in the movement. Despite his dubious non-aligned credentials, underscored by his ceaseless lobbying for the whole Soviet line, the Cuban leader in only six years would be selected the movement's chairman for the 1979 conference held in Havana.[4]

That honor, however, came at a price. At the Algiers conference, Castro was challenged by Muammar Qaddafi, in one of the Maximum Leader's most embarrassing moments on the international stage. The Libyan bluntly criticized Castro for being Moscow's faithful apologist. In short, the Cuban emperor had no neutralist clothes.

"We are against Cuba's presence in this conference of non-aligned nations," Qaddafi said at a press conference following Castro's address. "There is no difference between Cuba and any Eastern European country, or for that matter Uzbekistan and the Soviet Union itself."[5]

Stung by the Libyan's effrontery, Castro characteristically moved to cut his losses and recover the initiative—but not before two days of frantic maneuvering by the PLO and others to patch up their differences. It was a public spat that threatened to torpedo the whole conference. And so it nearly did, but, within an hour of its scheduled conclusion, Castro, in a form of self-criticism, changed the subject—it had been Qaddafi's charge that he was mere Soviet toady—by announcing Cuba's severing of all ties with Israel.[6]

The surprise move, which caught, among others, the Cuban foreign ministry off-balance, did the trick. According to eyewitnesses, both Qaddafi and Arafat rushed to embrace anti-Zionism's newest member.[7]

The warming Cuban-PLO relationship, not surprisingly, paralleled the Soviet Union's growing interest in the Palestinian cause. Until 1969, Moscow paid the PLO little attention, considering it too ineffectual for serious support. Five years later, however, the Kremlin did a dramatic turnabout, thanks to Israel's victory in the Yom Kippur War in October 1973. The Soviets, thanks to Henry Kissinger's astute diplomacy, feared their eclipse in the Middle East. As a consequence, they strengthened their ties with their remaining Arab clients, the PLO in particular. A year later, the Arab summit conference held in Rabat declared the PLO "the sole legitimate representative of the Palestinian people," a development that merely confirmed the wisdom of the Soviet decision to give the PLO a permanent office in Moscow, taken earlier in August.[8]

But while the PLO's relationship with the Kremlin was warming, it soon would become torrid with the Cubans. A month after the Rabat conference, Arafat paid, in effect, a state visit to Cuba where he was given full honors during his stay, which included the awarding of the country's highest decoration, the Playa Giron medal.[9]

Fidel Castro's embrace of the PLO would also result in cruelties visited upon the Jewish community in Cuba. When, for example, the PLO opened its office in Havana, it was offered the building that once housed the Cuban Zionist Center.[10]

Meanwhile, the handful of Palestinians being trained in Cuba in the 1960s rapidly increased in the 1970s, with 300 being reported in the camps by 1977.[11]

Cuban–PLO cooperation has taken other forms as well. In South Yemen, Cuban and Soviet military advisers arrived in March 1983 to serve as instructors for three-to-five-month courses in the basics of guerrilla and terrorist warfare taught in four PLO camps. Cuban presence in South Yemen as trainers dates from at least 1979. At those camps, a number of terrorist groups, many of them non-Arab, has reportedly received assistance, including the West German Red Army, the South Moluccans, and the Irish Republican Army.[12]

Cuban trainers have also been spotted working in PLO camps in southern Lebanon in the late 1970s, following Fidel Castro's early 1978 meeting with George Habash, one of the most intransigient of the PLO leaders.[13]

According to Kopilow:

> The Cuban presence [in Lebanon] was further confirmed in 1982 when the Israelis found . . . such papers as *"muy secreto"* ("very secret") Cuban training manual detailing how to conduct military operations, including blowing-up high-power electric transformers and railway stations.[14]

But if the PLO helped introduce Fidel Castro in a serious and sustained way to the Middle East, the Cubans have more than reciprocated. As a result, the PLO has built up an impressive presence in the Western Hemisphere, particularly Central America.

The basis of the Cuban–PLO relationship remains their shared belief that, while the PLO's enemy is Israel, the United States is the main adversary because it is the principal supporter of the Jewish state. What harms the United States ultimately harms Israel. On that basis, therefore, Fidel Castro and the PLO continue to cooperate.

That applies to Cuba's protégés as well, primarily the Sandinistas in Nicaragua and the Salvadoran FMLN. Indeed, the PLO–Sandinista relationship dates to the late 1960s. In 1969, top Sandinista leaders (including Tomas Borge Martinez, Managua's Minister of the Interior in charge of the secret police) were trained by Palestinians in Lebanon. In the same year, the Sandinistas also arranged for the joint Cuban–PLO training of 50–70 more guerrillas in Lebanon.[15]

As a result, several Sandinistas received "combat experience" by participating in a PLO terrorist operation in the summer of 1970. The operation involved in the successful and simultaneous air hijacking of three commercial jets, which were subsequently destroyed. A fourth attempt on an airliner belonging to Israel's El Al failed—the only fatality, a Sandinista shot by an Israeli sky marshall.[16]

One State Department report concluded:

From the PLO, the Sandinistas got training in guerrilla warfare and an opportunity to practice their skills by aiding the PLO in terrorist acts such as airline hijackings and a campaign against King Hussein in Jordan. The PLO got help from the Sandinistas in operations that brought the PLO to world attention and served as an example for countless other terrorists.[17]

Not surprisingly, the PLO, in turn, helped the Sandinistas win power in Nicaragua. The Palestinians acted as an intermediary to obtain assistance from Libya, North Korea, and Vietnam. They also directly sent arms from their own stocks to the FSLN in the final stages of its war against Somoza. But one 50-ton plane load of arms was intercepted and confiscated by Tunisian authorities in July 1979. However, in the end it would make no difference.[18]

Since the Sandinista takeover, the relationship with the PLO has continued to grow. In recognition of past Palestinian help, the new government in Managua immediately allowed the PLO an "embassy" in Nicaragua, a virtually unprecedented action. And in a similar action to that taken by the Cubans in 1974, Arafat was accorded the honor of a "state visit" in July 1980.[19]

The PLO continues to support the Sandinistas in power. The Palestinians have extended loans to Managua, sent military advisers to teach the Sandinista army how to handle the newly acquired sophisticated Soviet arms, and provided pilots to develop the infant air force. By 1982, there were also reports of PLO military officers providing special guerrilla training in Nicaragua as well.[20]

Nor has the PLO confined its efforts to Cuba or Nicaragua. In perfect tandem with both Castro and the Sandinista leadership, the Palestinians have also assisted the FMLN rebels in El Salvador, according to a direct admission made by Yasir Arafat in January 1982. The PLO, he said, provided training and weapons, mostly mortars and light arms, to the FMLN.[21]

The PLO–Sandinista–FMLN–Cuban nexus has almost perfectly suited Havana's interests. Not only has the high-profile PLO served as useful cutouts when it came to the more sordid aspects of training and equipping new terrorist cadres for any number of regional insurgencies, but the Palestinians, financed by other Arab states, have also provided real resources from other than Soviet bloc origin, thus lessening the burden on Moscow.

Cuban military involvement in the Middle East, of course, has not been confined to terrorist or terrorist-related activity. In 1973, for example, after the end of the October war, Cuban tank units were in place along the Syrian line, and the Cubans participated in the so-called war of attrition, suffering themselves heavy casualties.[22]

But the bulk of Cuban activity has been the training of a variety of terrorist groups who will, it is hoped, damage U.S. and related Western interests. Because both the PLO and Cuban aims are so similar, cooperation between the two has become especially close over the years. It remains, nevertheless, a remarkable development because of the topsy-turvy nature of Middle Eastern politics.

Cuba and Libya

On paper, they should be a good, if not a perfect, match. Both regimes are violently anti-American; each appreciates that terrorism can damage its enemy's interests.

Yet, unlike the PLO, the curious relationship that has evolved between Havana and Tripoli since the 1973 non-aligned conference cannot be labelled close or even friendly. It is often competitive, and there are reports that Castro in particular has been annoyed at the Libyan leader, especially when Qaddafi has meddled in Latin America and the Caribbean.

Nor is it very likely that Fidel has forgotten the Libyan strongman's comparing Cuba—"the first free territory in the Americas"—to a Soviet backwater republic. Even less is Castro willing to forgive that kind of canard coming from a younger man who came to power through an ordinary *golpe,* or from a leader who has squandered huge resources on futile adventures which call attention to himself and risk American armed retaliation for being caught, *flagrante delicto.*[23]

Still, even Castro can appreciate that the Libyans are not without their merit—at least up to a point. Qaddafi, for example, has been generous in his economic support of the Sandinistas. Before their victory, it was Libyan money which bought arms from the cash-starved Vietnamese and North Koreans. Later, in 1981, he extended a $100 million loan, supplied Managua with low cost oil, and invested in two major agricultural-pastoral projects, with at least two more on the drawing boards. Projected cost for the four: $256 million.[24]

Still Tripoli's generosity has had its downside for Havana. In April 1983, when the Reagan administration was trying to convince a doubting Congress that El Salvador was under attack by a network of foreign powers, four Libyan transport planes stuffed with arms arrived in Brazil. Suspicious officials quickly realized the manifests and the stated destination were false. The "medical supplies for Colombia," in fact, were 84 tons of arms, explosives, and dismantled fighter planes intended for the Sandinistas and their allies in the field, the Salvadoran FMLN.

The huge publicity generated by this fiasco, and the clumsiness of the deception followed by Qaddafi's public admission of the truth only confirmed the Reagan administration's charges, and it came at precisely the wrong time for Havana. As such, the Brazil affair is still considered a major turning point in the battle for El Salvador at least.[25]

But worse was to come. While Qaddafi merely embarrassed Castro by clumsily attempting to support the Cuban leader's protégés in Central America, the Libyan has also attempted to buy protégés of his own in the Caribbean.

According to U.S. intelligence, Tripoli has organized Islamic groups in Barbados and the Netherlands Antilles. It has also provided secret funds for Eastern Caribbean leftists in Antigua, Dominica, French Guiana, Guadeloupe, Martinique, and St. Lucia.

Moreover, Qaddafi has demanded a return for his investment. The State Department reports:

In the spring 1986, a Libyan official tried—apparently without success—to induce Caribbean nationalists to take violent action against U.S. interests in the region. Eugenia Charles, Prime Minister of Dominica, said on March 4, 1986, that her country is a major target of Qaddafi because of its support role in the Grenada rescue mission. "Anybody who is hand in glove with the Libyan regime is not spouting ideology. He is embracing terrorism."[26]

In addition, the State Department has also charged Libya with direct attempts at destabilization of an area dotted with democratic, but fragile governments.

Libya has also actively recruited members of leftist groups. Leftist leaders from Antigua, Barbados, Dominica, the Dominican Republic, Haiti, St. Lucia, St. Vincent, and the French "Departments" have been invited to Libya for "seminars" at which they are urged to undertake violent action rather than peacefully participate in the political process. Some have received paramilitary training in Libya.[27]

The Libyans have achieved little so far with their scatter-shot efforts. Moreover, there is no sign, whatever, in contrast to PLO efforts, of any attempt at coordination with the Cubans, a particularly grating development for Fidel Castro who considers the Americas his own turf.

There is, in fact, direct evidence that the Cubans have resented the Libyan intrusion. A Grenadian official, in a captured document, details in a memorandum Cuban guidance on how to act at a Libyan-sponsored "congress" held in Tripoli in June 1982. The Grenadian was told to give no support to any Libyan effort to make that country "the center of the World anti-imperialist struggle . . . and that we should only give solidarity expressions for the proposed World Center."[28]

Still, small scale Libyan meddling will go on, and it may continue to work at cross purposes to the more sophisticated designs of Havana.

Notes to Chapter 6

1. David J. Kopilow, *Castro, Israel, and the PLO* (Washington, D.C.; The Cuban American National Foundation, 1985), 20.

2. Ibid. Also Maurice Halperin, *The Taming of Fidel Castro* (Berkeley: University of California Press, 1981), 244.

3. *The PLO's Growing Latin American Base*, Heritage Foundation Backgrounder No. 281 (Washington, D.C., 2 August 1983), 2. Cited in unpublished manuscript by Yonah Alexander, 21–22.

4. Kopilow, 21. Castro's lobbying effort began early. On his way to Algiers, he collected Prime Ministers Michael Manley of Jamaica and Forbes Burnham of Guyana, and Guinea's President Sekou Toure. Halperin, *Taming of . . . Castro*, 249.

5. George Volsky, "Cuba 15 Years Later," *Current History* 66 (January 1974): 13. Also cited in Kapilow, 22 and M. Halperin, *Taming*, 251. The sources differ slightly on the Qaddafi quote, but the sense is always the same.

6. By way of contrast, in Castro's opening address which lashed out at the United States as well as Bolivia, Brazil, Portugal, and South Africa, Israel rated only one mildly critical reference. Moreover, as leader of a small country, Fidel broke his own rule of never being the first to break relations with another country. Even in the case of Chile after the fall of Allende, it was Pinochet, not Castro, who ended diplomatic ties. M. Halperin, *Taming*, 248; 251.

7. Ibid. Also *Le Monde*, 11 September 1973, and *Granma Weekly Review*, 16 September 1973. Despite the public *abrazo* with Qaddafi, it is likely that Castro has yet to forgive or forget the Libyan leader's action as will be seen. Still, at the time, Qaddafi's presence at the conference went unmentioned in the Cuban press (according to M. Halperin, *Taming*, 252). Nevertheless, Cuba's hos-

tility for Israel has remained consistent since Algiers. Among other things, Cuba was only one of three non-Arab regimes that co-sponsored the Zionism–is–racism U.N. resolution in 1975. After Israeli commandos rescued hostages held at Kampala's Entebbe airport, Cuba criticized Israel's violation of Ugandan sovereignty. The incident revealed not only how far Castro was willing to support "the Arab cause," it also showed Cuban unwillingness to condemn any act of terrorism, no matter how brutal or unwarranted, if committed against an adversary. See Kopilow, 27, and M. Halperin, *Taming,* 257.

8. Ray S. Cline and Yonah Alexander, *Terrorism: The Soviet Connection* (New York: Crane Russak, 1984), 31–34.

9. Kopilow, 23. *Granma Weekly Review* in its 24 November 1974 issue devoted three-quarters of its space to the Arafat visit.

10. Yoram Shapira, "Cuba and the Arab-Israeli Conflict," in *Cuba in the World,* Ed. Cole Blasier and Carmelo Mesa–LAGO (Pittsburgh, University of Pittsburgh Press, 1979), 159. Also cited in Kopilow, 28.

11. *Time,* 24 October 1977. Also Cline and Alexander, 71.

12. Ibid., 67–68, and "Foreign Report," *The Economist,* 24 March 1983.

13. Kopilow, 12.

14. Ibid. Also Raphael Israeli, ed, *PLO in Lebanon: Selected Documents* (London: Weidenfeld and Nicolson, Ltd., 1983), 158–167.

15. "The Sandinistas and Middle Eastern Radicals," Department of State, August 1985: 1. According to the State Department which cites a report in *Business Week,* 3 May 1983, Borge also acted as Castro's special envoy to the Middle East in those years.

16. The terrorist, Patrick Argeullo Ryan, has since become a Sandinista martyr.

17. "The Sandinistas and Middle Eastern Radicals," 2. Sandinista participation was first disclosed by a Sandinista officer to the Kuwaiti newspaper *al–Watan:* 7 August 1979, that is, almost three weeks *after* the FSLN had seized power in Managua. The spokesman, Jorge Mandi, also said that Sandinistas fought side-by-side with PLO gunmen in their Black September 1970 effort to overthrow King Hussein. "The Sandinistas and Middle Eastern Radicals," 2.

18. *Washington Post,* 29 May 1982, and *U.S. News and World Report,* 23 July 1979, and cited in the State Department's "The Sandinistas and Middle Eastern Radicals," 6.

19. "Sandinistas and Middle Eastern Radicals," 7. On the four-day visit to Nicaragua, Arafat pledged that "anyone who threatens Nicaragua will have to face Palestinian combatants." Quoted in *Foreign Broadcast Information Service,* 23 July 1980, P–8.

20. "The Sandinistas and Middle Eastern Radicals," 7. Also *Washington Post,* 29 May 1982: *Newsweek,* 15 March 1982; and Robert F. Lamberg, "The PLO in Latin America," *Swiss Review of World Affairs,* June 1982, 12.

21. Kopilow, 15. PLO links with one FMLN leader, Shafik Handal, of the Salvadoran Communist party and himself of Palestinian descent, go back more than a dozen years. Also see the *Wall Street Journal,* 14 January 1982. Two years earlier, in a gesture of solidarity, a Salvadoran terrorist group attacked the

Israeli embassy in San Salvador and afterwards demanded that the government establish ties with the PLO. Cline and Alexander, 65. The information was obtained by the authors from an Israeli foreign ministry briefing on 16 May 1982. The PLO has established relationships with other Cuban-supported Latin American terrorist groups, including the Argentine Montoneros and the Chilean MIR.

22. See "Foreign Report," *The Economist*, 1 March and 15 March 1978, for details of the first deployment of Cuban combat troops off the island, a decision which left 180 Cubans dead and 250 wounded. The operation preceded the better known Angolan adventure by nearly two years.

23. At the time of the 1973 Algiers conference of the non-aligned, the Cuban press suppressed all references to Libyan leader Muammar Qaddafi. M. Halperin, *Taming*, 252 (n).

24. "Libyan Activities in the Western Hemisphere," Department of State, August 1986: 1–3.

25. Ibid., 3–4. Also see the *Washington Post*, 26 April 1983. Qaddafi suffered another humilitation when Brazilian press reports detailed the activities of the Libyan crews during their enforced stay in Brazil—they spent their time on a very long "lost weekend" of drink and womanizing.

26. "Libyan Activities," 6.

27. Ibid. Elsewhere in Latin America, the Libyans have made contact and given support to Colombia's M-19, the Chilean MIR, and Ecuador's AVC. In Venezuela, they have so far unsuccessfully attempted to recruit would-be terrorists from the country's fringe leftist groups. Ibid., 4–7.

28. Quoted in Ledeen and Romerstein, Document 34-1. Despite Cuban disapproval, Libya continues to hold annual conferences at the "International Center for Combatting Imperialism" for approximately 1,000 members of radical left-wing and terrorist groups around the world. "Libyan Activities," 5–6.

Chapter 7

The Cubans in Sub-Saharan Africa

The Castro regime's ventures in Africa are not of recent origin, and they did not begin with the massive troop intervention in Angola in 1975. Havana, in fact, has intruded into the continent's affairs on numerous occasions, in an unconventional fashion pursuing interests it believes are wholly antithetical to those of the United States and its friends and allies. Although the instruments of force have varied, they have, as in Latin America, included the use of terrorism.

The Early Years

Cuba's interest in Africa dates to the first year of the revolution, namely, 1959 when "Che" Guevara toured the region. It would be the first of several African trips for the peripatetic Argentine.

The first African nation of interest to Cuba was not, in fact, sub-Saharan, but the military aid it provided the Algerian rebels in 1960 in their struggle against the French set a pattern for Cuban involvement throughout the continent. The warmth of that relationship continued after Algeria achieved independence in 1962, when Havana immediately sent a military mission to Algiers. In October 1963 during a brief border war with Morocco, Castro ordered a shipment of men and material to Algeria in the uncharacteristic glare of Cuban press publicity.[1]

The closeness of the relationship continued for two more years, but it would wither after a military coup removed Castro's close friend Ahmed Ben Bella from power.

Even before the disenchantment with Algeria set in, however, the Castro regime was already looking south. Maurice Halperin reports that "students" from the old Belgian Congo could be seen in Havana in the early 1960s. It seemed more than a straw in the wind.[2]

Cuba in Africa: Round One

Fidel Castro's fascination with Africa first flowered in the mid-1960s. As was the case ten years later, much of that interest came from frustration. The years 1964 and 1965 were times of reversal in Latin America for Cuba. The Venezuelan rebellion had been all but smashed; Salvador Allende had failed to win the election in Chile; the Brazilian military had overthrown the leftwing regime of Joao Goulart; Castro had been maneuvered by the Soviet Union into signing a compromise agreement with the Latin American communist parties which allowed revolution in only a handful of countries; and finally, a left-wing revolt in the Dominican Republic was put down with the help of U.S. military forces.[3]

Africa, on the other hand, despite the setback in Algeria, seemed to hold more promise for the Cubans, particularly in the old Belgian Congo, which, in 1965, appeared to be as unstable as ever after five years of independence.[4]

The way was paved with a secret trip to the country made by Ernesto Guevara in April 1965. He would be joined by 125 Cuban combat veterans who attempted to train guerrillas to fight Moise Tshombe in Katanga (now Shaba) province. This little known adventure, nevertheless, nearly had disastrous consequences for the Argentine physician.[5]

According to a defecting intelligence officer in the Cuban embassy in Paris, Guevara had to flee for his life from the Congo.

> Cubans had endured severe privations, . . . they were busy trying to keep the tribes from fighting among themselves. . . . There were angry arguments . . . Guevara and his Cubans had to flee through the jungles, pursued by enemy troops and their former allies.[6]

By December of that year, Guevara was safely out of the Congo, but it was a fiasco that would serve as an eerie precedent for the ill-fated adventure in Bolivia. But if stirring an Indian revolt in Bolivia seemed an improbable goal, fostering a Marxist insurrection in a tribal society was an even greater flight from reality. Nevertheless, it would not be the last time the Castro regime violently attempted to shape the Congo (now Zaire) and its mineral-rich southern province of Katanga to its own liking.

Or as Colombian writer Gabriel Garcia Marques, a long-time apologist for Castro and his support for other revolutions, would put it: in the Congo, Guevara "planted a seed that no one could uproot."[7]

The failure of this first major effort in black Africa, in fact, was so completely embarrassing to the regime that it was not acknowledged by Havana until 1977, a decade after Guevara's death in Bolivia and two years after Cuban troops had arrived in Angola. Even then, it was only in a highly censored form whose purpose was to justify Castro's 1975 decision to intervene in Angola.[8]

Cuba and Africa: Round Two

If the Cuban revolution's most salient attribute in its foreign adventures is persistence, its second is learning from past mistakes.

In the case of Africa, the Cubans did profit from their early failures and setbacks and reshaped their strategy and objectives regarding the continent. And most importantly, as they would do in Latin America, they stopped working at cross purposes with their sponsor and paymaster, the Soviet Union.

Fidel Castro first changed his mind about the strategic objective. From an intuitive and opportunistic feeling that the old Belgian Congo was of utmost interest, the focus shifted, first, to southern Africa, and, secondly, to the Horn of Africa. Not too surprisingly, these changes fitted exactly Soviet strategic requirements in the 1970s.[9]

One inkling of that strategy became apparent when Havana began training black Rhodesians in urban terrorism and rural guerrilla warfare in Tanzania and Mozambique in the mid-1970s. The estimates on the numbers of Cubans involved in that activity run to a 1,000 in Mozambique and 200–600 in Tanzania.[10]

Those activities, however, would be overshadowed entirely by Cuba's involvement in Angola. That initial commitment in the fall of 1975 of elite units to save an embattled and nascent minority Marxist government in Luanda has, of course, ballooned to a 12-year commitment of over 35,000 combat troops, with no end in sight.

The military history of that intervention need not be spelled out here, but Cuba's 1975 big leap into Africa requires some analysis.

As in 1965, the turn to Africa ten years later was to some degree rooted in failure in Latin America. By the mid-1970s, it was clear that Cuba's second round of intervention in the region had produced little in the way of results. Urban terrorist groups were either defeated or on the run in

Brazil, Chile, and Uruguay. Argentina's Montoneros and the People's Guerrillas were on the defensive. As for the *via pacifica,* which Castro tentatively endorsed for Chile, that too was in ashes after Allende's overthrow in September 1973.

As a result, Castro, in his 26 of July speech in 1972, offered an olive branch to Latin American governments, and by 1975, Havana had broken out of its isolation—a condition that would last as long as the support of subversives was kept at a relatively low level.

But these diplomatic successes in Latin America rang hollow. Despite his best efforts after 15 years, Castro had not been able to sponsor another successful revolution in Latin America. Furthermore, prospects were poor for promoting insurgency in the region. Nevertheless, with the serious economic problems of the early 1970's temporarily overcome, the restless Fidel Castro must have seen Africa as far richer in opportunities.[11]

One key decision, however, had to be made. For Castro to avoid the spectacle of another small contingent of Cuban guerrillas fleeing for their lives, intervention this time had to be massive (and militarily conventional), and that would have to depend on Soviet logistical support. In the case of Angola in the 1970s, in contrast to the Congo of the 1960s, Havana would receive the help from Moscow.

Propping up a would-be Marxist police state in Angola, however, was hardly the sole objective. Both the Soviets and Cubans were intent on solidifying friendly and dependent regimes in Angola, Mozambique, and Rhodesia (now Zimbabwe) in order to place pressure on South Africa, the ultimate prize.

Angola was of particular importance in this calculation. Unlike Mozambique and Zimbabwe, it was not so economically dependent on the South African republic and, therefore, was relatively immune to Pretoria's counter-pressures. Moreover, the former Portuguese colony bordered on Southwest Africa (Namibia), whose independence had already widespread world support outside the Soviet bloc. In addition, a guerrilla movement, the Southwest African People's Organization (SWAPO), was already in business by the early 1970s.

If SWAPO could achieve a victory in Namibia, the MPLA regime in Angola would be made secure, and the Soviet bloc could then concentrate its considerable resources on South Africa, with Cuban forces serving as useful auxiliaries.

The strategy is sound enough—certainly more so than the belief that Bolivia was the key to South America or the old Congo to sub-Saharan

Africa—but the course of events has not run as smoothly as the strategists in Havana and Moscow would have liked.

In the first place, South Africa has proved to be a tougher adversary than expected. The Republic has not been chased out of Namibia despite intense international pressures, and its forces have felt free to strike at SWAPO on Angolan soil.

Moreover, the MPLA's rival, Jonas Savimbi's UNITA, (National Union for the Total Independence of Angola) did not disappear after its defeat in 1975. Twelve years later, despite repeated attempts of the MPLA, the Soviets, and the Cubans to destroy Savimbi, his forces have grown and UNITA's areas of control and activity have steadily increased over the years.

Moreover, with the coming of the Reagan administration, American foreign policy became firmer, and in Angola, especially with the repeal of the Clark amendment, the United States is once again a player in southern Africa.

But the biggest disappointments for the Soviet bloc have been the inability to establish completely reliable client states in the region. In Zimbabwe, the regime is Marxist but has yet to forge the close links with the Soviet bloc that Nicaragua has, for example. Meanwhile, Harare continues to pick its way through a minefield in which it must denounce Pretoria regularly but do nothing that would lead the South Africans to impose economic sanctions on Zimbabwe's precarious economy.[12]

Mozambique, while supported by the Soviet Union (and Western nations too, including the United States), is under full-scale attack from its resistance movement, Renamo, and as a result is one of the shakiest regimes in black Africa. Maputo, in fact, has become so hardpressed by Renamo and suffers so acutely from its own self-made economic failures, that it was forced to sign a virtual non-aggression pact with Pretoria in 1985 and for the moment, at least, cannot contribute much to the long-term Soviet-Cuban strategy of placing military pressure on South Africa.

Still, some idea of what the Cubans could do under changed circumstances can be gathered from their support of two incursions into Zaire's mineral-rich Shaba province in 1977 and 1978.

On both occasions, Cuban instructors trained and equipped dissident former Katangan gendarmerie and led them, at least initially, into the province, causing enormous economic damage and frightening the skilled European community from the area.[13]

Each time, however, the ragtag insurgents were eventually run out of the province by a collection of French, Belgian, and Moroccan forces. After the second incursion, the French retrained elite Zairean units, as President Mobutu of Zaire and Agostino Neto of Angola concluded, in effect, a non-aggression pact where both sides would cease support of rebel forces. So far, that agreement, now nearly a decade old, has held.

But a failure on these fronts has not led to a reduction of the Soviet and Cuban effort in southern Africa. The more than 35,000 Cuban troops in Angola alone serve not only as a shield for the embattled MPLA regime, they provide the back-up muscle for SWAPO and the African National Congress. Indeed, Cuban direct involvement in the fighting in Angola is increasing because of the Angolan inability to use the more sophisticated weapons supplied to the MPLA by the Soviet Union in recent years. At the same time, present relations with SWAPO, in particular, and the ANC (African National Congress) are good, if not close.

According to one recent estimate:

> SWAPO leader Sam Nujoma makes frequent trips to Cuba and has met with Cuban Politburo member Jorge Risquet in Angola. The ANC's Oliver Tambo, while more cautious, continues to maintain strong ties of solidarity with Cuba. Though they know it may take years, Cuban leaders are banking on an eventual change of government that will bring these groups to power in their respective nations.[14]

In light of these contacts, and more importantly, the belief held in Moscow and Havana that their long-term strategy in southern Africa is the installation of a Marxist regime in South Africa, that shield will not be lifted.[15] And despite occasional flurries and hints that Cuban troops would be reduced in number, if not withdrawn, there is as yet no sign that that has ever been the true intention of Fidel Castro.[16]

Notes to Chapter 7

1. Maurice Halperin, *The Rise and Decline of Fidel Castro*, Berkeley, University of California Press, 1972. 276–277.

2. M. Halperin, *The Taming of Fidel Castro*, 122.

3. The point is made in ibid., 121.

4. Especially to the Cuban leadership who knew nothing about the tribal com-

plexities of Africa. They would soon learn, however, and later adapt to circumstances successfully.

5. For a detailed account of Guevara's adventure in the Congo, see Daniel James, *Che Guevara*, (London: George Allen and Unwin Ltd, 1970), 157–60. Also Martin Ebon, *Che: The Making of a Legend* (New York: Signet Books, 1969), 68–77. Among other problems Guevara encountered was an unwillingness to fight on the part of his Congolese allies and an inability to communicate with them in their language—the latter was a problem that would recur in Bolivia.

6. Castro Hidalgo, *Spy,* 54–55, and also quoted in M. Halperin, *The Taming of Fidel Castro,* 130. See also William E. Ratliff, *Follow the Leader in the Horn* (Washington, D.C.: Cuban American National Foundation, 1986), 6.

7. Mohammed Hassamein Heikel, a confidante of the Egyptian President Gamal Nasser, reports that Guevara informed Nasser of his plans to battle imperialism in the Congo on a visit to Cairo in February 1965. Nasser's reaction was negative. According to Heikel, the Egyptian told Guevara: "If you want to become another Tarzan, a white man coming among black men, leading and protecting them, . . . it can't be done." From Heikel's *The Cairo Documents* (New York: Doubleday, 1973), 348–349, and quoted in M. Halperin, *The Taming of Fidel Castro,* 123. The Marquez quote can also be found in Halperin, 131.

8. Ibid., 130–131. Castro also knew (as his audience did not) that most of Guevara's Congo band was reassigned to Guinea and Congo–Brazzaville where they trained the Angolan Popular Movement for the Liberation of Angola and the African Party for the Independence of Guinea–Bissau (PAIGC). This first material aid to the MPLA would, in fact, be "the seed" from which the later Angolan intervention would grow. See Samuels Michael A. Samuels et al., *Implications of Soviet and Cuban Activities in Africa for U.S. Policy* (Washington, D.C.: Center for Strategic and International Studies, 1979), 45. Also William M. LeoGrande, "Cuban-Soviet Relations and Cuban Policy in Africa," in *Cuba in Africa,* Ed. Carmelo Mesa-Lago and June S. Belkin (Pittsburgh: University of Pittsburgh, 1982), 20–21.

9. In fairness, and only a few years earlier, the Soviets, or at least Nikita Khrushchev, had similar notions about the Congo, or as long as Moscow's client, Patrice Lumumba stayed alive.

10. *Christian Science Monitor,* 23 February 1977, and *Sunday Telegraph* [London], 20 February 1977. Cited in Dan Humbert, "Cuba in Africa," in *Issues in Brief* (Washington, D.C.: ACU Education and Research Institute, 22 August 1977), 3.

11. A similar analysis can be found in Ratliff, *Follow the Leader in the Horn,* 4–5.

12. For a current and perceptive assessment of Cuban and Soviet problems in Africa, see. Pamela S. Falk, "Cuba in Africa," in *Foreign Affairs* 65 (Summer 1987): 1077–1096.

13. Castro heatedly denied involvement in the Shaba venture, but the Carter administration with President Carter in the lead said it had hard intelligence on Cuban participation based on human intelligence and intercepts. Mr. Carter, not known for his inordinate distrust of communists—the Soviet invasion of Af-

ghanistan would come more than a year later—was insistent on this point and, in the subsequent war of words with Havana, refused to back down, although Castro successfully cast doubt on the president's veracity within the American press. See Roger W. Fontaine, "Fidel Castro: Front and Center," in *The Washington Quarterly* 2 (Spring 1979): 78–79.

14. Falk, "Cuba in Africa," 1088.

15. For added insurance, Fidel Castro has recently announced another condition for his forces' withdrawal from Angola. In a speech at the eighth meeting of the non-aligned in Zimbabwe in September 1986, the Maximum Leader declared that, besides Namibian independence, Cuba would not leave until apartheid were completely erradicated in South Africa, even if it took a thousand years. The new condition, which, of course, is subject to unilateral Cuban interpretation, not only unfortunately smacks of a thousand year Cuban reich in Africa, it came as a surprise to the Angolans whose invitation was ostensibly the reason for Havana's being there in the first place. Ibid., 1091.

16. This, of course, is not a complete catalogue of Cuban activities in Africa, even of a violent nature. Indeed, the other major military intervention in the Horn of Africa deserves a brief comment. After the overthrow of Ethiopia's Emperor Haile Selassie in 1974, both Moscow and Havana entertained the notion of a confederation of Marxist states in the area, including principally Ethiopia, Somalia, Djibouti, and possibly South Yemen. Castro at one point engaged in shuttle diplomacy in 1977 to bring it about. But the attempt foundered on Somali insistence on a greater Somalia which included, among other things, a portion of Ethiopia. When the Somali army came to the assistance of Somali guerrillas operating in the Ogaden in June 1977, the Soviets and Cubans sided with Ethiopia with Moscow, pouring in over a billion dollars of arms, and the Cubans contributing 15,000 men in Addis Ababa's defense. As a result, the Somali army was routed in March 1978. Although the Cubans have since reduced their military presence in the Horn (to approximately 3,000 combat troops and 2,000 advisers), they continue to play an active part in keeping intact a Marxist regime beset by several internal revolts. Ironically, that assistance includes support for the war against Eritrean rebels who are former recipients of Cuban training in the 1960s. See Ratliff, *Follow the Leader,* 9–15, and LeoGrande, 36–42.

Chapter 8

Closer to Home: Cuban Terrorism in the United States

Cuban-sponsored terrorism does not occur simply in faraway places. It is a tactic that Fidel Castro has adopted in pursuit of his overall goal of damaging U.S. interests anywhere in the world. Those interests include, of course, the physical security of the continental United States, including the Commonwealth of Puerto Rico.

Cuban-linked acts of terrorism on the American mainland and Puerto Rico are inextricably bound together. Puerto Rican terrorist groups because of their members' U.S. citizenship can freely move and operate on the island as well as in American cities, especially New York and Chicago.

The first Puerto Rican terrorist group that made its appearance since Fidel Castro took power in 1959 was the Independent Revolutionary Armed Movement (MIRA) which began its campaign of terror in 1967 and hit its stride in 1968 and 1969. The MIRA was responsible for over 300 bombings, mostly in the San Juan and tourist resort areas, until it was broken up by the police in the early 1970s.[1]

The Puerto Rican terrorist group that has had the biggest impact, however, is the Armed Forces of National Liberation which made its appearance in 1974. Although the FALN is committed to winning Puerto Rican independence through violence, its activities, in contrast to the MIRA, have been almost entirely confined to the United States, principally New York and Chicago.

Furthermore, according to one recent study, the FALN is not even entirely Puerto Rican.

[It] comprises activists of mixed nationality (predominantly of Puerto Rican extraction, but also other Hispanics and some non-Hispanics) who are based

in New York and Chicago. Most of its Puerto Rican members were born
in the United States; some have never visited Puerto Rico; some do not
even speak Spanish. They know little about Puerto Rican history or culture.
*It is more appropriate to call the FALN a U.S. terrorist group which sup-
ports Puerto Rican independence with the aid of Fidel Castro.*[2]

Over the span of a decade, the FALN has specialized in bombings
beginning with a rash of explosions at the end of 1974 that culminated
in an act of pure terrorism—the bombing of the Fraunces Tavern in lower
Manhattan in late January 1975.

Until 1977, the FALN claimed responsibility, according to the *The New
York Times,* for 49 bombings which killed four persons and injured 65.
In recent years, however, it has become less active in its bomb throwing.
A more recent estimate lists six dead and more than 100 wounded because
of the FALN.[3]

FALN activity has not entirely ceased. Four FALN members, for example, were convicted in October 1985 for having planned the bombing
of two military installations two years earlier in Chicago.[4]

Nevertheless, the FALN in recent years has been eclipsed by a largely
Puerto Rico-based terrorist group styling itself the *Ejercito Popular Boricua* (EPB), more popularly known as the Macheteros. Like the FALN,
the EPB wants Puerto Rican independence, and it believes that using violent methods alone will achieve that goal. The Macheteros also are doc-
trinaire Marxist–Leninists; they first made their appearance in 1978. Since
then they have rapidly established themselves as the most active and dangerous of all the Puerto Rican terrorist groups.[5]

The Macheteros operate on the mainland and the island, and they began
their career in crime with the murder of a policeman in Puerto Rico in
August 1978. In December of 1979, the terrorists ambushed a U.S. Navy
bus, killing two sailors and wounding nine others. The Macheteros also
claimed responsibility for destroying nine Puerto Rican Air National Guard
fighters in January 1981 in a highly sophisticated attack similar to a Salvadoran FMLN raid on the Ilopongo airbase in El Salvador more than a
year later. In fact, 1981 was something of a banner year for the EPB. In
addition, they robbed a Wells Fargo armored car and repeatedly bombed
the Puerto Rican Electric Power Authority.[6]

More recently, the Macheteros held up a Wells Fargo Depot in West
Hartford, Connecticut, for $7 million—the nation's second largest rob-
bery—in September 1983 and rocket bombed the U.S. Court House in
San Juan (January 1985).[7]

The Cuban Connection

U.S. officials have long suspected that the Puerto Rican groups have had the active support of the Castro regime. But only in recent years have authorities amassed near certain proof of Havana's involvement.[8]

Fidel Castro, for example, has never made his championing of Puerto Rican independence a secret. Indeed, from the beginning of his rule in 1959, Puerto Rico has been an obsession with Cuba's Maximum Leader.

Publicly, Castro has long called for the island's independence from U.S. imperialism, citing as a reason for his position Cuba's long and close relationship with Puerto Rico, a declaration that has some historical validity, although Castro is the first Cuban leader to advance seriously that argument.[9]

The Cuban leader has backed his rhetoric with a diplomatic strategy that has earned him the support of the non-aligned movement, and he has used that as leverage in the United Nations, the General Assembly, in particular.

Castro's greatest success came in 1979 when the Cuban mission to the United Nations lobbied successfully for a UN Decolonization Committee resolution which "reaffirmed the right" of Puerto Rican independence. It also criticized the United States for not complying with earlier Committee resolutions, condemned the "persecution, harassment and repressive measures" against pro-independence supporters, and pledged to keep the issue under continuous review.[10]

With the victory of the Sandinistas in Nicaragua, Fidel Castro convinced himself that an anti-American momentum was beginning to build. The Puerto Rican campaign at the United Nations, therefore, was designed to keep the Carter administration off balance. As a consequence, a similar resolution was introduced in the same UN committee with the same results the following year. But Castro wanted more, and in the following year he won a Committee of 24 resolution recommending it be placed on the agenda of the UN General Assembly.[11]

That vote was the highwater mark to date for the Castro regime on the Puerto Rican question at the United Nations. Subsequently, Havana has had its share of reversals. In September 1982, for example, the Cubans attempted to pass another resolution (this time before the General Committee). That one asserted Puerto Ricans were unhappy with their political status. That Committee rejected the Cuban argument, and, when Havana appealed to the General Assembly for a vote, the U.S. delegation led by

Ambassador Jeane J. Kirkpatrick successfully sustained the Committee's decision by a crushing 70 to 30 margin with 43 abstentions.[12]

Despite that setback, the Castro regime continues its efforts at the United Nations within the non-aligned movement on behalf of Puerto Rican independence, but the scale and tone of the attack, especially on the United States, have diminished in recent years.

The diplomatic game, however, is not the only one that Havana has been playing in regard to Puerto Rico. The Castro regime, in fact, has had a long and close relationship with Puerto Rican terrorist groups, as well as the Marxist–Leninist element in the independence movement, particularly the Puerto Rican Socialist Party (PSP) led by Juan Mari Bras.[13]

The PSP, like the Palestine Liberation Organization, established a permanent office in Havana in 1973. Earlier, Juan Mari Bras played an important role at the 1967 OLAS meeting in Havana. The PSP itself grew out of an earlier organization run by Mari Bras, the Pro-Independence Movement (MPI), begun in 1959, the year of Castro's takeover in Cuba.[14]

The PSP has been both cagey and careful in its pronouncements on violence. For instance, the party's secretary general said in the PSP's house organ *Claridad:*

> Whoever seeks unity with us must not be anti-Communist or oppose armed struggle. That does not mean that our allies have to be Communists or advocates of armed struggle, but they must not be against these two things. And, logically, whoever seeks unity with us will be fully aware of the fact that he is dealing with Communists and revolutionaries.[15]

The PSP's at least propagandistic support for "armed struggle" in general and terrorism in particular is illustrated by a photo that appeared in *Claridad* in November 1974 during one wave of Puerto Rican violence in New York. The picture showed the results of one of the bomb blasts, and the caption read: "Puerto Rico must be the spearhead to bring the anti-imperialistic war to the very heart of the American society"[16]

But the precise link between the PSP and the various terrorist groups that have operated over the years has never been established.[17] The terrorist tie with Cuba, however, has been.

Although it has long been strongly suspected, the clearest evidence came to light as a result of the FBI's investigation of the September 1983 Wells Fargo robbery. The Bureau's work led to the arrests of 13 Puerto

Rican Macheteros in Puerto Rico, Texas, and Massachusetts. Subsequently, a federal grand jury in August 1985 charged 17 people with the robbery and transportation of the bulk of the funds to Cuba.[18]

Moreover, according to William Webster, one of those indicted, Victor Manuel Gerena, "has been given sanctuary in Cuba."[19]

In the course of its investigation, the Bureau collected intelligence, principally through wire taps, which showed that the Castro regime had provided training and sanctuary for Puerto Rican terrorist groups. The weapons, authorities discovered, included M–16s and anti-tank rocket launchers (LAWs) which were then traced to stocks left in South Vietnam at the time of its conquest by the North.[20]

The Cuban–Puerto Rican terrorist connection is well illustrated by the career of Filiberto Inocencio Ojeda–Rios, one of those indicted for the Wells Fargo robbery. Now 54, Ojeda–Rios has had a long career in terrorism and is believed to be the real leader of the attack on Wells Fargo.

He was a founding member of the MIRA, which conducted its bombing campaign in the late 1960s. Later, in the early 1970s, he joined the FALN, according to the Puerto Rican Information Service in Washington, D.C. In the early 1980s, Ojeda was reborn as a Machetero.[21]

His ties to the Castro regime date to 1961 when, as a member of a visiting Venceremos Brigade, he was recruited by Cuban intelligence (the DGI) who then turned him into an expert on explosives.

Daniel James, an authority on Cuban-sponsored terrorism, has outlined the rest of Ojeda's career in testimony to the Senate Subcommittee on Security and Terrorism:

> After a series of "bombings" the police finally broke up MIRA and Ojeda Rios was arrested. After jumping bail, he headed for New York and was assigned to the DGI station (which was operating under the auspices of the Cuban Mission to the United Nations) where he organized the FALN with remnants of the old MIRA group. . . .[22]

As for the Cuban UN mission in New York, James told the subcommittee:

> [It] is honeycombed with DGI and other Cuban intelligence personnel. An estimated 75 per cent of its normal 50-person staff, which is itself unusu-

ally large for a country the size of Cuba, is estimated to belong to the DGI
and other Cuban intelligence agencies. . . .[23]

   There is then, at least, strong circumstantial evidence that Havana over
the years has developed a cadre of Puerto Rican agents who, in turn,
organize terrorist groups that launch bombing and robbery campaigns until the recruits are arrested. Invariably, however, the cadre survives and
is provided sanctuary in Cuba until the time is considered ripe for the
forming of yet another terrorist group.[24]
   Why has the Castro regime been so persistent in its efforts to destablize
Puerto Rico?
   The use of the terrorist and diplomatic tracks in the war on Puerto Rico
is nothing new for Castro. Indeed, the diplomatic tactic not only provides
a diversion from Havana's sponsoring of terrorism, but it has always had
promising potential of its own. In making anti-colonial appeals in Third
World forums, including the United Nations, Castro knows that he has
a ready-made audience. Moreover, because so many regimes are undemocratic, if not actively anti-democratic, the fact that the overwhelming
majority of Puerto Ricans is not in favor of independence is not likely to
dissuade such governments from supporting the Cuban position.
   Tearing Puerto Rico away from the United States, especially by force,
serves a number of Cuban (and Soviet) interests. An independent (and
communist) Puerto Rico would be a major blow to the United States. It
would not only lose a major trade and investment partner, the U.S. would
no longer have the naval base at Roosevelt Roads, the largest such facility
in the Caribbean. Indeed, when Panama by treaty takes control of all
American military bases in the old Canal Zone, the Puerto Rican facilities
increase in importance. The right to reactivate Ramey Air Force Base in
an emergency situation also would be lost.
   The security of the Caribbean, a subject of increasing importance because of the establishment of a Soviet Nicaragua, will continue to be a
vital interest to the United States, a strategic consideration that Fidel Castro is intimately familiar with. The loss of Puerto Rico also would be a
devastating blow to American credibility. An inability to protect and defend the Commonwealth of Puerto Rico would be viewed by the rest of
the world as a sure and certain sign of an American lack of resolve. A
pro-Soviet Puerto Rico would also in time be one more support station
for subverting the remainder of the Caribbean, while offering yet another
prime location for additional intelligence collecting facilities.[25]

Terrorism in the United States

The possibilities for terrorism, particularly in the 1970s, on the U.S. mainland did not escape Fidel Castro's attention. And although much of the urban mayhem has been committed so far by Havana-supported Puerto Rican terrorists, they are not the only groups Castro has attempted to cultivate.

Twenty years ago, the Castro regime had great expectations regarding a black-led revolution in the United States. The hot summers of the late 1960s, in which the inner core of a number of major American cities were the scenes of serious rioting with its concomitant arson and looting, seemed to offer real potential for further, even more serious internal divisions.

Nor did Castro make an effort to conceal those hopes. A "Radio Free Dixie" broadcasting service aimed at southern blacks was set up beaming vitriolic propaganda decades before the Reagan administration set up its alternative radio service, Radio Marti, aimed at an on-island Cuban audience.

At the August 1967 premier meeting of the Latin American Solidarity Conference in Havana, Stokely Carmichael was placed at the right hand of Castro himself and given the privilege of delivering the longest speech at the conference.

At at later press conference, Carmichael said what the Cuban leadership undoubtedly very much wanted to hear: "We are moving toward urban guerrilla warfare within the United States since there is no other way to obtain our homes, our lands, and our rights. . . ."[26]

Castro, in turn, at the conference's closing session urged the OLAS participants to give "Stokely their utmost support as protection against the repression of the imperialists. . . ."[27]

But those bright hopes faded as black power groups began to collapse, sometimes, but not always, as the result of police action.[28]

Cuban success in rousing young white radicals into action proved even less successful. That the Cubans tried, however, is undeniable. Some members of American Venceremos Brigades (invariably young, white, "radical," and middle class), who came to Cuba to contribute to the "Revolution" much as a later generation would do for Sandinista Nicaragua, would in turn be recruited, if they volunteered, by the Cuban intelligence services for additional training in something more violent than chopping sugar cane or making propaganda.[29]

Those radicals who found themselves in the so-called Weather Underground were Havana's principal hope that homegrown and middle-class revolutionaries could contribute to the undoing of America.

Its members were laboriously dependent on foreign inspiration. For example, Bernadine Dorhn, a leader in the Students for a Democratic Society (SDS), said in a tape recorded in May 1970 what the new Weather Underground strategy would be:

> Now we are adapting the classic guerrilla strategy of the Tupamaros to our own situation here in the most technically advanced county in the world. Che taught us that "revolutionaries move like fish in the sea." The alienation and contempt that young people have for this country has [sic] created the ocean for this revolution.[30]

The Weather Underground, despite its involvement in a wave of bombings in the late 1960s and early 1970s, showed more talent in producing bombast than bombs. Nevertheless, the Underground and its sister west coast organization, New World Liberation Front, did manage to set off thousands of bombs in less than a decade.[31] Moreover, Weather Underground did not do so in complete isolation. It maintained close ties to the Puerto Rican Socialist Party and took credit for bombing a Puerto Rican-owned bank, the Banco de Ponce, in New York in June 1975.[32]

One small California-based group, the Zapata Unit, had been advised by a Cuban intelligence agent.[33] Such contacts, however, appear to have taken place more often outside the United States.

According to Possony and Bouchey:

> . . . Cuban espionage agents operating in the United States and Canada supplied aid to New Left organizations in the late 1960s and early 1970s. Through foreign meetings held in Hungary, Czechoslovakia and North Vietnam, the Cubans and North Vietnamese influenced SDS militants even before the Weather Underground split off in 1970s. Contacts assigned to the Cuban Mission to the United Nations arranged for American youths to be inculcated with revolutionary fervor and trained in weapons through the Venceremos units.[34]

Aside from the Puerto Rican groups, the Cuban efforts at promoting homestyle American terrorism, to date, have not proven successful on any front. Middle-class, college-educated white Americans, in particular, proved more adept at sloganeering than at committing acts of terrorism. A sense of both their ineptitude and their unreadiness to carry out anything significant is evident from the testimony of one former Weatherman. Asked about the Underground's ability to mount a serious commando-style military operation against Wright Patterson airbase, the ex-militant said in Senate hearings in 1974:

> No, no; they didn't, and this is, I think, one of the reasons why they decided against it. There were people in the Weathermen who told me that they had been trained in various kinds of guerrilla-type activities in other countries, but none to the extent—well, I will put it this way, as far as military knowledge and ability, I had more than any one of them, any 10 of them.[35]

Still, the Castro regime's efforts cannot be dismissed lightly. It is very unlikely that anyone in Havana thought a few half-trained radicals could, by themselves, do great damage to the United States. But, given enough time and the proper atmosphere, some disruption could prove helpful to Havana. Nor is it likely that Cuba will become disinterested in promoting terrorism in the U.S. if it would have tangible returns on the investment.

Notes to Chapter 8

1. Michael Ledeen et al., *Castro's Puerto Rican Obsession*, (Washington, D.C.: The Cuban–American National Foundation, 1987), 15–16. But it was not the first instance of bombing on the island since 1959. The first explosion occurred in 1964 with the destruction of a department store. The identity of the group involved is not certain. See Stefan T. Possony and L. Francis Bouchey, *International Terrorism—The Communist Connection*, (Washington, D.C.: American Council for World Freedom, 1978), 60. For a more benign view of Cuban policy on Puerto Rico, see Falk, *Cuban Foreign Policy*, 70.

2. Ledeen, et al., 14.

3. *The New York Times*, 20 February 1977, and quoted in Ledeen, et al., 14–15. See also *El Miami Herald*, 5 October 1985.

4. Ibid.

5. *Macheteros* means "machete wielders," although, in fact, their preferred weapon is the American M–16 and the Soviet AK–47. Janke, *Guerrilla*, 400.

6. Ledeen, et al., 18. Also see a Federal Bureau of Investigation press release, 30 August 1985, 1. The first robbery netted them $348,000.

7. FBI press release, 30 Aug. 1985.

8. See, for example, FBI Director William H. Webster's statement to the press in August 1985. He said: "Cuba's aggressive support of terrorism has not gone unnoticed. Let those who commit crimes here and then seek asylum in other nations know of our determination to bring criminal charges against them regardless of where they flee to avoid prosecution." *The Hartford Courant*, 31 August 1985.

9. There is a grain of truth in Castro's claim. Cuba and Puerto Rico alone remained within the American portion of the Spanish empire until the Spanish–American war of 1898. Puerto Ricans of the nineteenth century supported and fought for Cuban independence, and, before independence, the Cuban and Puerto Rican delegations worked together in the Spanish parliament, the *Cortes*. After Cuban independence, economic, cultural, and immigration links were maintained. But until Fidel Castro, no Cuban leader had ever made the status of Puerto Rico an issue between Havana and Washington. See Ledeen, etal., 8–11.

10. A resolution from the so-called Committee of 24 received 11 favorable votes and 12 abstentions. Quoted in ibid., 33.

11. Ibid., 34.

12. Ibid., 34–35. The Cubans never made their case for the simple reason that, in free elections in Puerto Rico, the supporters of independence in recent years have gotten less than five percent of the vote. That contrasts with a figure of nearly 20 percent in the 1952 elections. Ibid., 38.

13. According to Romerstein, *Soviet Support*, 25: "In October of 1979 four Puerto Rican terrorists were released after being imprisoned in the U.S. since the 1950s for the attempted murder of President Truman and for shooting up the U.S. House of Representatives. Soon after their release they visited Cuba, at the invitation of the Central Committee of the Communist Party. They were greeted at the plane by important Cuban government and party officials, where they declared over Cuban television that 'we are here to learn from Cuba.' Later, a televised state reception in their honor was held, at which Castro pinned medals on each of them. Soon after, terrorist activity in Puerto Rico increased significantly."

14. *Claridad*, 2 January 1975, and quoted in Possony and Bouchey, *International Terrorism*, 61; 66.

15. Quoted in Possony and Bouchey, 62. In 1973, however, the U.S. branch of the PSP was even more explicit. "Armed struggle [it declared] can contribute to the development and deepening of the Puerto Rican people and raise the mass struggle to higher levels. . . . The Puerto Rican Socialist Party believes that it is necessary to respond to the system's reactionary violence in accord with the objective conditions and to the extent that the objection conditions require it." *Political Declaration of the U.S. Branch of the Puerto Rican Socialist Party*, approved 1 April 1973, 25, and quoted in Romerstein, 25.

16. Quoted in Possony and Bouchey, 63.

17. Bras, however, in a speech in New York City in October 1974 said in reference to the FALN's setting off five bombs the previous day: "There is a diversity of forms and means by which the Puerto Rican people struggle for in-

dependence and national liberation. *This is one of them."* (Emphasis mine). Quoted in Romerstein, 26.

18. Ledeen, et al., 5.

19. Federal Bureau of Investigation, *Press Advisory,* 20 August 1985, 5.

20. *The Hartford Courant,* 4 September 1985. The phone conversations recorded were between members of the Macheteros and a Cuban agent in Mexico. The Cuban is identified only as "Coma." Also see *The Los Angeles Times,* 4 September 1985.

21. Cited in Ledeen, et al., 15, and Senate Subcommittee to Investigate the Administration of the Internal Security Act, Puerto Rico, *The Communist Threat to the U.S. Through the Caribbean,* 90th Cong. 2d sess., 1968, 1368–1373.

22. Senate Subcommittee on Security and Terrorism, Committee on the Judiciary, *The Role of Cuba in International Terrorism and Subversion,* 98th Cong., 1st, sess., 1983, 164–165, and quoted in Ledeen, et al., 18.

23. Ledeen, et al., 18.

24. In May 1976, before the National Press Club in Washington, D.C., then Governor of Puerto Rico Rafael Hernandez Colon said: "Terrorist activities in Puerto Rico are being sponsored and they are within the mantle of Castro's communist objectives in general. . . . There is a clear and undeniable link to Castro. . . . I don't think that the Cubans can realistically promote a successful revolution in Puerto Rico. . . . But they can make trouble for us. They can, as they have done in the past, train those people in terrorist activities." Quoted in *The San Juan Star,* 20 May 1976. Also cited in Ledeen, et al., 17.

25. See Ledeen, et al., 41–42.

26. Cited in the "First Conference of the Latin American Solidarity Organization," Pan American Union, 1967, 31. The report was prepared by the OAS's Special Consultative Committee on Security. Carmichael, eight months later, after the assassination of Martin Luther King, Jr., played a role in provoking the Washington, D.C., riots. His involvement, however, virtually ended his troublemaking career in the United States.

27. Quoted in ibid., 41.

28. As an example, the so-called Black Liberation Army, an off-shoot of the Black Panthers, began a campaign of robbery and cop killing with a heavy (albeit nearly illiterate) political propaganda campaign. By the early 1970s, however, most of its leadership was either dead, in jail, on the run, or in self-imposed exile. See Possony and Bouchey, 82–84.

29. Details of that recruitment can be found in the Federal Bureau of Investigation, *Report on Foreign Influence in the Weather Underground Organization,* 20 August 1976, 90; 120; 126, and quoted in Romerstein, 23.

30. Quoted in Possony and Bouchey, 73.

31. The Weather Underground's score from January 1969 to April 1970 alone was 4,330 bombs. Clutterbuck, *Protest,* 243.

32. *Possony and Bouchey. op. cit.* p. 76.

33. *Chicago Tribune,* 19 March 1976, and cited in Possony and Bouchey, 81.

34. Possony and Bouchey, 82.

35. U.S. Senate, Committee on the Judiciary, Subcommittee to Investigate the Administration of the Internal Security Act and other Internal Security Laws, 93rd Cong., 2d sess., 18 October 1974, 108.

Chapter 9

Conclusions

Cuba's involvement in terrorism is longstanding and has become a major instrument of its expansionary foreign policy. There are, therefore, compelling reasons for Cuban-sponsored terrorism to go on. Moreover, other factors will reinforce Havana's preference for terrorism—at least during the lifetime of the revolution's chief priest and prophet, Fidel Castro. Indeed, the chances of its actually increasing are high.

For one thing, terrorism is cheap compared to other forms of armed violence. Training and supporting small bands of terrorists, often with third country weapons (such as from Vietnam), are relatively low cost affairs. Substantial savings can also be made by sharing the burden with other countries and movements, and, as we have already seen, Cuba since 1968 has been firmly plugged into the international terrorist network. Moreover, because of Havana's chronic but now increasing economic failures, it is unlikely that the Castro regime will undertake major new commitments in foreign policy other than helping favored revolutionary (but operationally terrorist) groups.

Such then are the attractions of terrorism for Cuba, provided, of course, they are directed at the United States and its principal friends and allies.

On these matters, the testimony of a recent and high-level defector, Brigadier General Rafael del Pino Diaz, is relevent.

General del Pino left Cuba at the end of May 1987, flying with his family to safety at the Key West naval air station. In subsequent interviews with Radio Marti, the U.S. government-sponsored alternative radio service beamed at Cuba, the former deputy commander of Havana's anti-air defense command told of increasing discontent within the Cuban armed forces over Castro's open-ended commitment in Angola.

General del Pino traveled regularly to Angola in his duties in order to investigate aircraft and helicopter accidents and shootdowns by the pesky UNITA forces. From this experience and from conversations with his fellow officers, del Pino concluded:

Angola is a blind alley. Angola . . . is the Cuban Vietnam. If anyone has
some faith in victory, Fidel and Raul may be the only ones that think so.
But I believe that, at least I have talked with officers in my rank who have
the full conviction that [the war] is lost and that our presence there is causing a great problem for our people. . . . The Cuban family feels greatly
affected and it feels that its sons are going to die uselessly. And the high
command of the armed forces . . . among themselves say that this war is
lost and that we have been converted . . . into a mercenary army.[1]

If these views are as widespread as General del Pino indicates (and
circumstantial evidence suggests they exist), then the Castro brothers are
fully aware of them. And although the regime is a solid one-man tyranny,
long-lived dictators (and Fidel, if nothing else, is a survivor) know the
limits of their people's patience, and that of critical institutions, like the
military in particular.

Hence, the regime's reluctance to take on further large scale assignments such as Angola—or even Ethiopia—has been reinforced. In fact,
Havana has not done that since 1977—a full decade ago. Therefore, it
is all the more likely that promoting low-cost insurrectionist ventures—
at least, low-cost in Cuban blood and treasure—will continue to be the
favored instrument of Cuban foreign policy, where violence is the assumed means to a defined end. And as we have seen, Cuban-sponsored
violence has more and more been associated with the free use of terrorism, most prominently in major cities from New York to Santiago.

There is yet one more factor that should encourage Havana to continue
its support for terrorism, and that is the new restraints imposed on American policy, particularly those on its counter-terrorist program, over at
least the next few years.

It is virtually certain that the U.S. Congress, in the wake of the Iran–
Contra affair, will slap additional restrictions on the executive branch,
thus making it even more difficult for that cumbersome animal to react
even in emergencies. Moreover, because the counter-terrorist policy is
seen as part of the perceived pattern of abuses committed by the Reagan
administration, that program has been paralyzed since the original dis-
closures in November 1986. Short of an all-out assault on U.S. citizens
and property by terrorists, as was the case in the summer of 1985, counter-
terrorism is not likely to get much support.

Furthermore, the American anti-terrorist campaign at its most effective
was never directed at Cuba but at the more obvious offenders, mainly
Libya's Muammar Qaddafi. The Reagan administration, for example, has

always hesitated at pointing the finger at Syria or even Iran. Thus, Cuba will remain safely in the shadows.

Havana, of course, has provoked the administration into taking hostile measures. For example, the American trade embargo, weakened by President Carter, has been tightened up—a move that has added to the regime's economic distress. But for all that, Washington since 1981 has not "gone to the source," as former, Secretary of State Alexander Haig badly wanted to do. Nor will it or any future administration likely act to end Castro's terrorism, despite Havana's occasional attack of the jitters.

The last question concerns the human cost that Cuban terrorism has inflicted over the last generation.

Terrorism has always played a part in Castro's political life. The overthrow of Batista was made possible by the work of urban terrorist groups, although Castro and Guevara chose to deny it at the time. Yet, when the rural guerrilla strategy failed repeatedly in Latin America, Fidel Castro willingly (although privately) endorsed urban terrorism as a legitimate and practical way to win power.

In the case of the Cuban revolution, the cost in lives was relatively low because acts of terrorism were carefully circumscribed. What followed, however, was far different.

The Venezuelan FALN made no special effort to limit casualties—nor did the Brazilian ALN or the Uruguayan Tupamaros or the Argentine Montoneros or the Chilean MIR or the Colombian M–19. In that whole dreary list of organizations dedicated to murder and mayhem, there never once has been a sense that a human life was anything more than a potential target or victim. And in that coarse philosophy of the barbarian, Fidel Castro and his men fully concur.

The present (much less the final) toll in human life of Castro's reckless adventures in terrorism is not known and probably will never be known. Judging from the Nicaraguan experience alone, however, the number could well be in six figures. But the misery caused by Cuban-sponsored terrorism cannot in moral terms be measured simply in lives taken and lives destroyed.

In fact, there are others measures, and the list too is long and negative in nature. Democracies—long-standing and struggling alike—for example, have been undermined and some destroyed. Their political lives have been poisoned for a generation, at least. Authoritarian regimes, as a result of terrorist attacks, have become more brutal and more entrenched in power. When, as in the case of Argentina, the regime was replaced by a better one, it was not the work of the Cuban-supported terrorist groups, but the folly of the Buenos Aires generals in attempting to wrest the Falklands from Her Majesty's Government.

Meanwhile, with one single exception, no government has ever been overthrown and replaced by Cuban-sponsored terrorists. That exception, of course, is Sandinista Nicaragua. But for those who are seasoned observers of the movement and the regime (in contrast to the casual "revolutionary tourist"), the cruelties committed by the Sandinistas exceed anything done by the Somoza family. For that, there is ample testimony from the democratic opposition—many of whom were in the fight against Somoza—as well as the Roman Catholic Church and the much abused Miskito Indians.

Fidel Castro's empty rhetoric about the achivements of his revolution aside, his efforts at terrorism since 1968 have increasingly served the purposes of the Soviet elite. Thus, not only have Castro's ventures resulted in no benefit for the Cuban people, but increasingly less of what the aging Cuban leader does anymore serves any national purpose at all—including his own.

Moreover, the ostensible reason the Maximum Leader has aligned himself with the Soviet Union (and which morally excuses his free use of force on an international scale) is his self-imposed duty to help defeat a decadent and inferior socio-economic system (that is, American imperialism) and replace it with a superior one (that is, Soviet-style socialism).

Does Castro really believe the Soviet Union is a model for mankind anymore? Did he ever? That is difficult, if not impossible, to answer. But it is not vital to answer those questions. It is interesting to note, however, that all references by Russian leaders regarding the urgent need for reforming the Soviet system are forbidden in Cuba—in stark contrast to the rest of the Soviet bloc. Meanwhile, Castro recently has ordered a halt to and reversal of all examples of economic liberalism on the island—efforts with which his technocrats once beguiled innocent visitors.

Castro-fomented terrorism continues. Unfortunately, however, acts of terrorism soon become impersonal while judgment of them softens, and sometimes is never rendered.

As a consequence, it is useful to recall the deaths of two men: one Venezuelan, Julio Iribarren Borges; and one American, Chester Bitterman. They were murdered more than 15 years apart. Yet both crimes were similar in nature. They were committed by terrorists fully supported by Havana. Neither group gained anything by the killing, even by their shabby standards. The pain they inflicted on the victims' family and friends was enormous. Their deaths, by all accounts, were hideously cruel.

Still the crimes, needless and brutal as they were, were ardently and shamelessly defended by Havana.

In the case of Iribarren Borges, Castro himself personally offered a defense for the crime that was so apallingly ludicrous it received no support from the rest of the communist world, not otherwise known for its tender regard for human life.

As for Chester Bitterman, the young American who worked in Colombia translating the Bible into Indian languages, Castro's personally supervised propaganda apparatus repeated the *non sequitur* lie (it had originally invented) that Bitterman's institute was part of the American intelligence community.

The Cuban dictator's inhumanity, justified by no moral reason, in short, could only be disguised by a web of deceit.

By such, we measure Fidel Castro's contribution to the 20th century. And for that, history will not absolve him.

Notes to Chapter 9

1. The text of General del Pino's interview with Radio Marti was published in the Spanish-language edition of *The Miami Herald,* 11 and 12 July 1987. The quotation is taken from the July 11 portion of the interview, 11.

Appendix A:

Documents

Document 1. The Founding of the Revolutionary Coordinating Committee, February 1974[†]

It is the road of Vietnam; it is the road the people must follow; it is the road that America will follow, with the special characteristic that the armed groups may form something like coordinating committees [*juntas de coordinación*] to make more difficult the repressive task of the Yanqui imperialism and to facilitate our own cause.

Che Guevara, "Message to the Tricontinental"

The Revolutionary Coordinating Committee (Junta de Coordinación Revolucionaria, or JCR), made up of the Chilean Movement of the Revolutionary Left (Movimiento de Izquierda Revolucionaria, or MIR), the Uruguayan National Liberation Movement (Movimiento de Liberación Nacional, or MLN), which is to say the Tupamaros, the Bolivian National Liberation Army (Ejército de Liberación Nacional, or ELN), and the Argentine People's Revolutionary Army (Ejército Revolucionario del Pueblo, or ERP), announced its formation on 13 February 1974 in Buenos Aires. At that time the JCR released the following "joint declaration" which the Mexican leftist magazine *Por Que?* (20 June 1974) described as "the most important political document that has been published in Latin America since the 'Second Declaration of Havana'" twelve years earlier.[1]

The National Liberation Movement (Tupamaros) of Uruguay, the Movement of the Revolutionary Left (MIR) of Chile, the National Liberation Army (ELN) of Bolivia, and the People's Revolutionary Army (ERP) of Argentina sign this declaration to make known to the workers, the poor peasants, the poor in the cities, the students and intellectuals, the aborigines, and the millions of exploited workers of our long-suffering Latin American homeland, their decision to unite in a Revolutionary Coordinating Committee.

This important step is the result of a felt need, of the need to pull together our peoples in the area of organization, to unite the revolutionary forces against the imperialist energy, to carry out with greater effective-

---

†Reprinted with permission from *Castroism and Communism in Latin America, 1959–1976*, trans. William E. Ratliff. (Washington, D.C.: American Enterprise Institute for Public Policy Research, 1976), 209–215.
1. Complete text of JCR document translated by William Ratliff from *Por Que?* [Mexico City], 20 June 1974.

ness the political and ideological struggle against bourgeois nationalism and reformism.

This important step is the realization of one of the principal strategic ideas of Comandante Che Guevara, hero, symbol, and precursor of the continental socialist revolution. It is also a significant step toward reviving the fractured tradition of our peoples who were able to come together like brothers and fight as one man against the oppressors of the past century, the Spanish colonialists.

Our Struggle is Anti-Imperialist

The peoples of the world live under the permanent threat of the most aggressive and rapacious imperialism that has ever existed. They have seen, and not with indifference, the genocide organized and directed by Yankee imperialism against the heroic Vietnamese people. In this unequal war, whose flames have not yet been extinguished, the warlike and treacherous character of the imperialism of the North has been fully demonstrated. But this war has also shown once again the weakness of its system, in spite of all its military power, against a people resolved to fight and determined to be free at any price.

Since the last century the Latin American peoples have borne the antiquated colonial or neocolonial yoke of the imperialists; they have suffered successive military interventions and unjust wars fomented and executed by the North American army and multinational monopolies.

These include the despoliation of Mexico, the occupation of Puerto Rico, the interventions in Santo Domingo and Playa Girón, and many other bellicose acts that our America does not forget and will never forgive. And there is Shell, Esso, Standard Oil, United Fruit, ITT, the money of Mr. Rockefeller and Mr. Ford. And the CIA, which with "Papy" Shelton, Mitrione, and Siracusa, left an indelible mark on the enslaving and oppressive policies of the United States against the people's movement in Latin America.

Latin America Marches Toward Socialism

The First of January 1959, with the triumph of the Cuban Revolution, began the final march of the Latin American peoples toward socialism, toward true national independence, toward the collective well-being of the peoples. It is the just and open rebellion of the exploited people of Latin America against a barbaric colonial capitalist system imposed since the end of the last century by Yankee and European imperialism, which with force, deception, and corruption, seized our continent. The cowardly creole bourgeoisie and their armies did not know how to honor the revolutionary liberationist legacy of the glorious anti-colonial struggle of our people which, led by heroes like Bolívar, San Martín, Artigas, and many others, won independence, equality, and liberty.

The ruling classes, defending their petty group interests, joined forces with the imperialists, collaborated with them, facilitating their economic penetration, progressively handing over control of our economies to the insatiable voracity of foreign capital. Economic domination led to political and cultural control and subordination. So began the neocolonial capitalist system which for a hundred years has been exploiting, oppressing, and deforming the working classes of our continent.

From the beginning of the century the working class began to rise up against the system, unfurling the then-little-known banner of socialism, united indissolubly with the banner of national independence, striving to awaken the peasants, the students, all the healthy and revolutionary of our peoples. Anarchism, socialism, communism as organized movements of the working class led in the mobilization of the broad masses with energy and heroism and were indelible milestones in the revolutionary struggle. The legendary Nicaraguan leader, Augusto César Sandino, metalworker, led one of the most heroic of these battles in his own small country when his guerrilla army checked and defeated the interventionist North American troops in 1932. In the decade of the 1930s a formidable surge of the masses developed throughout the continent which checked the neocolonial domination built up by Yankee imperialism, the No. 1 enemy of all the peoples of the world.

But this formidable revolutionary mobilization of the masses was not crowned with victory. The active counterrevolutionary intervention, political and military, direct and indirect, by Yankee imperialism, taken with the deficiencies of anarchism, socialist currents, and the communist parties, were the causes of a temporary defeat. The majority of the communist parties, the most conscious, consistent, and organized groups of this period, fell into reformism. Some of them, like the heroic and battle-hardened Salvadorian Communist Party, suffered defeats with scores and even thousands of martyrs. For this reason, the impetuous surge of the masses was deflected from its revolutionary road and fell under the influence and direction of bourgeois nationalism, a dead-end for the revolution, a clever and demagogic means utilized by the ruling classes to prolong the life of the neocolonial capitalist system through deception.

After the formidable triumph of the Cuban people—under the skillful and far-sighted leadership of Fidel Castro and a group of Marxist–Leninist leaders—managed to defeat the army of Batista and establish on the island of Cuba, within the very beard of the imperialists, the first socialist state of Latin America, the people of the continent were strengthened in their revolutionary faith and initiated a new and profound general mobilization.

With steps forward and errors, our peoples and their vanguards hurled themselves resolutely into the struggle against imperialism and for socialism. The decade of the 1960s saw an uninterrupted succession of great popular struggles, violent guerrilla combats, and powerful mass insurrections. The April War, the general uprising of the Dominican people, required the direct intervention of Yankee imperialism which had to send 30,000 soldiers in order to choke out this magnificent insurrection with a massacre.

The legendary figure of Comandante Ernesto Guevara personified and symbolized this entire period of struggle just as his exemplary life and his clear Marxist–Leninist strategic conceptions illuminated the new revolutionary surge of our peoples which grew day by day in power and solidarity, beginning in the factories, in the towns, in the countryside, in the cities, and spreading out of control over the entire continent.

This is the definitive awakening of our peoples which has brought millions upon millions of workers to their feet and set them inexorably on the road toward the second independence, toward the definitive elimination of the unjust capitalist system, and the establishment of revolutionary socialism.

The Struggle for the Leadership of the Mass Movement

But the revolutionary road is neither simple nor harmless. We do not face only the barbarous military and economic force of imperialism. More subtle enemies and dangers lie in wait at each moment for the revolutionary forces, to prevent them from carrying out the anti-imperialist and anti-capitalist struggle effectively and victoriously.

Today, with respect to the particular situation of the continental revolutionary process, we must refer to two currents of thought and action which conspire powerfully against the revolutionary efforts of the Latin Americans. These are an enemy, bourgeois nationalism, and an erroneous conception in the people's camp, reformism.

The two—at times closely united—are trying to ride the revolutionary wave of our peoples, taking over its direction and imposing their own mistaken and selfish conceptions which unfailingly end in stopping and crushing the revolutionary impulse. Therefore there is a strategic dimension to the intransigent political and ideological struggle we revolutionaries must wage against these currents to win back the leadership of the broad masses, in order to give our peoples a consistent revolutionary leadership that will guide us with perseverance, intelligence, and effectiveness to the final victory.

Bourgeois nationalism is a current approved by imperialism which supports it as a demagogic variant to distract and divert the struggle of the peoples when counterrevolutionary violence loses its effectiveness. Its social nucleus is the pro-imperialist bourgeoisie or an embryo of it that seeks to enrich itself without limit by competing with the oligarchy and the traditional bourgeoisie for the favors of imperialism by presenting itself as the fireman to put out the revolutionary conflagration by means of its popular influence and capacity of negotiation with the mass movement. In their policy of deception they express a verbal anti-imperialism but seek to confuse the masses with their favorite nationalist thesis—the third position. In reality they are not anti-imperialists but smooth the way for new and more subtle forms of foreign economic penetration.

Reformism, on the other hand, is a current that nests in the very womb of the working people, reflecting the fear of a confrontation with the petit-bourgeois sectors and the labor aristocracy. It is characterized by its total rejection in practice of the just and necessary revolutionary violence as the fundamental method in the struggle for power, thus abandoning the Marxist concept of class struggle. Reformism spreads noxious pacifist and liberal ideas among the masses, beautifying the national bourgeoisie and the counterrevolutionary armies with whom they always seek alliances, exaggerating the importance of legality and parliamentarianism. One of their favorite arguments, that it is necessary to reject violence and link up with the bourgeoisie and "patriotic military" in search for a peaceful way that will spare the shedding of blood by the masses on the road to socialism, is circular and painfully refuted by the facts. Where reformism has been able to impose its conciliatory and pacifist policies, the class enemies and their armies have carried out the worst massacres against the people. The nearness of the Chilean experience with more than 20,000 men and women workers assassinated makes further commentary unnecessary.

Against bourgeois nationalism, reformism, and other less important currents, in constant ideological and political struggle against them, the armed people have risen up, a revolutionary pole that day by day consolidates its position among the masses, increasing its influence, improving its political and military capacity, converting itself more and more into a real option for national independence and socialism.

Precisely in order to contribute to the strengthening of this revolutionary pole on a continental scale, the four organizations that signed this document decided to form the present Committee for Revolutionary Coordination. We call upon all the revolutionary vanguard of people and workers in Latin America to organize themselves and fight together.

Naturally this means that the doors of this Committee of Coordination are open to the revolutionary organizations in the different Latin American countries.

The Experience of Our Organizations

In the course of their patriotic and revolutionary struggles, the MLN Tupamaros, the Movement of the Revolutionary Left, the National Liberation Army, and the People's Revolutionary Army have come to understand the need for unity, to affirm by their own experience their internationalist concepts, understanding that the united and organized imperialism and capitalist enemy must be confronted by the most hardened and tightly knit unity of our peoples.

Based on the similarities of our struggles and our lines, the four organizations first established fraternal bonds and an exchange of experiences, then increased active mutual collaboration to the point that today this decisive step which accelerates the coordination and collaboration that undoubtedly will result in greater practical effectiveness in the cruel struggle our people are waging against a fierce common enemy.

The greater development of our organization, the strengthening of our internationalist concepts and practice, will permit the greater utilization of our people's potentialities in order to build a powerful revolutionary force that can definitively defeat capitalist imperialist reaction, annihilate the counterrevolutionary armies, expel Yankee and European imperialism country by country from Latin American soil, and begin the construction of socialism in each of our countries to achieve the most complete Latin American unity.

Achieving that sacred objective will not be easy. The cruelty and power of imperialism will make necessary—as Comandante Guevara foresaw—the development of a bloody and prolonged revolutionary war that will make the Latin American continent the second or third Vietnam of the world. However, following the glorious example of the heroic Vietnamese people, the Latin American workers will be able to fight without dismay, with increasing effectiveness, unfolding in all their intensity the irresistible energies of the masses and crushing Yankee imperialism and its agents; it will win our happiness and contribute mightily to the definitive destruction of the principal enemy of the international working class, of socialism, and of all the peoples of the world.

Our Program

We have united with the understanding that there is no other viable strategy in Latin America than the strategy of revolutionary war. This revolutionary war is a complex process of mass struggle—armed and unarmed, peaceful and violent—in which all forms of struggle develop harmoniously, converging around the axis of armed struggle. In order for this whole process of revolutionary war to unfold victoriously, it is necessary to mobilize the entire people under the leadership of the revolutionary proletariat. The proletarian leadership of the war must be exercised by a Marxist–Leninist combat party of the proletarian character, which is capable of centralizing and directing the popular struggle, guaranteeing a proper strategic leadership, and uniting all aspects in a single and powerful matrix. Under the leadership of the party it is necessary to build a powerful popular army, the iron core of the revolutionary forces. This army, closely united with the masses and nurtured by them, will grow from small to large, erect an impenetrable wall against which the military designs of the reactionaries will be smashed, and have the material quality to assure the total annihilation of the counterrevolutionary armies. At the same time, it is necessary to build a broad mass front of workers and the people that can mobilize all the progressive and revolutionary people, the separate people's parties, the unions, and other similar organizations—in short, the broadest masses whose own struggle parallels and continually converges with the military activities of the people's army and the clandestine political activities of the party of the proletariat.

The response must be clear and none other than armed struggle as the main factor in the polarization, agitation, and, finally, the defeat of the enemy: this is the only possibility for victory. This is not to say that we do not use all forms of organization and struggle possible—legal and clandestine, peaceful and violent, economic and political—all converging with the greatest effectiveness in the armed struggle according to the peculiarities of each region and country.

The character of the struggle is marked fundamentally by the presence of a common enemy. North American imperialism is carrying out an international strategy to stop the Socialist Revolution in Latin America. It is not by chance that fascist regimes have been imposed in countries where the rising mass movement threatens the stability of oligarchical power. The continental strategy of the revolutionaries is in response to the international strategy of the imperialists.

The road to travel in this struggle is not short. The international bourgeoisie is determined to impede the revolution, by whatever method, even if it arises in a single country. It has all the means to employ against the people—official and bureaucratic, military and propagandistic. For this reason, in its first phase, our revolutionary war is one of wearing down the enemy until we can form a people's army that is more powerful than the armies of the enemy. This process is a slow one but, paradoxically, the shortest and least costly road to achieve the strategic objectives of the disadvantaged classes.

Latin American People, to arms! We are living through decisive moments in our history. With this awareness, the MLN Tupamaros, the Movement of the Revolutionary Left, the National Liberation Army, and the People's Revolutionary Army call upon the exploited toilers of Latin America, on the working class, on the poor peasants, on the poor in the cities, on the students and intellectuals, on the revolutionary Christians and all those emerging elements of the exploited classes who are prepared to support the people's just cause, to take up arms with determination and to join actively the revolutionary struggle against imperialism and for socialism, that is already under way on our continent under the banner and example of Comandante Guevara.

Liberty or Death (MLN, Tupamaros)
Win or Die for Argentina (ERP)
Fatherland or Death, We Will Win (MIR)
Victory or Death (ELN)

Document 2. Minimanual of the Urban Guerrilla†

A Definition of the Urban Guerrilla

The chronic structural crisis characteristic of Brazil today, and its resultant political instability, are what have brought about the upsurge of revolutionary war in the country. The revolutionary war manifests itself in the form of urban guerrilla warfare, psychological warfare, or rural guerrilla warfare. Urban guerrilla warfare or psychological warfare in the city depends on the urban guerrilla.

The urban guerrilla is a man who fights the military dictatorship with arms, using unconventional methods. A political revolutionary and an ardent patriot, he is a fighter for his country's liberation, a friend of the people and of freedom. The area in which the urban guerrilla acts is in the large Brazilian cities. There are also bandits, commonly known as outlaws, who work in the big cities. Many times assaults by outlaws are taken as actions by urban guerrillas.

The urban guerrilla, however, differs radically from the outlaw. The outlaw benefits personally from the action, and attacks indiscriminately without distinguishing between the exploited and the exploiters, which is why there are so many ordinary men and women among his victims. The urban guerrilla follows a political goal and only attacks the government, the big capitalists, and the foreign imperialists, particularly North Americans.

Another element just as prejudicial as the outlaw and also operating in the urban area is the right-wing counterrevolutionary who creates confusion, assaults banks, hurls bombs, kidnaps, assassinates, and commits the worst imaginable crimes against urban guerrillas, revolutionary priests, students, and citizens who oppose fascism and seek liberty.

The urban guerrilla is an implacable enemy of the government and systematically inflicts damage on the authorities and on the men who dom-

---

†Reprinted with permission from *Terror and Urban Guerrillas: A Study of Tactics and Documents*, ed. Jay Mallin. (Coral Gables, FL: University of Miami Press, 1971), 71–73; 77–81; 83; 91–104; 112–115.

inate the country and exercise power. The principal task of the urban guerrilla is to distract, to wear out, to demoralize the militarists, the military dictatorship and its repressive forces, and also to attack and destroy the wealth and property of the North Americans, the foreign managers, and the Brazilian upper class.

The urban guerrilla is not afraid of dismantling and destroying the present Brazilian economic, political, and social system, for his aim is to help the rural guerrilla and to collaborate in the creation of a totally new and revolutionary social and political structure, with the armed people in power.

The urban guerrilla must have a certain minimal political understanding. To gain that he must read certain printed or mimeographed works such as:

Guerrilla Warfare by Che Guevara
Memories of a Terrorist
Some Questions about the Brazilian Guerrilla Operations and Tactics
On Strategic Problems and Principles
Certain Tactical Principles for Comrades Undertaking Guerrilla Operations
Organizational Questions
O Guerrilheiro, newspaper of the Brazilian revolutionary groups.

Personal Qualities of the Urban Guerrilla

The urban guerrilla is characterized by his bravery and decisive nature. He must be a good tactician and a good shot. The urban guerrilla must be a person of great astuteness to compensate for the fact that he is not sufficiently strong in arms, ammunition, and equipment.

The career militarists or the government police have modern arms and transport, and can go about anywhere freely, using the force of their power. The urban guerrilla does not have such resources at his disposal and leads to a clandestine existence. Sometimes he is a convicted person or is out on parole, and is obliged to use false documents.

Nevertheless, the urban guerrilla has a certain advantage over the conventional military or the police. It is that, while the military and the police act on behalf of the enemy, whom the people hate, the urban guerrilla defends a just cause, which is the people's cause.

The urban guerrilla's arms are inferior to the enemy's, but from a moral point of view, the urban guerrilla has an undeniable superiority.

This moral superiority is what sustains the urban guerrilla. Thanks to it, the urban guerrilla can accomplish his principal duty, which is to attack and to survive.

The urban guerrilla has to capture or divert arms from the enemy to be able to fight. Because his arms are not uniform, since what he has are expropriated or have fallen into his hands in different ways, the urban guerrilla faces the problem of a variety of arms and a shortage of ammunition. Moreover, he has no place to practice shooting and marksmanship.

These difficulties have to be surmounted, forcing the urban guerrilla to be imaginative and creative, qualities without which it would be impossible for him to carry out his role as a revolutionary.

The urban guerrilla must possess initiative, mobility, and flexibility, as well as versatility and a command of any situation. Initiative especially is an indispensable quality. It is not always possible to foresee everything, and the urban guerrilla cannot let himself become confused, or wait for orders. His duty is to act, to find adequate solutions for each problem he faces, and not to retreat. It is better to err acting than to do nothing for fear of erring. Without initiative there is no urban guerrilla warfare.

Other important qualities in the urban guerrilla are the following: to be a good walker, to be able to stand up against fatigue, hunger, rain, heat. To know how to hide and to be vigilant. To conquer the art of dissembling. Never to fear danger. To behave the same by day as by night. Not to act impetuously. To have unlimited patience. To remain calm and cool in the worst conditions and situations. Never to leave a track or trail. Not to get discouraged.

In the face of the almost insurmountable difficulties of urban warfare, sometimes comrades weaken, leave, give up the work.

The urban guerrilla is not a businessman in a commercial firm nor is he a character in a play. Urban guerrilla warfare, like rural guerrilla warfare, is a pledge the guerrilla makes to himself. When he cannot face the difficulties, or knows that he lacks the patience to wait, then it is better to relinquish his role before he betrays his pledge, for he clearly lacks the basic qualities necessary to be a guerrilla.

How the Urban Guerrilla Lives and Subsists

The urban guerrilla must know how to live among the people and must be careful not to appear strange and separated from ordinary city life.

He should not wear clothes that are different from those that other people wear. Elaborate and high fashion clothing for men or women may often be a handicap if the urban guerrilla's mission takes him into working class neighborhoods or sections where such dress is uncommon. . . .

The Urban Guerrilla's Arms

The urban guerrilla's arms are light arms, easily exchanged, usually captured from the enemy, purchased, or made on the spot.

Light arms have the advantage of fast handling and easy transport. In general, light arms are characterized as short barrelled. This includes many automatic arms.

Automatic and semiautomatic arms considerably increase the fighting power of the urban guerrilla. The disadvantage of this type of arm for us is the difficulty in controlling it, resulting in wasted rounds or in a prodigious use of ammunition, compensated for only by optimal aim and firing precision. Men who are poorly trained convert automatic weapons into an ammunition drain.

Experience has shown that the basic arm of the urban guerrilla is the light machine gun. This arm, in addition to being efficient and easy to shoot in an urban area, has the advantage of being greatly respected by the enemy. The guerrilla must know thoroughly how to handle the machine gun, now so popular and indispensable to the Brazilian urban guerrilla.

The ideal machine gun for the urban guerrilla is the Ina 45 calibre. Other types of machine guns of different calibres can be used—understanding, of course, the problem of ammunition. Thus it is preferable that the industrial potential of the urban guerrilla permit the production of a single machine gun so that the ammunition used can be standardized.

Each firing group of urban guerrillas must have a machine gun managed by a good marksman. The other components of the group must be armed with .38 revolvers, our standard arm. The .32 is also useful for those who want to participate. But the .38 is preferable since its impact usually puts the enemy out of action.

Hand grenades and conventional smoke bombs can be considered light arms, the defensive power for cover and withdrawal.

Long barrel arms are more difficult for the urban guerrilla to transport and attract much attention because of their size. Among the long barrel arms are the FAL, the Mauser guns or rifles, hunting guns such as the Winchester, and others.

Shotguns can be useful if used at close range and point blank. They are useful even for a poor shot, especially at night when precision isn't much help. A pressure airgun can be useful for training in marksmanship. Bazookas and mortars can also be used in action but the conditions for using them have to be prepared and the people who use them must be trained.

The urban guerrilla should not try to base his actions on the use of heavy arms, which have major drawbacks in a type of fighting that demands lightweight weapons to insure mobility and speed.

Homemade weapons are often as efficient as the best arms produced in conventional factories, and even a cut-off shotgun is a good arm for the urban guerrilla.

The urban guerrilla's role as gunsmith has a fundamental importance. As gunsmith he takes care of the arms, knows how to repair them, and in many cases can set up a small shop for improvising and producing efficient small arms.

Work in metallurgy and on the mechanical lathe are basic skills the urban guerrilla should incorporate into his industrial planning, which is the construction of homemade weapons.

This construction and courses in explosives and sabotage must be organized. The primary materials for practice in these courses must be obtained ahead of time to prevent an incomplete apprenticeship—that is to say, so as to leave no room for experimentation.

Molotov cocktails, gasoline, homemade contrivances such as catapults and mortars for firing explosives, grenades made of tubes and cans, smoke bombs, mines, conventional explosives such as dynamite and potassium chloride, plastic explosives, gelatine capsules, ammunition of every kind are indispensable to the success of the urban guerrilla's mission.

The method of obtaining the necessary materials and munitions will be to buy them or to take them by force in expropriation actions especially planned and carried out.

The urban guerrilla will be careful not to keep explosives and materials that can cause accidents around for very long, but will try always to use them immediately on their destined targets.

The urban guerrilla's arms and his ability to maintain them constitute his fire power. By taking advantage of modern arms and introducing innovations in his fire power and in the use of certain arms, the urban guerrilla can change many of the tactics of city warfare. An example of this was the innovation made by the urban guerrillas in Brazil when they introduced the machine gun in their attacks on banks.

When the massive use of uniform machine guns becomes possible, there will be new changes in urban guerrilla warfare tactics. The firing group that utilizes uniform weapons and corresponding ammunition, with reasonable support for their maintenance, will reach a considerable level of efficiency. The urban guerrilla increases his efficiency as he improves his firing potential.

The Shot: the Urban Guerrilla's Reason for Existence

The urban guerrilla's reason for existence, the basic condition in which he acts and survives, is to shoot. The urban guerrilla must know how to shoot well because it is required by his type of combat.

In conventional warfare, combat is generally at a distance with long range arms. In unconventional warfare, in which urban guerrilla warfare is included, the combat is at close range, often very close. To prevent his own extinction, the urban guerrilla has to shoot first and he cannot err in his shot. He cannot waste his ammunition because he doesn't have large amounts, so he must save it. Nor can he replace his ammunition quickly, since he is part of a small group in which each guerrilla has to take care of himself. The urban guerrilla can lose no time and must be able to shoot at once.

One fundamental fact which we want to emphasize fully and whose particular importance cannot be overestimated is that the urban guerrilla must not fire continuously, using up his ammunition. It may be that the enemy is not responding to the fire precisely because he is waiting until the guerrilla's ammunition is used up. At such a moment, without having time to replace his ammunition, the urban guerrilla faces a rain of enemy fire and can be taken prisoner or be killed.

In spite of the value of the surprise factor which many times makes it unnecessary for the urban guerrilla to use his arms, he cannot be allowed the luxury of entering combat without knowing how to shoot. And face to face with the enemy, he must always be moving from one position to another, because to stay in one position makes him a fixed target and, as such, very vulnerable.

The urban guerrilla's life depends on shooting, on his ability to handle his arms well and to avoid being hit. When we speak of shooting, we speak of marksmanship as well. Shooting must be learned until it becomes a reflex action on the part of the urban guerrilla.

To learn how to shoot and to have good aim, the urban guerrilla must train himself systematically, utilizing every apprenticeship method, shooting at targets, even in amusement parks and at home.

Shooting and marksmanship are the urban guerrilla's water and air. His perfection of the art of shooting makes him a special type of urban guerrilla—that is, a sniper, a category of solitary combatant indispensable in isolated actions. The sniper knows how to shoot, at close range and at long range, and his arms are appropriate for either type of shooting.

The Firing Group

In order to function, the urban guerrillas must be organized in small groups. A group of no more than four or five is called *the firing group*.

A minimum of two firing groups, separated and sealed off from other firing groups, directed and coordinated by one or two persons, this is what makes a *firing team*.

Within the firing group there must be complete confidence among the comrades. The best shot and the one who best knows how to manage the machine gun is the person in charge of operations.

The firing group plans and executes urban guerrilla actions, obtains and guards arms, studies and corrects its own tactics.

When there are tasks planned by the strategic command, these tasks take preference. But there is no such thing as a firing group without its own initiative. For this reason it is essential to avoid any rigidity in the organization in order to permit the greatest possible initiative on the part of the firing group. The old-type hierarchy, the style of the traditional left doesn't exist in our organization.

This means that, except for the priority of objectives set by the strategic command, any firing group can decide to assault a bank, to kidnap or to execute an agent of the dictatorship, a figure identified with the reaction, or a North American spy, and can carry out any kind of propaganda or war of nerves against the enemy without the need to consult the general command.

No firing group can remain inactive waiting for orders from above. Its obligation is to act. Any single urban guerrilla who wants to establish a firing group and begin action can do so and thus become a part of the organization.

This method of action eliminates the need for knowing who is carrying out which actions, since there is free initiative and the only important point is to increase substantialy the volume of urban guerrilla activity in order to wear out the government and force it onto the defensive.

The firing group is the instrument of organized action. Within it, guerrilla operations and tactics are planned, launched, and carried through to success.

The general command counts on the firing groups to carry out objectives of a strategic nature, and to do so in any part of the country. For its part, it helps the firing groups with their difficulties and their needs.

The organization is an indestructible network of firing groups, and of coordinations among them, that functions simply and practically with a general command that also participates in the attacks; an organization which exists for no purpose other than pure and simple revolutionary action.

Characteristics of the Urban Guerrilla's Technique

The technique of the urban guerrilla has the following characteristics:

a) it is an aggressive technique, or in other words, it has an offensive character. As is well known, defensive action means death for us. Since we are inferior to the enemy in fire power and have neither his resources nor his power force, we cannot defend ourselves against an offensive or a concentrated attack by the gorillas. And that is the reason why our urban technique can never be permanent, can never defend a fixed base nor remain in any one spot waiting to repel the circle of reaction;

b) it is a technique of attack and retreat by which we preserve our forces;

c) it is a technique that aims at the development of urban guerrilla warfare, whose function will be to wear out, demoralize, and distract the enemy forces, permitting the emergence and survival of rural guerrilla warfare which is destined to play the decisive role in the revolutionary war.

On the Types and Nature of Action Models for the Urban Guerrilla

In order to achieve the objectives previously enumerated, the urban guerrilla is obliged, in his technique, to follow an action whose nature is as different and as diversified as possible. The urban guerrilla does not arbitrarily choose this or that action model. Some actions are simple, others are complicated. The urban guerrilla without experience must be incorporated gradually into actions and operations that run from the simple to the complex. He begins with small missions and tasks until he becomes a completely experienced urban guerrilla.

Before any action, the urban guerrilla must think of the methods and the personnel at his disposal to carry out the action. Operations and actions that demand the urban guerrilla's technical preparation cannot be carried out by someone who lacks that technical skill. With these cautions, the action models which the urban guerrilla can carry out are the following:

a) assaults;
b) raids and penetrations;
c) occupations;
d) ambush;
e) street tactics;
f) strikes and work interruptions;
g) desertions, diversions, seizures, expropriations of arms, ammunition, explosives;
h) liberation of prisoners;
i) executions;
j) kidnappings;
k) sabotage;
l) terrorism;
m) armed propaganda;
n) war of nerves.

Assaults

Assault is the armed attack which we make to expropriate funds, liberate prisoners, capture explosives, machine guns, and other types of arms and ammunition.

Assaults can take place in broad daylight or at night.

Daytime assaults are made when the objective cannot be achieved at any other hour, as for example, the transport of money by the banks, which is not done at night.

Night assault is usually the most advantageous to the urban guerrilla.

The ideal is for all assaults to take place at night when conditions for a surprise attack are most favorable and the darkness facilitates flight and hides the identity of the participants. The urbᴀ guerrilla must prepare himself, nevertheless, to act under all conditions, daytime as well as nighttime.

The most vulnerable targets for assault are the following:

a) credit establishments;
b) commercial and industrial enterprises, including the production of arms and explosives;
c) military establishments;
d) commissaries and police stations;
e) jails;
f) government property;
g) mass communication media;
h) North American firms and properties;
i) government vehicles, including military and police vehicles, trucks, armored vehicles, money carriers, trains, ships, and planes.

The assaults on establishments are of the same nature because in every case the property and buildings represent a fixed target.

Assaults on buildings are conceived as guerrilla operations, varied according to whether they are against banks, a commercial enterprise, industries, military camps, commissaries, prisons, radio stations, warehouses for imperialist firms, etc.

The assaults on vehicles—money-carriers, armored cars, trains, ships, airplanes—are of another nature since they are moving targets. The nature of the operations varies according to the situation and the possibility—that is, whether the target is stationary or moving.

Armored cars, including military cars, are not immune to mines. Obstructed roads, traps, ruses, interception of other vehicles, Molotov cocktails, shooting with heavy arms, are efficient methods of assaulting vehicles.

Heavy vehicles, grounded planes, anchored ships can be seized and their crews and guards overcome. Airplanes in flight can be diverted from their course by guerrilla action or by one person.

Ships and trains in movement can be assaulted or taken by guerrilla operations in order to capture the arms and munitions or to prevent troop deployment.

The Bank Assault as Popular Model

The most popular assault model is the bank assault. In Brazil, the urban guerrilla has begun a type of organized assault on the banks as a guerrilla operation. Today this type of assault is widely used and has served as a sort of preliminary examination for the urban guerrilla in his apprenticeship for the techniques of revolutionary warfare.

Important innovations in the technique of assaulting banks have developed, guaranteeing flight, the withdrawal of money, and the anonymity of those involved. Among these innovations we cite shooting the tires of cars to prevent pursuit; locking people in the bank bathroom, making them sit on the floor; immobilizing the bank guards and removing their arms, forcing someone to open the coffer or the strong box; using disguises.

Attempts to install bank alarms, to use guards or electronic detection devices of U.S. origin, prove fruitless when the assault is political and is carried out according to urban guerrilla warfare technique. This technique tries to utilize new resources to meet the enemy's tactical changes, has access to a fire power that is growing every day, becomes increasingly astute and audacious, and uses a larger number of revolutionaries every time; all to guarantee the success of operations planned down to the last detail.

The bank assault is a typical expropriation. But, as is true in any kind of armed expropriatory action, the revolutionary is handicapped by a twofold competition:

a) competition from the outlaw;
b) competition from the right-wing counterrevolutionary.

This competition produces confusion, which is reflected in the people's uncertainty. It is up to the urban guerrilla to prevent this from happening, and to accomplish this he must use two methods:

a) he must avoid the outlaw's technique, which is one of unnecessary violence and appropriation of goods and possessions belonging to the people;
b) he must use the assault for propaganda purposes, at the very moment it is taking place, and later distribute material, leaflets, every possible means of explaining the objectives and the principles of the

urban guerrilla as expropriator of the government, the ruling classes, and imperialism.

Raids and Penetration

Raids and penetrations are quick attacks on establishments located in neighborhoods or even in the center of the city, such as small military units, commissaries, hospitals, to cause trouble, seize arms, punish and terrorize the enemy, take reprisal, or rescue wounded prisoners, or those hospitalized under police vigilance.

Raids and penetrations are also made on garages and depots to destroy vehicles and damage installations, especially if they are North American firms and property.

When they take place on certain stretches of the highway or in certain distant neighborhoods, the raids can serve to force the enemy to move great numbers of troops, a totally useless effort since he will find nobody there to fight.

When they are carried out in certain houses, offices, archives, or public offices, their purpose is to capture or search for secret papers and documents with which to denounce involvements, compromises, and the corruption of men in government, their dirty deals and criminal transactions with the North Americans.

Raids and penetrations are most effective if they are carried out at night.

Occupations

Occupations are a type of attack carried out when the urban guerrilla stations himself in specific establishments and locations for a temporary resistance against the enemy or for some propaganda purpose.

The occupation of factories and schools during strikes or at other times is a method of protest or of distracting the enemy's attention.

The occupation of radio stations is for propaganda purposes.

Occupation is a highly effective model for action but, in order to prevent losses and material damage to our ranks, it is always a good idea to count on the possibility of withdrawal. It must always be meticulously planned and carried out at the opportune moment.

Occupation always has a time limit and the faster it is completed the better.

Street Tactics

Street tactics are used to fight the enemy in the streets, utilizing the participation of the masses against him.

In 1968 the Brazilian students used excellent street tactics against police troops, such as marching down streets against traffic, utilizing slings and marbles as arms against the mounted police.

Other street tactics consist in constructing barricades; pulling up paving blocks and hurling them at the police; throwing bottles, bricks, paperweights, and other projectiles from the tops of apartment and office buildings against the police; using buildings under construction for flight, for hiding, and for supporting surprise attacks.

It is equally necessary to know how to respond to enemy tactics. When the police troops come protected with helmets to defend themselves against flying objects, we have to divide ourselves into two teams: one to attack the enemy from the front, the other to attack him in the rear, withdrawing one as the other goes into action to prevent the first from becoming a target for projectiles hurled by the second.

By the same token it is important to know how to respond to the police net. When the police designate certain of their men to go into the masses to arrest a demonstrator, a larger group of urban guerrillas must surround the police group, disarming and beating them and at the same time letting the prisoner escape. This urban guerrilla operation is called the *net within the net.*

When the police net is formed at a school building, a factory, a place where the masses assemble, or some other point, the urban guerrilla must not give up or allow himself to be taken by surprise. To make his net work the enemy is obliged to transport the police in vehicles and special cars to occupy strategic points in the streets in order to invade the building or chosen locale. The urban guerrilla, for his part, must never clear a building or an area and meet in it without first knowing its exits, the way to break the circle, the strategic points that the police might occupy, and the roads that inevitably lead into the net, and he must hold other strategic points from which to strike at the enemy.

The roads followed by the police vehicles must be mined at key points along the way and at forced stopping points. When the mines explode, the vehicles will fly into the air. The police will be caught in the trap and will suffer losses or will be victims of ambush. The net must be broken by escape routes unknown to the police. The rigorous planning of the retreat is the best way of frustrating any encircling effort on the part of the enemy.

When there is no possibility of a flight plan, the urban guerrilla must not hold meetings, assemblies, or do anything else since to do so will prevent him from breaking through the net the enemy will surely try to throw around him.

Street tactics have revealed a new type of urban guerrilla, the urban guerrilla who participates in mass demonstrations. This is the type we designate as the urban guerrilla demonstrator, who joins the ranks and participates in popular marches with specific and definite aims.

These aims consist in hurling stones and projectiles of every type, using gasoline to start fires, using the police as a target for their fire arms, capturing police arms, kidnapping agents of the enemy and provocateurs, shooting with careful aim at the henchmen torturers and the police chiefs who come in special cars with false plates in order not to attract attention.

The urban guerrilla demonstrator shows groups in the mass demonstration the flight route if that is necessary. He plants mines, throws Molotov cocktails, prepares ambushes and explosions.

The urban guerrilla demonstrator must also initiate the *net within the net,* going through government vehicles, official cars, and police vehicles before turning them over or setting them on fire, to see if any of them have money and arms.

Snipers are very good for mass demonstrations and, along with the urban guerrilla demonstrators, can play a valuable role.

Hidden at strategic points, the snipers have complete success, using shotguns, machine guns, etc. whose fire and ricocheting easily cause losses among the enemy.

Strikes and Work Interruptions

The strike is a model of action employed by the urban guerrilla in work centers and schools to damage the enemy by stopping work and study activities. Because it is one of the weapons most feared by the exploiters and oppressors, the enemy uses tremendous fighting power and incredible violence against it. The strikers are taken to prison, suffer beatings, and many of them wind up assassinated.

The urban guerrilla must prepare the strike in such a way as to leave no tracks or clues that identify the leaders of the action. A strike is successful when it is organized through the action of a small group, if it is carefully prepared in secret and by the most clandestine methods.

Arms, ammunition, Molotovs, homemade weapons of destruction and attack, all this must be supplied beforehand in order to meet the enemy. So that it can do the greatest possible damage, it is a good idea to study and put into effect a sabotage plan.

Work and study interruptions, although they are of brief duration, cause severe damage to the enemy. It is enough for them to crop up at different points and in different sections of the same area, disrupting daily life, occurring endlessly one after the other, in authentic guerrilla fashion.

In strikes or simple work interruptions, the urban guerrilla has recourse to occupation or penetration of the locale or can simply make a raid. In that case his objective is to take hostages, to capture prisoners, or to kidnap enemy agents and propose an exchange for the arrested strikers.

In certain cases, strikes and brief work interruptions can offer an excellent opportunity for preparing ambushes or traps whose aim is the physical liquidation of the cruel, bloody police.

The basic fact is that the enemy suffers losses and material and moral damage, and is weakened by the action.

Desertions, Diversions, Seizures, Expropriations of Arms, Ammunition, Explosives

Desertion and the diversion of arms are actions effected in military camps, ships, military hospitals, etc. The urban guerrilla soldier, chief, sergeant, subofficial, and official must desert at the most opportune moment with modern arms and ammunition to hand them over for the use of the Brazilian revolution.

One of the opportune moments is when the military urban guerrilla is called upon to pursue and to fight his guerrilla comrades outside the military quarters. Instead of following the orders of the gorillas, the military urban guerrilla must join the revolutionaries by handing over the arms and ammunition he carries, or the military plane he pilots.

The advantage of this method is that the revolutionaries receive arms and ammunition from the army, the navy, and the air force, the military police, the civilian guard, or the firemen without any great work, since it reaches their hands by government transport.

Other opportunities may occur in the barracks, and the military urban guerrilla must always be alert to this. In case of carelessness on the part of the commanders or in other favorable conditions, such as bureaucratic attitudes and behavior or relaxation of discipline on the part of sublieutenants and other internal personnel, the military urban guerrilla must no longer wait but must try to advise the organizations and desert alone or accompanied, but with as large a supply of arms as possible.

With information from and participation of the military urban guerrilla, raids on barracks and other military establishments for the purpose of capturing arms can be organized.

When there is no possibility of deserting and taking arms and ammunition, the military urban guerrilla must engage in sabotage, starting explosions and fires in munitions and gunpowder.

This technique of deserting with arms and ammunition, of raiding and sabotaging the military centers, is the best way of wearing out and demoralizing the gorillas and of leaving them confused.

The urban guerrilla's purpose in disarming an individual enemy is to capture his arms. These arms are usually in the hands of sentinels or others whose task is guard duty or repression.

The capture of arms may be accompanied by violent means or by astuteness and by tricks or traps. When the enemy is disarmed, he must be searched for arms other than those already taken from him. If we are careless, he can use the arms that were not seized to shoot the urban guerrilla.

The seizure of arms is an efficient method of acquiring machine guns, the urban guerrilla's most important arms.

When we carry out small operations or actions to seize arms and ammunition, the material captured may be for personal use or for armaments and supplies for the firing groups.

The necessity to provide firing power for the urban guerrilla is so great that in order to take off from zero point we often have to purchase one weapon, divert or capture a single arm. The basic point is to begin, and to begin with a great spirit of decisiveness and of boldness. The possession of a single arm multiplies our forces.

In a bank assault, we must be careful to seize the arm or arms of the bank guard. The remainder of the arms we find with the treasurer, the bank teller, or the manager must also be seized ahead of time.

The other method we can use to capture arms is the preparation of ambushes against the police and the cars they use to move around in.

Quite often we succeed in capturing arms in the police commissaries as a result of raids from outside.

The expropriation of arms, ammunition, and explosives is the urban guerrilla's goal in assaulting commercial houses, industries, and quarries.

Liberation of Prisoners

The liberation of prisoners is an armed operation designed to free the jailed urban guerrilla. In daily struggle against the enemy, the urban guerrilla is subject to arrest and can be sentenced to unlimited years in jail. This does not mean that the revolutionary battle stops here. For the guerrilla, his experience is deepened by prison and continues even in the dungeons where he is held.

The imprisoned urban guerrilla views jail as a terrain he must dominate and understand in order to free himself by a guerrilla operation. There is no prison, either on an island, in a city penitentiary, or on a farm, that is impregnable to the slyness, the cleverness, and the firing potential of the revolutionaries.

The urban guerrilla who is free views the penal establishments of the enemy as the inevitable site of guerrilla action designed to liberate his ideological brothers from prison.

It is this combination of *the urban guerrilla in freedom and the urban guerrilla in jail* that results in the armed operations we refer to as the liberation of prisoners.

The guerrilla operations that can be used in liberating prisoners are the following:

a) riots in penal establishments, in correctional colonies and islands, or on transport or prison ships;
b) assaults on urban or rural penitentiaries, houses of detention, commissaries, prisoner depots, or any other permanent, occasional, or temporary place where prisoners are held;
c) assaults on prisoner transport trains and cars;
d) raids and penetrations of prisons;
e) ambushing of guards who are moving prisoners.

Execution

Execution is the killing of a North American spy, of an agent of the dictatorship, of a police torturer, of a fascist personality in the government involved in crimes and persecutions against patriots, of a stool pigeon, informer, police agent, or police provocateur.

Those who go to the police of their own free will to make denunciations and accusations, who supply clues and information and finger people, must also be executed when they are caught by the urban guerrilla.

Execution is a secret action in which the least possible number of urban guerrillas are involved. In many cases, the execution can be carried out by one sniper, patiently, alone and unknown, and operating in absolute secrecy and in cold blood.

Kidnapping

Kidnapping is capturing and holding in a secret spot a police agent, a North American spy, a political personality, or a notorious and dangerous enemy of the revolutionary movement.

Kidnapping is used to exchange or liberate imprisoned revolutionary comrades, or to force suspension of torture in the jail cells of the military dictatorship.

The kidnapping of personalities who are known artists, sports figures, or are outstanding in some other field, but who have evidenced no political interest, can be a useful form of propaganda for the revolutionary and patriotic principles of the urban guerrilla provided it occurs under special circumstances, and the kidnapping is handled so that the public sympathizes with it and accepts it.

The kidnapping of North American residents or visitors in Brazil constitutes a form of protest against the penetration and domination of United States imperialism in our country.

Sabotage

Sabotage is a highly destructive type of attack using very few persons and sometimes requiring only one to accomplish the desired result. When the urban guerrilla uses sabotage the first phase is isolated sabotage. Then comes the phase of dispersed and generalized sabotage, carried out by the people.

Well-executed sabotage demands study, planning, and careful execution. A characteristic form of sabotage is explosion using dynamite, fire, and the placing of mines.

A little sand, a trickle of any kind of combustible, a poor lubrication, a screw removed, a short circuit, pieces of wood or of iron, can cause irreparable damage.

The objective of sabotage is to hurt, to damage, to make useless, and to destroy vital enemy points such as the following:

a) the economy of the country;
b) agricultural or industrial production;
c) transport and communication systems;
d) the military and police systems and their establishments and deposits;
e) the repressive military-police system;
f) the firms and properties of North Americans in the country.

The urban guerrilla should endanger the economy of the country, particularly its economic and financial aspects, such as its domestic and foreign commercial network, its exchange and banking systems, its tax collection systems, and others.

Public offices, centers of government services, government warehouses, are easy targets for sabotage.

Nor will it be easy to prevent the sabotage of agricultural and industrial production by the urban guerrilla, with his thorough knowledge of the local situation.

Industrial workers acting as urban guerrillas are excellent industrial saboteurs since they, better than anyone, understand the industry, the factory, the machine, or the part most likely to destroy an entire operation, doing far more damage than a poorly informed layman could do.

With respect to the enemy's transport and communications systems, beginning with railway traffic, it is necessary to attack them systematically with sabotage arms.

The only caution is against causing death and fatal injury to passengers, especially regular commuters on suburban and long-distance trains.

Attacks on freight trains, rolling or stationary stock, stoppage of military transport and communication systems, these are the major sabotage objectives in this area.

Sleepers can be damaged and pulled up, as can rails. A tunnel blocked by a barrier after an explosion, an obstruction by a derailed car, cause tremendous harm.

The derailment of a cargo train carrying fuel is of major damage to the enemy. So is dynamiting railway bridges. In a system where the weight and the size of the rolling equipment is enormous, it takes months for workers to repair or rebuild the destruction and damage.

As for highways they can be obstructed by trees, stationary vehicles, ditches, dislocation of barriers by dynamite, and bridges blown up by explosion.

Ships can be damaged at anchor in seaports and river ports or in the shipyards. Airplanes can be destroyed or sabotaged on the ground.

Telephonic and telegraphic lines can be systematically damaged, their towers blown up, and their lines made useless.

Transport and communications must be sabotaged at once because the revolutionary war has already begun in Brazil and it is essential to impede the enemy's movement of troops and munitions.

Oil lines, fuel plants, depots for bombs and ammunition, powder magazines and arsenals, military camps, commissaries must become targets par excellence in sabotage operations, while vehicles, army trucks, and other military and police cars must be destroyed wherever they are found.

The military and police repression centers and their specific and specialized organs, must also claim the attention of the urban guerrilla saboteur.

North American firms and properties in the country, for their part, must become such frequent targets of sabotage that the volume of actions directed against them surpasses the total of all other actions against vital enemy points.

Terrorism

Terrorism is an action, usually involving the placement of a bomb or fire explosion of great destructive power, which is capable of effecting irreparable loss against the enemy.

Terrorism requires that the urban guerrilla should have an adequate theoretical and practical knowledge of how to make explosives.

The terroristic act, apart from the apparent facility with which it can be carried out, is no different from other urban guerrilla acts and actions whose success depends on the planning and determination of the revolutionary organization. It is an action the urban guerrilla must execute with the greatest cold bloodedness, calmness, and decision.

Although terrorism generally involves an explosion, there are cases in which it may also be carried out by execution and the systematic burning of installations, properties, and North American depots, plantations, etc. It is essential to point out the importance of fires and the construction of incendiary bombs such as gasoline bombs in the technique of revolutionary terrorism. Another thing is the importance of the material the urban guerrilla can persuade the people to expropriate in moments of hunger and scarcity resulting from the greed of the big commercial interest.

Terrorism is an arm the revolutionary can never relinquish.

Armed Propaganda

The coordination of urban guerrilla actions, including each armed action, is the principal way of making armed propaganda.

These actions, carried out with specific and determined objectives, inevitably become propaganda material for the mass communications system.

Bank assaults, ambushes, desertions and diverting of arms, the rescue of prisoners, executions, kidnappings, sabotage, terrorism, and the war of nerves, are all cases in point.

Airplanes diverted in flight by revolutionary action, moving ships and trains assaulted and seized by guerrillas, can also be solely for propaganda effects.

But the urban guerrilla must never fail to install a clandestine press and must be able to turn out mimeographed copies using alcohol or electric plates and other duplicating apparatus, expropriating what he cannot buy in order to produce small clandestine newspapers, pamphlets, flyers, and stamps for propaganda and agitation against the dictatorship.

The urban guerrilla engaged in clandestine printing facilitates enormously the incorporation of large numbers of people into the revolutionary struggle, by opening a permanent work front for those willing to carry on revolutionary propaganda, even when to do so means acting alone and risking their lives as revolutionaries.

With the existence of clandestine propaganda and agitational material, the inventive spirit of the urban guerrilla expands and creates catapults, artifacts, mortars, and other instruments with which to distribute the antigovernment pamphlets at a distance.

Tape recordings, the occupation of radio stations, and the use of loud speakers, drawings on walls and in other inaccessible places are other forms of propaganda.

In using them, the urban guerrilla should give them the character of armed operations.

A consistent propaganda by letters sent to specific addresses, explaining the meaning of the urban guerrillas' armed actions, produces considerable results and is one method of influencing certain segments of the population.

Even this influence exercised in the heart of the people by every possible propaganda device revolving around the activity of the urban guerrilla does not indicate that our forces have everyone's support.

It is enough to win the support of a part of the people and this can be done by popularizing the following slogan: "Let he who does not wish to do anything for the revolutionaries, do nothing against them."

Urban Guerrilla Warfare, School for Selecting the Guerrilla

Revolution is a social phenomenon that depends on men, arms, and resources. Arms and resources exist in the country and can be taken and used, but to do this it is necessary to count on men. Without them, the arms and the resources have no use and no value. For their part, the men must have two basic and indispensable obligatory qualities:

a) they must have a politico-revolutionary motivation;
b) they must have the necessary technical-revolutionary preparation.

Men with a politico-revolutionary motivation are found among the vast and clearheaded contingents of enemies of the military dictatorship and of the domination of U.S. imperialism.

Almost daily such men gravitate to urban guerrilla warfare, and it is for this reason that the reaction no longer announces that it has thwarted the revolutionaries and goes through the unpleasantness of seeing them rise up again out of their own ashes.

The men who are best trained, most experienced, and dedicated to urban guerrilla warfare and at the same time to rural guerrilla warfare, constitute the backbone of the revolutionary war and, therefore, of the Brazilian revolution. From this backbone will come the marrow of the revolutionary army of national liberation, rising out of guerrilla warfare.

This is the central nucleus, not the bureaucrats and opportunists hidden in the organizational structure, not the empty conferees, the clichéd writers of resolutions that remain on paper, but rather the men who fight. The men who from the very first have been determined and ready for anything, who personally participate in revolutionary actions, who do not waver or deceive.

This is the nucleus indoctrinated and disciplined with a long-range strategic and tactical vision consistent with the application of Marxist theory, of Leninism, and of Castro–Guevara developments applied to the specific conditions of the Brazilian situation. This is the nucleus that will lead the rebellion through its guerrilla phase.

From it will come men and women with politico-military development, one and indivisible, whose task will be that of future leaders after the triumph of the revolution, in the construction of the new Brazilian society.

As of now, the men and women chosen for urban guerrilla warfare are workers; peasants whom the city has attracted as a market for manpower and who return to the countryside indoctrinated and politically and technically prepared: students, intellectuals, priests. This is the material with which we are building—starting with urban guerrilla warfare—the armed alliance of workers and peasants, with students, intellectuals, priests.

Workers have infinite knowledge in the industrial sphere and are best for urban revolutionary tasks. The urban guerrilla worker participates in the struggle by constructing arms, sabotaging and preparing saboteurs and dynamiters, and personally participating in actions involving hand arms, or organizing strikes and partial paralysis with the characteristics of mass violence in factories, workships, and other work centers.

The peasants have an extraordinary intuition for knowledge of the land, judgment in confronting the enemy, and the indispensable ability to communicate with the humble masses. The peasant guerrilla is already participating in our struggle and it is he who reaches the guerrilla core, establishes support points in the countryside, finds hiding places for individuals, arms, munitions, supplies, organizes the sowing and harvesting of grain for use in the guerrilla war, chooses the points of transport, cattle-raising posts, and sources of meat supplies, trains the guides that show the rural guerrillas the road, and creates an information service in the countryside.

Students are noted for being politically crude and coarse and thus they break all the taboos. When they are integrated into urban guerrilla warfare, as is now occurring on a wide scale, they show a special talent for revolutionary violence and soon acquire a high level of political-technical-military skill. Students have plenty of free time on their hands because they are systematically separated, suspended, and expelled from school by the dictatorship and so they begin to spend their time advantageously, in behalf of the revolution.

The intellectuals constitute the vanguard of resistance to arbitrary acts, social injustice, and the terrible inhumanity of the dictatorship of the gorillas. They spread the revolutionary call and they have great influence on people. The urban guerrilla intellectual or artist is the most modern of the Brazilian revolution's adherents.

Churchmen—that is to say, those ministers or priests and religious men of various hierarchies and persuasions—represent a sector that has special ability to communicate with the people, particularly with workers, peasants, and the Brazilian woman. The priest who is an urban guerrilla is an active ingredient in the ongoing Brazilian revolutionary war, and constitutes a powerful arm in the struggle against military power and North American imperialism.

As for the Brazilian woman, her participation in the revolutionary war, and particularly in urban guerrilla warfare, has been marked by an unmatched fighting spirit and tenacity, and it is not by chance that so many women have been accused of participation in guerrilla actions against banks, quarries, military centers, etc., and that so many are in prison while others are sought by the police.

As a school for choosing the guerrilla, urban guerrilla warfare prepares and places at the same level of responsibility and efficiency the men and women who share the same dangers fighting, rounding up supplies, serving as messengers or runners, as drivers, sailors, or airplane pilots, obtaining secret information, and helping with propaganda and the task of indoctrination.

Carlos Marighella

June 1969

Appendix B:

Photographs

Photographs supplied courtesy of and with permission from the government of Chile.

Figure 1. Captured photograph depicts members of the Chilean terrorist group the Manuel Rodriguez Patriotic Front, the armed wing of the Chilean Communist Party, waiting to receive Cuban-supplied arms that were disembarked on the north coast of Chile in 1986.

Figure 2. Japanese-made communications equipment used by Chilean terrorists to stay in touch with arms-supplying Cuban fishing boats.

Figure 3. The arms bundles were destined for terrorist units in Santiago and Valparaiso and contained American-made M–16 rifles from Vietnam and Soviet RPG–7 rocket launchers, hand grenades, and ammunition.

Figure 4. The fishing boat *Astrid Sue* used by the Chilean terrorists to off-load arms and explosives from larger Cuban vessels hovering off the coast of Chile.

Figure 5. One part of the 3,115 M-16s captured by Chilean police in August 1986.

Figure 6. Captured Soviet-made RPG-7 rocket launchers, a favorite weapon of Soviet bloc-assisted terrorists.

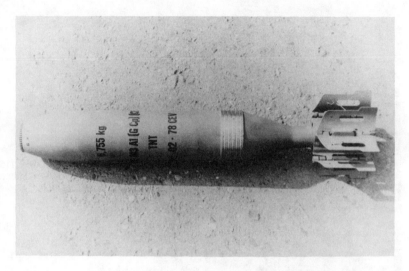

Figure 7. U.S.-made, Cuban-supplied .81 millimeter mortar bomb destined for the armed wing of the Chilean Communist Party.

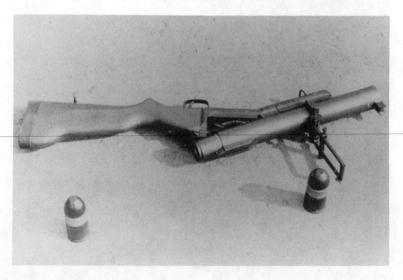

Figure 8. One of five U.S.-made M–79 grenade launchers captured by Chilean security forces. U.S. intelligence believes they came from stocks captured by the North Vietnamese in 1975.

Figure 9. 102 captured Belgian-made FAL rifles destined for the Chilean terrorist group the Manual Rodriguez Patriotic Front. The FALs probably came directly from Cuban stocks.

Figure 10. It is estimated by U.S. and Chilean intelligence that the arms captured would have equipped a 5,000 man army of terrorists.

Acronyms

ABC . . . . Cuban group of the 1930's. It is not known what the initials
        signify.
AD . . . . America Department. CUBA
ALN . . . . National Liberation Action. BRAZIL
ANAPO . . . . . . National Popular Alliance. COLOMBIA
ANC . . . . African National Congress. SOUTH AFRICA
APRA . . . . American Popular Revolutionary Alliance. PERU
AVC . . . . Alfaro Vive Carajo. ECUADOR
CGR . . . . General Revolutionary Command. GUATEMALA
CPJ . . . . Communist Party of Jamaica
CUTCh . . . . . . Chilean Communist Party's Central Organization of Workers
DGI . . . . General Directorate of Intelligence. CUBA
DGRE . . . . . . General Directorate of Foreign Relations. CUBA
DGSE . . . . General Department of State Security. NICARAGUA
DNU–MRH . . . National Unity Directorate of the Revolutionary Movement
        of Honduras
DOE . . . . Special Operations Directorate. CUBA
DR . . . . Revolutionary Directorate. CUBA
DRU . . . . United Revolutionary Directorate. EL SALVADOR
EGP . . . . Guerrilla Army of the Poor. GUATEMALA
ELN . . . . National Liberation Army. BOLIVIA
ELN . . . . National Liberation Army. COLOMBIA
ELN . . . . National Liberation Army. PERU
EPB . . . . Ejercito Popular Boricua. PUERTO RICO
ERP . . . . Popular Revolutionary Army. ARGENTINA
ERP . . . . Popular Revolutionary Army. EL SALVADOR
ETA . . . . Basque Nation and Liberty. SPAIN
FALN . . . . Armed Forces of National Liberation. PUERTO RICO
FALN . . . . Armed Forces of National Liberation. VENEZUELA
FAR . . . . Rebel Armed Forces. GUATEMALA
FARC . . . . Colombian Revolutionary Armed Forces
FARN . . . . . . Armed Forces of National Resistance. EL SALVADOR
FIR . . . . Left Revolutionary Front. PERU
FLN . . . . National Liberation Front. VENEZUELA
FMLN . . . . . . Farabundo Marti National Liberation Front. EL SALVADOR
FMR . . . . Manuel Rodriguez Patriotic Front. CHILE
FPL . . . . Popular Forces of Liberation. EL SALVADOR
FPR . . . . Popular Revolutionary Forces. HONDURAS

FSLN . . . . Sandinist Front of National Liberation. NICARAGUA
JCR . . . . Junta of Revolutionary Coordination. ARGENTINA
JLP . . . . Jamaican Labour Party
M–19 . . . . April 19 Movement. COLOMBIA
MIR . . . . Revolutionary Left Movement. CHILE
MIR . . . . Revolutionary Left Movement. ECUADOR
MIR . . . . Revolutionary Left Movement. PERU
MIRA . . . . Independent Revolutionary Armed Movement. PUERTO RICO
MLN . . . . National Liberation Movement (Tupamaros) URUGUAY
MPI . . . . Pro-Independence Movement. PUERTO RICO
MPLA . . . . . . Popular Movement for the Liberation of Angola
MRP . . . . Revolutionary Movement of the People. COSTA RICA
NJM . . . . New Jewel Movement. GRENADA
OAS . . . . Organization of American States
OLAS . . . . Latin American Solidarity Organization
OPR–33 . . . . . . Revolutionary Popular Organization. URUGUAY
OSPAAAL . . . . First Conference of Solidarity of the Peoples of Africa, Asia,
            and Latin America
PAIGC . . . . African Party for the Independence of Guinea-Bissau
PCC . . . . Colombian Communist Party
PCC . . . . Cuban Communist Party
PCCh . . . . Chilean Communist Party
PCD . . . . Dominican Communist Party. DOMINICAN REPUBLIC
PCES . . . . Salvadoran Communist Party. EL SALVADOR
PCH . . . . Honduran Communist Party
PCV . . . . Venezuelan Communist Party
PGT . . . . Guatemalan Workers Party
PGT/D . . . . . . Dissident faction of the Guatemalan Workers Party
PLO . . . . Palestine Liberation Organization
PNP . . . . People's National Party. JAMAICA
PRD . . . . Dominican Revolutionary Party. DOMINICAN REPUBLIC
PRTC . . . . Central American Revolutionary Workers Party. EL
            SALVADOR
PSP . . . . Popular Socialist Party. DOMINICAN REPUBLIC
PSP . . . . Puerto Rican Socialist Party
PVP . . . . People's Vanguard Party. COSTA RICA
SDS . . . . Students for a Democratic Society. UNITED STATES
SWAPO . . . . . . Southwest African People's Organization
UIR . . . . Insurrectional Revolutionary Union. CUBA
UNITA . . . . . . National Union for the Total Independence of Angola
UNRG . . . . National Revolutionary Union. GUATEMALA
URP/MLP . . . . People's Revolutionary Union/Popular Liberation Movement
            HONDURAS
WJP . . . . Workers Party of Jamaica

Selected Bibliography

Books

Alexander, Yonah, and Robert A. Kilmarx. *Political Terrorism and Business*. New York: Praeger, 1979.

Bell, J. Bowyer. *Transnational Terror*. Washington, D.C.: American Enterprise Institute, 1975.

Berry, R. Albert, Ronald G. Hellman, and Mauricio Solaun, eds. *Politics of Compromise: Coalition Government in Colombia*. New Brunswick, New Jersey: Transaction Books, 1980.

Blasier, Cole, and Carmelo Mesa-Lago, eds. *Cuba in the World*. Pittsburgh: University of Pittsburgh Press, 1979.

Bonachea, Ramon L., and Marta San Martin. *The Cuban Insurrection, 1952–1959*. New Brunswick, New Jersey: Transaction Books, 1974.

Bonachea, Rolando E., and Nelson P. Valdes, eds. *Che: Selected Works of Ernesto Guevara*. Cambridge, MA: MIT press, 1969.

―――. *Revolutionary Struggle: The Selected Works of Fidel Castro*. Vol. 1. Cambridge, MA: MIT Press, 1972.

Burton, Anthony M. *Urban Terrorism: Theory, Practice and Response*. New York: The Free Press, 1975.

Carlos Marighella. Havana: Tricontinental, Colleccion/los hombres, [1970].

Castro, Orlando Hildago. *Spy for Fidel*. Miami: E. A. Seeman Publishing, Inc., 1971.

Christian, Shirley. *Nicaragua: Revolution in the Family*. New York: Random House, 1985.

Cline, Ray S., and Yonah Alexander. *Terrorism: The Soviet Connection*. New York: Crane Russak, 1984.

Clutterbuck, Richard. *Protest and the Urban Guerrilla*. New York: Abelard Schuman, 1973.

Debray, Regis. *Revolution Within the Revolution*. New York: Grove Press, 1967.

―――. *The Chilean Revolution: Conversations with Allende*. New York: Vintage Books, 1971.

Dennis, Colin. *The Road Not Taken: Memoirs of a Reluctant Guerrilla*. Kingston: Kingston Publishers, Ltd., 1985.

Dobson, Christopher, and Ronald Payne. *The Terrorists: Their Weapons, Leaders and Tactics*. New York: Facts on File, 1979.

Draper, Theodore. *Castroism, Theory and Practice*. New York: Praeger, 1965.

Dreier, John C. *The Organization of American States and the Hemisphere Crisis*. New York: Harper and Row, 1962.

Ebon, Martin. *Che: The Making of a Legend*. New York: Signet Books, 1969.

Falk, Pamela S. *Cuban Foreign Policy: Caribbean Tempest*. Lexington, MA: Lexington Books, D.C. Heath and Co., 1986.

Goure, Leon, and Morris Rothenberg. *Soviet Penetration of Latin America*, Miami: Miami Center for Advanced International Studies, University of Miami, 1975.

Gott, Richard. *Guerrilla Movements in Latin America*. New York: Doubleday, 1971.

Guillen, Abraham. *Estrategia de la Guerrilla Urbana*. Montevideo: Ediciones Liberacion, 1966.

Gutteridge, William, ed. *Contemporary Terrorism*. New York: Facts on File, 1986.

Halperin, Ernst. *Nationalism and Communism in Chile*. Cambridge, MA: MIT Press, 1965.

———. *Terrorism in Latin America*. Beverly Hills, CA: Sage Publications, 1976.

Halperin, Maurice. *The Rise and Decline of Fidel Castro*. Berkeley: University of California Press, 1972.

———. *The Taming of Fidel Castro*. Berkeley: University of California Press, 1980.

Heikel, Mohammed Hassamein. *The Cairo Documents*. New York: Doubleday, 1973.

Hendriksen, Thomas H., ed. *Communist Powers and Sub-Saharan Africa*. Stanford: Hoover Institution Press, 1981.

Hodges, Donald C., ed. *Philosophy of the Urban Guerrilla: The Revolutionary Writings of Abraham Guillen*. New York: William Morrow and Company, 1973.

Israeli, Raphael, ed. *PLO in Lebanon: Selected Documents*. London: Weidenfeld and Nicolson Ltd., 1983.

Jackson, D. Bruce. *Castro, The Kremlin, and Communism in Latin America*. Baltimore: The Johns Hopkins Press, 1969.

James, Daniel. *Che Guevara.* London: George Allen and Unwin Ltd., 1970.

Janke, Peter. *Guerrilla and Terrorist Organizations: A World Directory.* New York: MacMillan, 1983.

Kopilow, David J. *Castro, Israel, and the PLO.* Washington, D.C.: The Cuban American National Foundation, 1985.

Lacquer, Walter, ed. *The Terrorism Reader: A Historical Anthology.* New York: New American Library, 1978.

Lacquer, Walter. *Terrorism.* Boston: Little, Brown, and Company, 1977.

Ledeen, Michael, et al. *Castro's Puerto Rican Obsession.* Washington, D.C.: The Cuban American National Foundation, 1987.

Lowy, Michael. *The Marxism of Che Guevara.* New York: Monthly Review Press, 1973.

Mallin, Jay, ed. *Terror and Urban Guerrillas.* Coral Gables: University of Miami Press, 1971.

Martin, John Bartlow. *Overtaken by Events.* Garden City, NY: Doubleday, 1966.

Matthews, Herbert L. *Fidel Castro.* New York: Simon and Schuster, 1969.

Mesa-Lago, Carmelo. *Cuba in Africa.* Pittsburgh: Center for Latin American Studies, University of Pittsburgh Press, 1982.

Moss, Robert. *Chile's Marxist Experiment.* New York: Halstead Press, 1973.

———. *Urban Guerrillas.* London: Temple Smith, 1972.

Possony, Stefan T., and L. Francis Bouchey. *International Terrorism: The Communist Connection.* Washington, D.C.: American Council for World Freedom, 1978.

Ratliff, William E. *Castroism and Communism in Latin America, 1959–1976.* Washington, D.C.: American Enterprise Institute, 1976.

———. *Follow the Leader in the Horn.* Washington, D.C.: The Cuban American National Foundation, 1986.

Robbins, Carla Anne. *The Cuban Threat.* New York: McGraw Hill, 1983.

Romerstein, Herbert. *Soviet Support for International Terrorism.* Washington, D.C.: The Foundation for Democratic Education, Inc., 1981.

Samuels, Michael A., et al. *Implications of Soviet and Cuban Activities in Africa for U.S. Policy.* Washington, D.C.: Center for Strategic and International Studies, 1979.

Seabury, Paul, and Walter A. McDougall, eds. *The Grenada Papers.* San Francisco: ICS Press, 1984.

Sterling, Claire. *The Terror Network: The Secret War of International Terrorism.* New York: Holt, Rinehart and Winston, 1985.

Suarez, Andres. *Cuba: Castroism and Communism 1959–1966.* Cambridge, Massachusetts: MIT Press, 1967.

Szulc, Tad. *Fidel: A Critical Portrait.* New York: William Morrow and Company, 1986.

Theberge, James D. *The Soviet Presence in Latin America.* New York: Crane Russak and Company, 1974.

Thomas, Hugh. *Cuba: The Pursuit of Freedom.* New York: Harper and Row, 1971.

Articles, U.S. Government Documents and Other Publications

Castro, Fidel. *Fidel in Chile.* New York: International Publishers, 1972.

Castro and the Narcotics Connection. Washington, D.C.: The Cuban American National Foundation, 1983.

Falk, Pamela S. "Cuba in Africa." *Foreign Affairs* Vol. 65 (Summer 1987): 1077–1096.

First Conference of the Latin American Solidarity Organization. Washington, D.C.: Pan American Union, 1967.

Fontaine, Roger W. "Fidel Castro: Front and Center." *The Washington Quarterly* Vol. 2 (Spring 1979): 75–84.

Francis, Samuel T. *Latin American Terrorism: The Cuban Connection.* Washington, D.C.: Heritage Foundation Backgrounder No. 104, 1979.

Humbert, Dan. "Cuba in Africa." *Issues in Brief.* Washington, D.C.: ACU Education and Research Institute, 22 August 1977.

Ledeen, Michael, and Herbert Romerstein, eds. *Grenada Documents: An Overview and Selection.* Washington, D.C.: Department of State and Department of Defense, 1984.

Marin, Juan de Dios. "Inside a Castro 'Terror School'. " *Readers Digest,* Vol. 85 (December 1964): 119–123.

The PLO's Growing Latin American Base. Washington, D.C.: Heritage Foundation Backgrounder No. 281, 1983.

Report on the First Afro-Asian-Latin American People's Solidarity Conference and Its Projections; Council of the Organization of American States. Washington, D.C.: The Pan American Union, 1966.

Sterling, Claire. "The Terrorist Network." *The Atlantic Monthly* Vol. 242 (November 1978): 37–43.

U.S. Congress. *Communist Threat to the United States through the Caribbean part 20, U.S. Senate Internal Sub-Committee, United States Senate.* 90th Cong., 2d sess. 1969.

U.S. Congress. *The Role of Cuba in International Terrorism and Subversion—U.S. Congress Senate Sub-Committee on Security and Terrorism of the Committee on the Judiciary, United States Senate.* 98th Cong., 1st sess. 1984.

U.S. Congress. *The Role of Cuba in International Terrorism—Hearings before the Sub-Committee on Security and Terrorism of the Committee on the Judiciary, United States Senate.* 97th Cong., 2d sess. 1982.

U.S. Congress. *U.S. Response to Cuban involvement in Narcotics Trafficking and Review of Worldwide Illicit Narcotics Situation—Hearings before the House Foreign Affairs Committee on February 21 and 23, 1984, United States Senate.* 98th Cong., 2d sess. 1984.

U.S. Department of State. *Cuba's Renewed Support for Violence in Latin America.* Special Report No. 90. 14 December 1981.

U.S. Department of State. *Libyan Activities in the Western Hemisphere.* August 1986.

U.S. Department of State. *Patterns of Global Terrorism: 1983.* September 1984.

U.S. Department of State. *Revolution Beyond Our Borders.* Special Report No. 132. September 1985.

U.S. Department of State. *The Sandinistas and Middle Eastern Radicals.* August 1985.

U.S. Department of State and Department of Defense. *Background Paper: Central America.* 27 May 1983.

U.S. Department of State and Department of Defense. *Background Paper: Nicaragua's Military Build-Up and Support for Central American Subversion.* 18 July 1984.

U.S. Department of State and Department of Defense. *Grenada. A Preliminary Report.* 16 December 1983.

U.S. Department of State and Department of Defense. *Intelligence Information on External Support of the Guerrillas in El Salvador.* August 1984.

U.S. Department of State and Department of Defense. *The Soviet-Cuban Connection in Central America and the Caribbean.* March 1985.

U.S. Federal Bureau of Investigation. *Report on Foreign Influence in the Weather Underground Organization, Federal Bureau of Investigation.* 20 August 1976.

Volsky, George. "Cuba 15 Years Later." *Current History* Vol. 66 (1974): 10–14.

About the Author

Roger W. Fontaine has had a distinguished career as a journalist, diplomatic advisor, and scholar.

From December 1983 until March 1987, Mr. Fontaine was the chief diplomatic correspondent for *The Washington Times*. His articles have also appeared in *The New York Times, The Christian Science Monitor, The Los Angeles Times,* and *The Miami Herald,* as well as in the journals *Foreign Policy, The New Leader,* and *Strategic Review*. In addition, he has appeared as a political analyst on North and South American television—on such shows as "The MacNeil–Lehrer Report," "Canada A.M.," and "The NBC Nightly News"—and on National Public and BBC Television and Radio.

Prior to his work at *The Washington Times,* from February 1981 until December 1983, Mr. Fontaine served on the National Security Council staff at the White House. There he shared responsibility for day-to-day national security policy for Latin America. While an NSC staff officer, he and Carnes Lord drew up the original plans for Radio Marti, the alternative radio service for the Cuban people.

Mr. Fontaine earned a B.A. from Valparaiso University and an M.A. and Ph.D. from Johns Hopkins University. Among his academic achievements, he has served as Director of Latin American Studies, Georgetown University Center for Strategic and International Studies (1974–1980); and Assistant Professor of Political Science at Middlebury College (1969–72). He is the author of several previous works, including *Brazil and the United States: Toward a Maturing Relationship* (1976) and *On Negotiating with Cuba* (1975).

Mr. Fontaine is married and the father of a son, Matthew.